Beyond Mechanical Markets

Beyond Mechanical Markets

ASSET PRICE SWINGS, RISK, AND THE ROLE OF THE STATE

*Roman Frydman
and Michael D. Goldberg*

PRINCETON UNIVERSITY PRESS • PRINCETON AND OXFORD

Published by Princeton University Press, 41 William Street,
Princeton, New Jersey 08540
In the United Kingdom: Princeton University Press, 6 Oxford Street,
Woodstock, Oxfordshire OX20 1TW
press.princeton.edu

Jacket Art: W. Jan Zakrzewski, *Eighteen Battlefields* project, 2010.
Courtesy of the artist.

Library of Congress Cataloging-in-Publication Data

Frydman, Roman, 1948–
    Beyond mechanical markets : asset price swings, risk, and
  the role of the state / Roman Frydman and Michael D. Goldberg.
        p.   cm.
    Includes bibliographical references and index
    ISBN 978-0-691-14577-8 (hardcover : alk. paper)
    1. Rational expectations (Economic theory).   2. Global
Financial Crisis, 2008–2009.   3. Economic forecasting.
4. Risk.   5. Keynesian economics.   6. Securities—Prices.
I. Goldberg, Michael D., 1958–   II. Title.
HB3731.F79   2011
339—dc22   2010044395
British Library Cataloging-in-Publication Data is available

This book has been composed in Warnock by
Princeton Editorial Associates Inc., Scottsdale, Arizona
Printed on acid-free paper.
Printed in the United States of America

10   9   8   7   6   5   4   3   2   1

To Halina, Julia, and Marcella
  R.F.

To Sybille and Ben
  M.G.

Contents

PART II
AN ALTERNATIVE

Acknowledgments

We ARE ENORMOUSLY grateful to Peter Dougherty of Princeton University Press for encouraging us to write this book. His guidance inspired us to rethink and extend an article on how placing imperfect knowledge at the center of macroeconomics and finance theory could help us to better understand the issues posed by the financial crisis that began in 2007. His unstinting belief that the technical findings from *Imperfect Knowledge Economics: Exchange Rates and Risk* (Princeton University Press, 2007) could, if presented in nonspecialist language, contribute to the public debate was the crucial catalyst for this book.

We have benefited tremendously from illuminating discussions about modern macroeconomics, stretching over decades, with Edmund Phelps. We have likewise been stimulated and sustained over the years by George Soros's ideas about the role of imperfect knowledge and reflexivity in the workings of financial markets and historical change.

Robert Skidelsky and Michael Woodford read most of the chapters in this book in draft form. Their penetrating insights on Keynes's thought as well as contemporary macroeconomic theory led us to important revisions of our ideas. Anatole Kaletsky took an early interest in our work and its broader implications for understanding the relative role of the market and the state in modern economies. Anatole's intellectual breadth has inspired our work.

Many discussions over the years at the Center on Capitalism and Society at Columbia University have nurtured us in our pursuit of an approach that recognizes the crucial importance of imperfect knowledge for understanding market outcomes. Richard Robb's early incisive comments on Imperfect Knowledge Economics, and on drafts of the initial chapters, helped us to clarify our arguments about contemporary finance theory and improve their presentation.

The recent creation of the Institute for New Economic Thinking (INET) has already greatly encouraged us in our ongoing efforts to develop an alternative approach to macroeconomics and finance. Reactions to our presentations at INET's inaugural conference at King's College, Cambridge, as well as many stimulating discussions about financial reform with its executive director, Robert Johnson, enabled us to sharpen a number of our key arguments.

Niels Thygesen also generously shared with us his extensive knowledge of various contemporary approaches to financial reform. His critique of our policy proposals saved us from many omissions and misconceptions. An enlightening conversation with Adair Turner in the early phase of the development of our policy framework enabled us to improve substantially our comparison of the policy proposals based on Imperfect Knowledge Economics with those advanced by public bodies in the wake of the crisis.

Thought-provoking discussions with many other colleagues and friends have led us to numerous revisions of our ideas and arguments. Many years of joint research with Andrzej Rapaczynski on the post-communist transition served as the basis for our arguments concerning the similarities between the economics of central planning and contemporary macroeconomics and finance. We benefited greatly from the historian's perspective on the early parts of the manuscript provided by Jan Gross. Peter Jungen's insightful reading of the manuscript, as well as a number of extensive discussions with him, helped us to refine our analysis of the connection between entrepreneurship, other key features of modern economies, and the allocative role of financial markets.

We are indebted to Bruce Elmslie, Lejb Fogelman, Irena Grudzinska-Gross, Helena Hessel, Soren Johansen, Katarina Juselius, Henri Kowalski, Jonathan Schell, Peter Sullivan, Josh Stillwagon, Klaudiusz Weiss, and Emre Yoldas for taking the time to read parts of an early version of the manuscript. Their queries and astute suggestions led to refinements and revisions of some of our key arguments.

We are grateful to Matthew Winkler for his interest in our work and his generosity in making available the electronic record of Bloomberg's "Market Wrap" stories. The evidence from these stories has been crucial to our analysis of the relative role of psychological and fundamental considerations in driving movements in asset prices and risk. In this book, we present early findings from this analysis. We are indebted to Nicholas Mangee for his extraordinary effort in analyzing the Bloomberg stories and in his work with us to develop an approach to the empirical analysis of asset markets that combines traditional econometric methodology with narrative evidence.

We are deeply grateful to Jonathan Stein for his extraordinary editorial work, which has greatly improved the book's style, presentation, and readability. Jonathan's efforts went well beyond those of a first-rate editor: our many stimulating discussions with him led to substantial rethinking of a number of arguments in this book. We were also very fortunate to have had Marcella Frydman and Kenneth Murphy involved in the editorial process. Cyd Westmoreland provided expert copyediting, and Peter Strupp and his staff at Princeton Editorial Associates were instrumental in accomplishing the rare feat of making the book's production a painless process.

Turning to institutional sponsors, we are pleased to acknowledge support for editorial assistance from the C. V. Starr Center for Applied Economics at New York University and the University of New Hampshire. We are grateful to Robert Litan from the Ewing Marion Kauffman Foundation for his interest in this book. The foundation's grant enabled us to devote the summer of 2010 to its completion.

Finally, we thank Halina, Sybille, Ben, Julia, and Marcella for their patience and warm support.

Beyond Mechanical Markets

What Went Wrong and
What We Can Do about It

Quite apart from the fact that we do not know the future, the future is objectively not fixed. The future is open: objectively open.

—Karl R. Popper, *A World of Propensities*

I confess that I prefer true but imperfect knowledge . . . to a pretense of exact knowledge that is likely to be false.

—Friedrich A. Hayek,
"The Pretence of Knowledge," *Nobel Lecture*

The Fatal Flaw

Instability is an inherent feature of capitalist economies, perhaps nowhere more markedly so than in modern financial markets. Asset prices and risk tend to fluctuate, and, as recent experience in housing, equity, currency, and commodity markets around the world has shown, upswings in prices sometimes become excessive, eventually ending in abrupt and dramatic reversals.

These boom-and-bust fluctuations in asset values often lead to painful shifts in consumption and investment patterns that can trigger or prolong economic downturns and sharply increase unemployment. Many observers have pointed to excessive up-swings in housing and equity prices as key factors behind the global financial crisis that began in 2007, with devastating conse-quences for people worldwide. Thus, understanding asset-price swings, their connection to financial risk, and their impact on the broader economy is crucial to assessing the causes of the crisis, as well as to evaluating the various policy proposals aimed at rectify-ing the system's failures.

The central premise of this book is that the conceptual framework underpinning the debate triggered by the global finan-cial crisis is grossly inadequate for understanding what went wrong with our economies and what should be done to reform them. The reason is simple: contemporary macroeconomic and finance theory attempts to account for risk and swings in asset prices with models that suppose that nonroutine change is irrele-vant, as if nothing genuinely new can ever happen.

As Frank Knight (1921, p. 198) put it, "if all changes were to take place in accordance with invariable and universally known laws, [so that] they could be foreseen for an indefinite period in advance of their occurrence, ... profit or loss would not arise." And yet contemporary models assume that such laws exist. At issue, then, is what motivates economic activity and guides the allocation of resources in capitalist economies. For Knight—and for us—"it is our imperfect knowledge of the future, a consequence of change, not change as such, which is crucial to the understand-ing" of how profit-seeking market participants make decisions and how prices and risk unfold over time.

ASSUMING AWAY WHAT MATTERS MOST

Of course, economists must always make some assump-tions as they build their models. But to assume, as contemporary economic models do, that movements in asset prices and risk can be understood as if the future followed mechanically from the past is to assume that, except for "shocks," all change is fully predictable. Were this self-deception confined to the world of academic economics, it would remain a puzzling but harmless intellectual conceit. But economists' mechanistic accounts of markets wield significant real-world influence over policymakers, financial market participants, and the wider public. Moreover, they have led to seemingly polarized views of financial markets: they are either rational and nearly perfect at allocating society's capital or irrational casino-like institutions that allocate capital haphazardly.

Both these extreme views share an irreparable flaw, which stems from contemporary economic models' portrayal of individuals as little more than robots. In one camp, conventional economists presume that rational individuals make decisions as if they adhered strictly and permanently to overarching mechanical rules that economists themselves fully specify in advance. In the other camp, behavioral economists, despite their critique of rational market models as lacking psychological realism, also presume that irrational individuals' decisions, and their implications for asset prices and risk, can be adequately portrayed with mechanical rules.[1]

These theories presuppose that market participants and policy officials never search for genuinely new ways of using their resources and never revise the way they think about the future. Moreover, the social context within which individuals make decisions—including economic policies, institutions, and global economic and political developments—is also supposed to unfold in ways that can be adequately portrayed with prespecified mechanical rules.

Beginning in the last four decades of the twentieth century, nearly all macroeconomists and finance theorists have spent their careers constructing such fully predetermined models. Indeed, these models have become the cornerstone of the contem-

[1]For a notable exception, see Akerlof and Shiller (2009). They rely on a narrative mode of analysis, and thus ipso facto avoid mechanical formalizations of behavioral insights, unlike widely used mathematical behavioral finance models. For further discussion, see Chapter 2.

porary approach to economic analysis. Because they presume that change and its consequences can be fully foreseen, such models purport to provide an overarching account of asset prices and risk in the past, present, and future all at once. In contrast, all other types of models have come to be viewed by the academic mainstream as unscientific and thus unworthy of serious consideration.

Remarkably, this bias persists despite the dismal record of fully predetermined models in explaining how profit-seeking individuals make decisions in financial markets and thus how asset prices and risk unfold over time. The recent crisis is merely a glaring addition to the massive evidence of such models' empirical failures.

In this book, we explore how economists came to believe that they could provide an exact, overarching account of individual decisions and market outcomes. We show how they construct their fully predetermined models and explain why, in their attempts to portray rational individuals' behavior and market outcomes, they must imagine a world in which nonroutine change and imperfect knowledge are unimportant. Indeed, we argue that, by ruling out novelty, contemporary macroeconomic and finance models assume away financial markets' raison d'être—namely, to help allocate society's capital in the face of nonroutine change and the imperfect knowledge that it engenders in modern economies.

Our aim, in short, is to persuade readers that extant economic models fail to account for swings in asset prices and risk because they rest on irreparably flawed foundations. Thus, their use by market participants (including investment banks and other financial institutions) to assess prices—whether of mortgage-backed securities or other assets, new or old—has no scientific basis. Indeed, the crisis has painfully demonstrated the gross inadequacy of mechanical finance models' estimates of prices of innovative financial products and the risks entailed by holding and trading them.

Most importantly, we show that contemporary models miss the integral role that swings in asset prices and risk play in the process by which financial markets evaluate prior investments and

foster new companies and projects—the key to modern economies' dynamism. And yet, owing to the imperfection of knowledge, these swings can sometimes become excessive, implying
huge economic and social costs.

What, then, should be the role of the state in asset markets? Contemporary macroeconomic and finance theory, which,
by design, disregards imperfect knowledge on the part of
policymakers and market participants, has been of little help in
thinking about this question. Indeed, despite widespread dis-
illusionment with unfettered markets, the debate on reform
and ensuing proposals and measures have largely continued to
reflect the precrisis ideological belief that, except for setting
and enforcing the rules of the game, the state should stay out of
financial markets.[2]

As a result, the current reforms—the Dodd-Frank Act,
Basel 3, and European Union proposals—are largely focused on
strengthening the banking and credit system's resilience to adverse
aggregate developments. Macro-prudential measures, such as
countercyclical capital buffers, the Volcker rule, and pro-transparency rules, will help limit the buildup of risks in the system. But
these reforms offer precious little in the way of attacking one of the
main causes of financial crises, namely, excessive upswings in key
asset markets—such as those for equity, housing, and currencies
—and the sharp and prolonged downturns that time and again follow these upswings.

The framework proposed in this book accounts for the
essential role that financial markets play in modern economies,

---

[2]Policy economists, notably at the Bank for International Settlements, as
well as academic researchers engaged in studying the historical evidence on financial
crises, are well aware of the connection between asset-price swings and these crises.
See, for example, Borio and Lowe (2002a), Borio (2003), and Reinhart and Rogoff
(2009). Borio and Lowe (2002a) stress that viewing wide price swings as bubbles is
unhelpful. However, lacking an adequate conceptual framework for understanding
such swings in capitalist economies, Cecchetti et al. (2000, 2002) and others interpret them as bubbles and propose using monetary policy to "prick" them—though
most economists, arguing on the basis of fully predetermined models, oppose such
use of monetary policy. See, for example, Bernanke and Gertler (2001).

while recognizing a role for the state in dampening their excesses. We use this framework to propose refinements of current systemic reforms, particularly of financial markets, which should be accorded much higher priority on the reform agenda. We suggest new ways of thinking about such reforms and consider a panoply of measures aimed at dampening financial market excess without hampering capitalist economies' ability to spur innovation and sustained growth (see Chapter 12).

The Imperfect Knowledge Alternative

Our critique of contemporary economic theory has led us to develop an alternative approach to modeling asset markets, which we call Imperfect Knowledge Economics (IKE) (Frydman and Goldberg, 2007). In contrast to contemporary approaches, Imperfect Knowledge Economics places nonroutine change and imperfect knowledge—the conditions under which financial markets evolved—at the center of economic analysis. We show that doing so implies that swings in asset prices and risk are inherent to the process by which financial markets help society allocate its capital. Thus, Imperfect Knowledge Economics provides an appropriate framework for evaluating and refining current plans and proposals for reform, while suggesting a new policy framework for state regulation and active prudential intervention in financial markets.

The type of economics that economists practice, and the ideas on which it depends, are of crucial significance to the public. With this in mind, we examine Imperfect Knowledge Economics and contemporary approaches—and their implications for understanding financial markets and state regulation—in nontechnical language. Our hope is to enable nonspecialists to take a more informed and active part in the public debate concerning post-crisis financial reform—the outcome of which is likely to affect vitally everyone's well-being and the health of economies around the world.

Fishermen and Financial Markets

The ability of a society's institutions to allocate savings among alternative investment projects and monitor their progress is among the main determinants of innovation and growth. In principle, no individual can compute these projects' prospects—the stream of future returns. Nevertheless, financial markets allocate society's savings to alternative investment projects every day.

To grasp the importance of nonroutine change and imperfect knowledge for investment decisions, and why ignoring them assumes away financial markets' essential role in modern economies, consider a fisherman who must decide in the morning whether to spend the day fishing for flounder or haddock. On a typical day, he has a fairly good basis for estimating the probable catch and price for each type of fish. If, however, he must decide whether to buy a flounder boat or a haddock boat, he must worry about an enormous number of other possibilities: someone might invent a new technology for fishing, people's tastes might change, sea pollution or other environmental factors might affect flounder and haddock differently, or fishing in general might not, in the long run, be the career that he should pursue.

Economists have developed an approach that purports to account for how our fisherman would make his investment decision: if he is self-interested and rational, he will calculate the consequences of each alternative for his well-being, along with the probabilities of their occurrence, and pick the one that he expects to be best for him. But making a decision solely on the basis of such calculation is not merely complicated; strictly speaking, it is impossible, because certain outcomes are inherently indeterminate. Either their existence or importance for the problem at hand will become apparent only with the passage of time, or the uncertainty surrounding them is so great that the fisherman cannot confidently assign any useful values to the probability that they will occur.

The fisherman's problem is emblematic of many investment decisions in modern economies. In the vast majority of cases, the prospects of investment projects can be known only imperfectly, which in turn gives rise to financial markets' essential role. These markets translate individuals' myriad bundles of knowledge and intuition about the prospects of projects and companies into prices of equities and other financial claims. As market prices unfold over time, they provide a better assessment of the changing values of alternative investment projects than any estimate of those values that an individual could produce on her own. Thus, they provide a better guide in society's search for new ways of using its savings.

But even though financial markets are the best institution available to help society allocate its savings, the very reasons that they are essential to modern economies—nonroutine change and ever-imperfect knowledge—also make them imperfect assessors of asset values. As a result, they do not allocate capital perfectly, even in the course of their normal functioning. Moreover, the recurrence of excessive fluctuations in asset prices—and the great costs that these swings ultimately inflict on the financial system and the broader economy—is evidence that financial markets sometimes grossly misallocate capital.

THE SURVIVAL OF THE RATIONAL MARKET MYTH

Economic theory based on the presumption that nothing genuinely new ever happens has survived even a crisis that few predicted. Indeed, it continues to shape the debate about fiscal stimulus, financial reform, and, more broadly, the future of capitalism—which means that it remains a danger to us all. Policymakers in central banks and treasuries around the world continue to analyze macroeconomic policy options using these fully predetermined models as if they had reliable scientific underpinnings.[3]

[3]The fully predetermined accounts of macroeconomic outcomes that frequently guide policymaking are the Dynamic Stochastic General Equilibrium models. Even in the aftermath of the crisis (May 2010), researchers at the

In fact, by giving rise to two extreme and opposing views of the relative roles of the market and the state, contemporary economic theory has obfuscated policy analysis and public debate. One view, ascendant for almost four decades prior to the crisis, is that markets allocate capital nearly perfectly, because they are populated by rational individuals who can supposedly ascertain the true prospects of projects and companies. According to this view, the state's role should be limited to providing the basic framework for the operation of competitive financial markets.

Unfortunately, many officials worldwide came to embrace this belief, resulting in the massive wave of deregulation that emerged in the 1980s and accelerated in the late 1990s and early 2000s. Official faith in this view also encouraged governments to turn a blind eye to the dramatic upswings in housing, equity, and other asset prices that occurred in the run-up to the crisis, which made the crisis that began in 2007 more likely, if not inevitable.

In the wake of the crisis, however, the rationality of the market began to be widely referred to as a "myth." The weight of professional and nonacademic opinion swung from faith in unfettered markets' magical power to set prices according to the "true" prospects of projects and companies to the other extreme. Markets now were deemed grossly inefficient in allocating capital, as supposedly proved by the occurrence of market distortions, such as informational asymmetries, and large and prolonged asset-price swings, characterized as bubbles.

To be sure, woefully insufficient transparency and distorted incentives for key participants in the financial system contributed significantly to the unfolding crisis. Many observers have emphasized the opacity of structured assets, the close relationship

---

European Central Bank referred to the bank's general equilibrium model as "designed for use in the Macroeconomic Projection Exercises *regularly* undertaken by ECB/Eurosystem staff and for policy analysis" (Christoffel et al., 2010, p. 5, emphasis added). For an example of how the staff macroeconomic projections are used in communicating the policies of the European Central Bank to the public, see Trichet (2010).

between investment banks and credit-rating agencies, and the dizzying rise of financial institutions' leverage ratios.

But as damaging as such market distortions are, they alone cannot account for the asset-price swings that played a central role in triggering the crisis. Treating these swings as bubbles that are largely unrelated to fundamental factors—such as economic policy, overall growth, industrial trends, and the prospects of projects and companies—was supposed to provide a dose of behavioral realism to economic analysis of individual decisionmaking and market outcomes.

Bubbles are thought to arise because, instead of trading rationally on the basis of movements in fundamental factors, many market participants succumb to waves of market psychology, indulge in irrationalities of various kinds, or engage in technical trading based on charts of asset-price movements. According to bubble models, markets behave like casinos, often allocating society's capital haphazardly. Thus, rather than recognizing that asset-price swings are inherent to how financial markets allocate society's capital, bubble models suggest that such fluctuations are socially pernicious and should be extinguished as soon as they arise.

It is difficult to imagine two views of markets that could be farther apart. On the one hand, markets are rational, allocate capital nearly perfectly, and require only a narrowly delimited role for the state. On the other hand, markets are grossly inefficient, prone to bubbles, and compel an extremely powerful role for the state.

Given such profound differences, it is striking that these extreme positions share the same fatal flaw: the core belief that nonroutine change and imperfect knowledge are unimportant for understanding market prices and risk. As a result, both strands of contemporary macroeconomic and finance theory attempt to account for market outcomes with fully predetermined models that presume that the future will unfold mechanically from the past.

Paradoxically, market-failure and bubble models, which were supposed to expose the rational market as a myth, ended up reinforcing its mythic significance. If only informational distortions and deficiencies of market competition were minimized, psychology eliminated from individual decisionmaking, and irrational speculators banned from influencing outcomes, the rational participants would supposedly regain the upper hand, and the "rational market" would again set prices at nearly "true" fundamental values.

The rational market, in fact, is a myth in the strict sense of the word: it is, as the *Oxford English Dictionary* puts it, a "widely held but false belief." It cannot be turned into reality by any means, including regulatory policy, no matter how wise or efficacious. The reason, again, is simple: the underlying values of assets unfold over time in ways that no one can fully foresee. In principle, there can be no true values of assets that competition among rational participants could possibly establish.

Opening Economics to Nonroutine Change and Imperfect Knowledge

By presuming that fully predetermined accounts of market prices and risk are within reach of economic analysis, contemporary economists have abandoned the profound insights of John Maynard Keynes (1921, 1936), Frank Knight (1921), Friedrich Hayek (1948), and other early modern economic thinkers. Whatever their differences, these theorists all placed nonroutine change and imperfect knowledge at the center of their accounts of economic outcomes—and of their thinking about the rationale and scope of public policy.

To be sure, the crisis thrust to the foreground Keynes's theory concerning the key role of fiscal stimulus in averting depressions. But even though the effects of fiscal (and monetary) policies were built into the fully predetermined models used by central banks and treasuries to analyze policy options, Keynes's emphasis on the centrality of imperfect knowledge for understanding financial markets simply did not fit the contemporary conception of economic science. To be sure, many observers have cited the instability of these markets as one of the proximate causes of the crisis. But, with few notable exceptions (Soros, 2008; Phelps, 2009; Skidelsky, 2009; Kaletsky, 2010; Volcker, 2010), the nexus between imperfect knowledge and movements in asset prices and risk has not featured prominently in the formulation of proposed reforms or in the analysis of their consequences. Some have even suggested that Keynes's ideas in this regard are largely irrelevant for understanding the causes of the crisis (Stiglitz, 2010).

In jettisoning fully predetermined accounts of outcomes, Imperfect Knowledge Economics builds on and incorporates into mathematical models the early modern economists' key premise: given the inescapability of imperfect knowledge—for market partici-pants, policymakers, and economists themselves—individual behav-ior cannot be adequately captured with overarching mechanical rules. As with any scientific theory, Imperfect Knowledge Economics must presume that purposeful behavior exhibits regularities, even if they are context dependent and become or cease to be relevant at times that cannot be fully specified in advance. Nonetheless, Imperfect Knowledge Economics explores the possibility that these contingent regularities—the ways in which market participants make and alter their decisions—may be formalized with qualitative conditions.

By establishing this alternative framework for analysis, Imperfect Knowledge Economics offers economists and practitio-ners a rigorous way to account for individual behavior, and thus asset prices and risk, without presuming that anyone can fully pre-determine how the future will unfold. Because it aims for only qual-itative predictions of market outcomes, its mathematical models remain open to nonroutine change and imperfect knowledge.

IMPERFECT KNOWLEDGE ECONOMICS AND ITS IMPLICATIONS

To model individual behavior, Imperfect Knowledge Eco-nomics draws on behavioral economists' empirical findings about how individuals actually behave. However, in contrast to behavioral finance models, which formalize these findings with mechanical rules, Imperfect Knowledge Economics formalizes them as qualitative and contingent regularities. And, whereas behavioral economists have interpreted the importance of psychology in individual decisionmaking as a symptom of irrationality, an emphasis on imperfect knowledge enables an economist to incorporate psychological factors in ways that are compatible with market participants' rationality.

Indeed, given that nonroutine change and ever-imperfect knowledge are key features of real-world financial markets, self-interested, profit-seeking market participants (however extraordinary their analytical abilities) cannot afford to base their assessments of the future, and thus their trading decisions, only on calculation and fundamental considerations, let alone on overarching mechanical rules. As Keynes pointed out in his much-neglected discussion of rational decisionmaking in modern economies,

> We are merely reminding ourselves that human decisions affecting the future, whether personal or political or economic, cannot depend on strict mathematical expectation, since the basis for making such calculations does not exist; and that . . . our *rational selves* [are] choosing between alternatives as best as we are able, calculating where we can, but often falling back for our motive on whim or sentiment or chance. [Keynes, 1936, pp. 162–63, emphasis added]

In contrast to behavioral economists, who interpret individuals' reliance on psychological factors in decisionmaking as a symptom of irrationality, Keynes's description makes clear that rational individuals in the real world use knowledge of facts ("calculating where we can"), but that, because knowledge is imperfect, they must supplement their computations with auxiliary psychological considerations. Even though such considerations play a role in individual decisionmaking, Keynes (1936, p. 162) stressed that "we should *not* conclude from this that everything depends on *waves* of irrational psychology." If fundamentals pointed the other way, "waves of irrational psychology" could not by themselves sustain the long swings in asset prices that we observe.

In fact, fundamental factors underpin changes in confidence and other market sentiments, which implies that they mediate the influence of psychological factors on asset prices and risk over time. New empirical evidence that we present in this book, based on Bloomberg's daily market wrap reports, shows that in virtually no cases do psychological considerations or technical trading alone move the market. Although psychological factors matter in nonroutine ways (as Imperfect Knowledge Economics predicts), this and other, more formal, empirical evidence points unambiguously to the importance of economic fundamentals, such as company earnings and interest rates, in sustaining swings in asset prices and risk.

We develop an IKE account in which fundamental considerations play the key role in driving such swings (see Chapters 7–9). However, our account also incorporates behavioral economists' psychological findings to model how market participants might revise their thinking about the importance of movements of fundamentals for forecasting outcomes. We show that such revisions are crucial to understanding sustained reversals of an upswing or downswing (see Chapter 10).

A New Understanding of Asset-Price Swings, Risk, and the Role of the State

Recognizing that asset-price swings are driven to a large extent by trends in fundamental factors suggests that they lie at the heart of financial markets' ability to monitor the results of prior investments and select new projects and companies for financing. Thus, policies aimed at extinguishing price swings as soon as policy officials believe that they have detected them would undermine the very process by which financial markets allocate capital.

The imperfection of knowledge, however, implies that price swings can sometimes become excessive. This possibility is enhanced by what George Soros (1987) has called "reflexive" relationships, or channels through which, for a time, asset-price swings and fundamental trends reinforce each other.

As the housing- and equity-price booms of the 2000s show, markets eventually correct excessive swings on their own. However, the self-correction came too late, and neither the banking sector nor financial markets were sufficiently prepared for it. As a result, the reversal had a severe impact on the financial system and on broader economic activity, with investment spending dropping to historically low levels and unemployment rates soaring to highs not seen for a quarter-century or more.

By early 2000, market participants understood that housing and equity prices had already reached historically high levels. Yet as fundamental factors continued to trend in bullish directions, they continued to bid up prices. Their concern was with profits, and so, in their trading, they did not internalize the economic and social costs associated with such excess. This externality, then, rationalizes a role for the state in asset markets beyond setting the rules of the game. Society has an interest in instituting a policy framework that dampens excessive swings in financial markets and regulates financial institutions' risk exposure to them before they reach crisis levels. Our IKE account of swings in asset prices and risk provides a new way of addressing both these objectives.

Because standard models relate financial risk to the volatility of asset prices over a month or a quarter, they obscure its inherent connection to long swings in asset prices—to how far prices have moved in one direction or another. In contrast, our IKE model relates risk to participants' perceptions of the gap between an asset price and its range of historical benchmark levels: as asset prices rise well above or fall well below most participants' perceptions of these levels, those who are betting on further movement away from the benchmark perceive an increased

risk in doing so. We extend this insight, which can be traced to
Keynes, and formalize it as a qualitative regularity.

Our IKE account of risk in financial markets suggests that
excessive overall price swings in equity and housing markets, as
well as in the key sectors to which bank loan portfolios or trading
books are heavily exposed, provide complementary indicators of
risk both for individual banks and for the system as a whole.
Dynamically relating bank capital buffers to these indicators provides regulators with an additional tool for managing systemic
risk. However, we argue that regulation best protects banks—and
the broader economy—from the consequences of sharp reversals
in asset prices by targeting excessive asset-price swings directly.

The policy framework suggested by Imperfect Knowledge
Economics aims to weaken market participants' incentives to prolong price swings beyond levels that are consistent with their
own assessments of the longer-term prospects of projects and
companies. However, the inherent connection between asset-
price swings and the process by which financial markets allocate
capital suggests that prudential intervention in markets should
not aim to minimize their instability. Cutting off price swings early
is likely to impede innovation, thereby reducing society's dynamism and growth potential.

In our proposed scheme, so long as asset-price fluctuations remain within reasonable bounds, the state's involvement is
limited to setting the rules of the game: ensuring transparency and
adequate competition, and eliminating other market distortions
(such as those that the recent crisis exposed). But officials should
also devise guidance ranges for asset prices. In doing so, they
should not rely solely on historically based valuations, which,
because they ignore nonroutine change, are unreliable as a guide
to likely thresholds of excess during asset-price swings. Once
prices move beyond such a nonroutine guidance range, Imperfect
Knowledge Economics suggests that policy officials should cautiously and gradually implement dampening measures, as well as
requiring banks to prepare for the eventual reversal by increasing
their loan-loss provisions.

Our proposed regulatory framework recognizes that policy officials, like everyone else, must cope with ever-imperfect knowledge. Imperfect Knowledge Economics nonetheless provides a rationale for active prudential intervention, which we hope may also help restore much-needed balance to the public debate concerning what should be left to the market and what only the state and collective action can accomplish.

PART I

The Critique

Indeed, the chief point was already seen by those
remarkable anticipators of modern economics, the
Spanish schoolmen of the sixteenth century, who
emphasized that what they called the mathematical
price depended on so many particular circumstances
that it could never be known to man but was known
only to God.

—Friedrich A. Hayek,
"The Pretence of Knowledge," *Nobel Lecture*

1

The Invention of Mechanical Markets

ALTHOUGH THE raison d'être for financial markets implies that they cannot assess asset values perfectly, over the last four decades of the twentieth century, economists developed an approach to macroeconomics and finance that implied that financial markets allocate society's capital almost perfectly. To reach this conclusion, economists constructed probabilistic models that portray an imaginary world in which nonroutine change ceases to be important; indeed, it becomes irrelevant.

An economic theory of the world that starts from the premise that nothing genuinely new ever happens has a particularly simple—and thus attractive—mathematical structure: its models are made up of fully specified mechanical rules that are supposed to capture individual decisionmaking and market outcomes at all times: past, present, and future. As one of the pioneers of contemporary macroeconomics put it, "I prefer to use the term 'theory' . . . [as] something that can be put on a computer and run . . . the construction of a mechanical artificial world populated by interacting robots that economics typically studies" (Lucas, 2001, p. 21).

To portray individuals as robots and markets as machines, contemporary economists must select one overarching rule that relates asset prices and risk to a set of fundamental factors, such as corporate earnings, interest rates, and overall economic activity, in all time periods. Only then can participants' decisionmaking process "be put on a computer and run." But this portrayal grossly distorts our understanding of financial markets. After all, participants' forecasts drive the movements of prices and risk in these markets, and market participants revise their forecasting strategies at times and in ways that they themselves cannot ascertain in advance.

To be sure, with insightful selection of the causal variables and a bit of luck, a fully predetermined model might adequately describe—according to statistical or other, less stringent, criteria —the past relationship between causal variables and aggregate outcomes in a selected historical period. As time passes, however, market participants eventually revise their forecasting strategies, and the social context changes in ways that cannot be fully foreseen by anyone. The collapse of the hedge fund Long Term Capital Management in 1998, and the failure of ratings agencies to provide adequate risk assessments in the run-up to the financial crisis that began in 2007, shows that models assuming that the future follows mechanically from the past eventually become inadequate. Trading in financial markets cannot, in the end, be reduced to mere financial engineering.

Economists' Rationality or Markets?

Ignoring such considerations, contemporary macroeconomic and finance theory developed models of asset prices and risk as if asset markets, and the broader economy, could be adequately portrayed as a fully predetermined mechanical system. And, recognizing that reducing economics and finance to engineering requires some justification, contemporary economists developed a mechanistic notion of rationality that they then claimed provided plausible individual foundations for their mechanical models.

Lucas hypothesized that the predictions produced by an economist's own fully predetermined model of market outcomes adequately characterizes the forecasts of rational market participants. The normative label of rationality has fostered the belief, among economists and noneconomists alike, that this so-called

Rational Expectations Hypothesis (REH) really does capture the way reasonable people think about the future.

Of course, hypothesizing that any fully predetermined model can adequately characterize reasonable decisionmaking in markets is fundamentally bogus. Assuming away nonroutine change cannot magically eliminate its importance in real-world markets. Profit-seeking participants simply cannot afford to ignore such change and steadfastly adhere to any overarching forecasting strategy, even if economists refer to it as "rational."[1]

The Soviet experiment in central planning clearly shows that even the vast and brutal powers of the state cannot compel history to follow a fully predetermined path.[2] Change that cannot be fully foreseen, whether political, economic, institutional, or cultural, is the essence of any society's historical development.[3]

Such arguments were, however, completely ignored. Once an economist hypothesizes that his model generates an exact account of how an asset's prospects are related to available information about fundamental factors and adopts the Rational Expectations Hypothesis as the basis for "rational" trading decisions, it is only a short step to a model of the "rational market."

Such a model implies that prices reflect the "true" prospects of the underlying assets nearly perfectly. An economist merely needs to assume that the market is populated solely by this sort of rational individuals, who all have equal access to informa-

---

[1]For a rigorous demonstration of this claim, see Frydman (1982). For other early arguments that the Rational Expectations Hypothesis is fundamentally flawed, see Frydman and Phelps (1983) and Phelps (1983). For a recent discussion and analytical results, see Frydman and Goldberg (2007, 2010a). For further discussion, see Chapter 3.

[2]Frydman (1983) formalized Hayek's (1948) arguments that central planning is impossible in principle and showed that these arguments imply the fundamental flaws of Rational Expectations models of market outcomes with decentralized information, such as those in Lucas (1973).

[3]For seminal arguments, see Popper (1946, 1957). Building on Frydman (1982, 1983) and Frydman and Rapaczynski (1993, 1994), we discuss in Chapters 2 and 3 the parallels between the contemporary approach to macroeconomics and finance, REH-based rationality, and the theory and experience of central planning.

tion when making trading decisions. In the context of such a model, "competition . . . among the many [rational] intelligent participants [would result in an] efficient market at any point in time." In such a market, "the actual price of a security will be a good estimate of its . . . ['true'] value" (Fama, 1965, p. 56).

Economists and many others thought that the theory of the rational market provided the scientific underpinning for their belief that markets populated by rational individuals set asset prices correctly on average. In fact, this theory is the proverbial castle in the air: it rests on the demonstrably false premises that the future unfolds mechanically from the past, and that market participants believe this as well.

Was Milton Friedman Really Unconcerned about Assumptions?

Fully predetermined models presume that nonroutine change can be completely ignored when searching for adequate accounts of outcomes. These models offer an extreme response to the daunting challenge that such change poses for economic analysis. In contrast, relying on largely narrative analysis, Hayek, Knight, Keynes, and their contemporaries focused on the inextricable connection between nonroutine change, imperfect knowledge, and the pursuit of profit in capitalist economies.

As insightful and rich as these narrative accounts were, most contemporary economists probably felt that jettisoning them in favor of the clarity and transparent logic of mathematical models was a move in the right direction. After all, any explanation of the real world, let alone of the highly complex interdependence between individuals and the market, must necessarily abstract radically from its numerous characteristics. Even the detailed narrative accounts of Hayek, Keynes, Knight, and others left out many features of this interdependence.

But to instruct economists to embrace models that are constrained to portray capitalist economies as a world populated by interacting robots was not merely to call for more clarity and transparent logic in economic analysis. Economists were being asked to adopt an approach that went well beyond useful abstraction, because what it left out was actually the essential feature of capitalist economies.

Of course, most economists would readily agree that assuming away the importance of nonroutine change is not realistic. But they nonetheless cling to this core assumption in the belief that it transforms economics into an exact science. They also would agree that the Rational Expectations Hypothesis is not realistic, often describing it as a convenient assumption.[4] When confronted with criticism that their assumptions are unrealistic, contemporary economists brush it off by invoking the dictum put forth by Milton Friedman (1953, p. 23) in his well-known essay on economic methodology: "theory cannot be tested by the 'realism' of its assumptions."

Our criticism, however, is not that the core assumptions of the contemporary approach are unrealistic. Useful scientific models are those that abstract from features of reality. The hope is that the omitted considerations really are relatively unimportant to understanding the phenomenon. The fatal flaw of contemporary economic models is their omission of considerations that play a crucial role in driving the outcomes that they seek to explain.

In fact, at no point did Friedman suggest that economists should not be concerned about the inadequacy of their models' assumptions.[5] Indeed, at the time that he wrote his essay, examining assumptions was an important aspect of the discourse among economists. Friedman (1953, p. 23) recounted a "strong tendency that we all have to speak of the assumptions of a theory and to

[4]Even the most prominent critics of the orthodox theory of efficient markets use the Rational Expectations Hypothesis as a matter of "convenience." See, for example, Stiglitz (2010), and our discussion below.

[5]Of course, on strictly logical grounds, Friedman's focus on the predictive test of a theory does not imply that he was arguing that economists should be unconcerned about their models' assumptions.

compare assumptions of alternative theories. There is too much smoke for there to be no fire."

Consequently, Friedman devoted substantial parts of his essay to an effort aimed at reconciling a "strong tendency" among economists of his time to discuss assumptions with his main conclusion that a theory cannot be tested by the realism of its assumptions. Using a variety of arguments and examples, he reiterated the essential point: an economist's success in devising a model that is likely to predict reasonably well crucially depends on the assumptions that are selected to construct it. As Friedman (1953, p. 26) put it, "The particular assumptions termed 'crucial' are selected [at least in part] on the grounds of . . . intuitive plausibility, or capacity to suggest, if only by implication, some of the considerations that are relevant in judging or applying the model."

The need to exclude many potentially relevant considerations is particularly acute if one aims to account for outcomes with mathematical models, which ipso facto make use of a few assumptions to explain a complex phenomenon. So the bolder an abstraction that one seeks, the more important it is to scrutinize the assumptions that one selects "on the grounds [of their] intuitive plausibility."

Even more pertinent is Friedman's emphasis on the importance of understanding when the theory applies and when it does not. As he emphasizes throughout his essay, economists should scrutinize whether the assumptions they select are relevant in judging or applying the model.

Viewed from this perspective, the contemporary approach's core assumptions—that nonroutine change and imperfect knowledge on the part of market participants and economists are unimportant for understanding outcomes—strongly "suggest, if only by implication" that models based on them cannot adequately account for asset prices and risk. As we have seen, these assumptions imply that financial markets do not play an essential role in capitalist economies. Moreover, reliance on fully predetermined models and the Rational Expectations Hypothesis to specify decision-making assumes obviously irrational behavior in real-world markets (see Chapters 3 and 4). Friedman would surely consider assumptions that yield such implications unsuitable to serve as the crucial foundation of a theory that purports to account for how profit-seeking individuals make decisions and how modern financial markets set asset prices and allocate capital.[6]

Re-reading Friedman's essay makes it clear why he wanted to alert economists to the dangers of interpreting his methodological position as a lack of concern about the assumptions underpinning economic models. As a superb empirical economist, Friedman understood that basing economic models, as abstract as they must be, on bogus premises is a recipe for predictive failure.

For various reasons, contemporary economists typically do not mention the parts of Friedman's essay in which he acknowledges that careful selection and scrutiny of assumptions is the crucial aspect of building successful scientific models. Instead, they invoke a selective reading of his essay to justify their steadfast refusal to consider that the core assumptions underpinning their approach could be irreparably flawed.

It is not surprising that, as Friedman cautioned, models that place such assumptions at their core repeatedly failed what he considered the ultimate test of a good theory: its ability to provide adequate predictions. Nowhere is this failure more apparent than in asset markets. Indeed, after considering many empirical studies, Maurice Obstfeld and Kenneth Rogoff (1996, p. 625) con-

---

[6]Friedman's views on the relationship between the market and the state draw on Hayek's, and thus he held an ambivalent position on the Rational Expectations Hypothesis and its implications. Those who knew Friedman were aware that, on the one hand, he was not prepared to criticize this hypothesis. After all, it delivered the "scientific proof" that markets are perfect and that government intervention is undesirable and ineffective. On the other hand, Friedman (1961, p. 447) understood that fully predetermined models and the Rational Expectations Hypothesis were inconsistent with his argument that the state should not actively intervene because the effects of such actions are highly uncertain and "affect economic conditions after a lag that is long and variable." In an interview with John Cassidy (2010a), James Heckman, Friedman's colleague at the University of Chicago at the time of the ascendancy of the Rational Expectations Hypothesis, recounts Friedman's ambivalence.

cluded in their magisterial book on international macroeconomics that "the undeniable difficulties that international economists encounter in empirically explaining nominal exchange rate movements are an embarrassment, but one shared with virtually any other field that attempts to explain asset price data."

Interestingly, however, this sober assessment—and the hundreds of studies that underpinned it—has not shaken economists' belief in the foundational principles of contemporary macroeconomics and finance. Despite their abject predictive record (indeed, despite the global financial crisis), fully predetermined accounts of economic outcomes are still held up as the only scientific kind, and the Rational Expectations Hypothesis remains the only widely accepted method for portraying how rational individuals forecast these outcomes.[7]

THE POST-CRISIS LIFE OF INTERACTING ROBOTS

One might have thought that the crisis that began in 2007 would have precipitated widespread questioning of the core assumptions of the contemporary approach to economic analysis. On the contrary, nearly all arguments about the causes of the crisis, and about the reforms needed to guard against the recurrence of such a catastrophe, take for granted the relevance of Lucas's conception of macroeconomics as a science of interacting robots whose rationality is based on the Rational Expectations Hypothesis.

[7]In a recent interview published by the Federal Reserve Bank of Minneapolis, Sargent (2010) has argued, rather unequivocally, that even the crisis has not undermined the broad consensus among macroeconomists concerning the usefulness of REH-based fully predetermined models. Recounting his visit to Princeton's Economics Department in the spring of 2009, Sargent (2010, p. 1) reminisced: "There were interesting discussions of many aspects of the financial crisis. But the sense was surely *not* that modern macro needed to be reconstructed. On the contrary, seminar participants were in the business of using the tools of modern macro, especially *rational expectations theorizing,* to shed light on the financial crisis." See also Sims (2010).

Imperfectly Informed Robots

To be sure, insistence on fully predetermined models and the use of the Rational Expectations Hypothesis does not necessarily imply that the market sets asset prices at their supposedly true values—the key claim behind the so-called "Efficient Market Hypothesis."[8] This implication of the Rational Expectations Hypothesis applies only if one assumes that all market participants have the proper incentives to search for the relevant information and are not somehow denied access to it. To preserve "rational expectations" and yet conclude that the Efficient Market Hypothesis is false, economists exploited the key distinction between information on fundamental variables, which serves as an input to the forecasting process, and the formal and informal knowledge that participants rely on to interpret that information and arrive at their forecasts.

In a seminal contribution to the Rational Expectations approach to the analysis of markets with informational imperfections, Grossman and Stiglitz (1980) pointed out that if all participants understood the supposedly true process driving asset prices, they would not devote the necessary resources to gathering information about the prospects of underlying assets.[9] Thus, perfectly efficient markets (which, according to the Efficient Market Hypothesis, incorporate all available information into prices) are impossible.

Moreover, for various reasons, participants may not have equal access to information that is relevant to their decisionmak-

---

[8]Strictly speaking, this claim is an implication of the Efficient Market Hypothesis, which postulates that asset prices reflect all available information. See Chapter 5.

[9]The argument runs roughly as follows: if some market participants did devote the necessary resources, others, who are presumed by the Rational Expectations Hypothesis to understand the true process through which this information is incorporated into prices, could glean the payoff from costly information simply by looking at prices. This free-rider problem would create a strong disincentive to gather information in the first place.

ing. Formalizations of this idea in Rational Expectations models with so-called "asymmetric information" produce market prices that substantially deviate from the supposedly "true" values generated by their perfect-information analogs.[10] These conclusions were generally viewed as providing the scientific underpinning needed to interpret important aspects of the crisis as stemming from distorted and asymmetric information, inadequate incentives, and imperfect market competition.

This helps explain why Rational Expectations models with asymmetric information have become ascendant in the public debate about the crisis that began in 2007. After all, woeful lack of transparency, glaring informational asymmetries, and distorted incentives for key market participants played significant roles in bringing the financial system to the brink of collapse.

Undoubtedly, Rational Expectations models with asymmetric information achieved "their aim [in showing] that the standard [Rational Expectations, 'perfect information'] paradigm was no longer valid when there was even this seemingly small and obviously reasonable change in assumptions" (Stiglitz, 2010, p. 17). Such models' demonstration of the gross informational inefficiency of markets remains a profound conclusion—not because it is a statement about the real world, but because it shows that Efficient Market Hypothesis claim that markets are nearly perfect does not hold up even under the Rational Expectations Hypothesis.

Rational Expectations models with asymmetric information were widely thought to provide a scientific explanation of the severe informational problems exposed by the crisis that began in 2007. However, the claim that these models' conclusions are relevant for understanding real-world markets during the crisis is no less problematic than the Efficient Market Hypothesis claim— which rests on Rational Expectations models that assume away

---

[10]For an overview of seminal contributions to the Rational Expectations approach to the analysis of markets with asymmetric information, see Akerlof (2001), Spence (2001), and Stiglitz (2001).

informational problems—that unfettered markets allocate capital perfectly.

Regardless of their informational assumptions, Rational Expectations models assume away the importance of nonroutine change and the imperfect knowledge that it engenders. Thus, if regulation and other measures could extinguish market distortions, the trading decisions of rational participants would result in asset prices that fluctuate randomly around their "true" underlying values, the truth being defined by how the economist's particular Rational Expectations model characterizes the process driving prices. Rational Expectations models with asymmetric information share with their orthodox perfect-information analogs —and also with behavioral finance models—this illusion of stability.

Asset-Price Swings as Bubbles?

Beyond colossal market failures, the crisis that started in 2007 highlighted another flaw of the Efficient Market Hypothesis: according to orthodox "rational market" models, excessive upswings in asset prices, such as those that occurred in housing and equity markets in the run-up to the crisis, should not really occur.[11] To be sure, as price swings were gathering momentum in the run-up to the crisis, informational difficulties and other distortions in credit markets were apparent. But few would suggest that market distortions alone drive long swings in currency, equity, and other major financial markets around the world. On the contrary, in most respects, these large, organized exchanges are prototypes of the markets for which standard macroeconomic and finance theory was designed. They are characterized by a large number of buyers and sellers, few if any barriers to entry and exit, no impediments to price adjustments, and a plethora of available information

---

[11]Financial economists' attempts to reconcile the Efficient Market Hypothesis with the persistence and magnitude of the observed long swings have not been successful. See Chapter 5.

that is quickly disseminated around the world. And yet asset prices in these markets often undergo long and wide swings that revolve around historical benchmark levels.

Linking Market Psychology to Fundamentals

The inability of Rational Expectations models to account for long-swing movements of asset prices and risk has not eroded the belief that an economist's Rational Expectations model adequately portrays the mechanism driving the true value of every asset. This belief has led economists to model long price swings in financial markets as departures from their supposedly "true" REH-based values. In keeping with the contemporary approach, they portrayed these so-called "bubbles" with mechanical rules, and assumed that if psychological considerations and other irrationalities could be eliminated, the market would return to its "normal" state: rational participants' trading decisions would result in asset prices that reflect the supposedly true prospects of projects and companies.[12]

The kind of speculative fever envisioned by the bubble view of asset-price swings—with asset purchases reflecting only individuals' emotions and confidence that they can quickly unload their investments to the next fellow at a higher price—may play a role in some markets at some times.[13] For example, evidence of such behavior can be found in real estate markets in several U.S. metropolitan areas, such as Phoenix and Miami, in the first half of the 2000s. As Figure 1.1 shows, housing prices in twenty metropolitan areas in the United States rose dramatically from the late 1990s to 2006. Accounts of this episode typically emphasize non-

---

[12]In a book titled *The Myth of the Rational Market,* Justin Fox (2009) popularized the idea that the crisis had ended the myth of the rational market. But, as we noted in the introduction, contemporary market-failure and bubble models in fact perpetuate the belief that perfect markets are possible.

[13]Economists construct many types of bubble models, including those based on so-called "momentum trading." See Chapter 6.

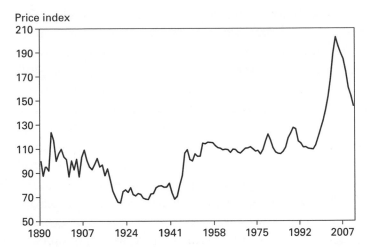

Fig. 1.1. U.S. real home price index, 1890—2009

Source: Data kindly provided by Robert Shiller.

Notes: The figure uses the Case-Shiller index, which is based on single-family home price indexes for the nine U.S. census divisions.

fundamental factors, such as emotions, get-rich-quick schemes, psychological biases (overconfidence), and house-flipping, which led individuals to bid up house prices (e.g., see Shiller, 2000; Cassidy, 2009). Indeed, the long upswing in Figure 1.1 is widely referred to as a "housing bubble."

Many nonacademic commentators have interpreted such observations as providing vivid support for the view that asset-price swings are largely unrelated to economic fundamentals. Bubble models are widely considered to provide a scientific underpinning for this view. But these models overlook the key point: fundamental factors do play an important and pronounced role in driving asset-price swings, but their influence cannot be captured with mechanical rules.[14]

[14]To be sure, some behavioral finance models allow for fundamental considerations to influence prices. See Shleifer (2000). But even though these models purport to capture psychological considerations, they do so with fully predetermined non-REH-based rules. In addition to the oddity of representing

Fundamental considerations matter in two ways: they have a direct effect on individuals' forecasting and trading decisions, and they indirectly influence and sustain market psychology. Indeed, the key role of fundamentals is implicit in much of the discussion of the upswing in real estate prices in the run-up to the crisis that started in 2007. Although this upswing is usually referred to as a "bubble" and interpreted by many in purely psychological terms, some observers have also pointed out that the easing of credit, falling mortgage rates, and rising income levels during the 1990s and 2000s had direct effects on most individuals' decisions to buy and led to a sustained growth in market demand.

Behavioral economists focus on psychological factors in their attempts to explain why their "irrational" individuals ignore fundamentals. But this focus overlooks the important role that fundamental considerations play in sustaining market participants' optimism and confidence during the upswing.[15] After all, if the trends in fundamentals had run in the opposite direction during the decade prior to 2007, the swing away from historical ranges of prices displayed in Figure 1.1 most likely would not have started, let alone lasted as long as it did.

The idea that fundamental factors can have an indirect effect on price movements through their influence on psychological factors was highlighted in a recent study of the U.S. housing market by Federal Reserve Bank of New York researcher James Kahn. He argued that the "resurgence in productivity that began in the mid-1990s contributed to a sense of optimism about future in-

---

psychology with mechanical rules, these models presume—as do all behavioral finance models—that psychology leads market participants to forgo obvious profit opportunities endlessly. See Chapters 6 and 7 for an extensive discussion of bubble models and the relative roles of fundamental and psychological factors in driving asset-price swings.

[15]Shiller (2000) and Akerlof and Shiller (2009) interpret psychological factors, particularly the notion of animal spirits, to suggest that market participants are irrational. However, in their narrative analysis of bubbles, they often discuss changes in fundamentals as triggering shifts in animal spirits.

come that likely encouraged many consumers to pay high prices for housing" (Kahn, 2009, p. 1).

To be sure, the upswing in house prices in many markets around the country in the 2000s did reach levels that history and the subsequent long downswings tell us were excessive. But, as we show in Part II, such excessive fluctuations should not be interpreted to mean that asset-price swings are unrelated to fundamental factors.

In fact, even if an individual is interested only in short-term returns—a feature of much trading in many markets—the use of data on fundamental factors to forecast these returns is extremely valuable. And the evidence that news concerning a wide array of fundamentals plays a key role in driving asset-price swings is overwhelming.[16]

Missing the Point in the Economists' Debate

Economists concluded that fundamentals do not matter for asset-price movements because they could not find one overarching relationship that could account for long swings in asset prices. The constraint that economists should consider only fully predetermined accounts of outcomes has led many to presume that some or all participants are irrational, in the sense that they ignore fundamentals altogether. Their decisions are thought to be driven purely by psychological considerations.

The belief in the scientific stature of fully predetermined models, and in the adequacy of the Rational Expectations Hypothesis to portray how rational individuals think about the future, extends well beyond asset markets. Some economists go as far as to argue that the logical consistency that obtains when this hypoth-

---

[16]See Chapters 7–9 for an extensive discussion of the role of fundamentals in driving price swings in asset markets and their interactions with psychological factors.

esis is imposed in fully predetermined models is a precondition of the ability of economic analysis to portray rationality and truth.

For example, in a well-known article published in *The New York Times Magazine* in September 2009, Paul Krugman (2009, p. 36) argued that Chicago-school free-market theorists "mistook beauty . . . for truth." One of the leading Chicago economists, John Cochrane (2009, p. 4), responded that "logical consistency and plausible foundations are indeed 'beautiful' but to me they are also basic preconditions for 'truth.'" Of course, what Cochrane meant by plausible foundations were fully predetermined Rational Expectations models. But, given the fundamental flaws of fully predetermined models, focusing on their logical consistency or inconsistency, let alone that of the Rational Expectations Hypothesis itself, can hardly be considered relevant to a discussion of the basic preconditions for truth in economic analysis, whatever "truth" might mean.

There is an irony in the debate between Krugman and Cochrane. Although the New Keynesian and behavioral models, which Krugman favors,[17] differ in terms of their specific assumptions, they are every bit as mechanical as those of the Chicago orthodoxy. Moreover, these approaches presume that the Rational Expectations Hypothesis provides the standard by which to define rationality and irrationality.[18]

---

[17] For example, in discussing the importance of the connection between the financial system and the wider economy for understanding the crisis and thinking about reform, Krugman endorses the approach taken by Bernanke and Gertler. (For an overview of these models, see Bernanke et al., 1999.) However, as pioneering as these models are in incorporating the financial sector into macroeconomics, they are fully predetermined and based on the Rational Expectations Hypothesis. As such, they suffer from the same fundamental flaws that plague other contemporary models. When used to analyze policy options, these models presume not only that the effects of contemplated policies can be fully prespecified by a policymaker, but also that nothing else genuinely new will ever happen. Supposedly, market participants respond to policy changes according to the REH-based forecasting rules. See footnote 3 in the Introduction and Chapter 2 for further discussion.

[18] The convergence in contemporary macroeconomics has become so striking that by now the leading advocates of both the "freshwater" New Classical

Behavioral economics provides a case in point. After uncovering massive evidence that the contemporary economics' standard of rationality fails to capture adequately how individuals actually make decisions, the only sensible conclusion to draw was that this standard was utterly wrong. Instead, behavioral economists, applying a variant of Brecht's dictum, concluded that individuals are irrational.[19]

To justify that conclusion, behavioral economists and nonacademic commentators argued that the standard of rationality based on the Rational Expectations Hypothesis works—but only for truly intelligent investors. Most individuals lack the abilities needed to understand the future and correctly compute the consequences of their decisions.[20]

In fact, the Rational Expectations Hypothesis requires no assumptions about the intelligence of market participants whatsoever (for further discussion, see Chapters 3 and 4). Rather than imputing superhuman cognitive and computational abilities to individuals, the hypothesis presumes just the opposite: market participants forgo using whatever cognitive abilities they do have. The Rational Expectations Hypothesis supposes that individuals do not engage actively and creatively in revising the way they think about the future. Instead, they are presumed to adhere steadfastly

approach and the "saltwater" New Keynesian approach, regardless of their other differences, extol the virtues of using the Rational Expectations Hypothesis in constructing contemporary models. See Prescott (2006) and Blanchard (2009). It is also widely believed that reliance on the Rational Expectations Hypothesis makes New Keynesian models particularly useful for policy analysis by central banks. See footnote 7 in this chapter and Sims (2010). For further discussion, see Frydman and Goldberg (2008).

[19]Following the East German government's brutal repression of a worker uprising in 1953, Bertolt Brecht famously remarked, "Wouldn't it be easier to dissolve the people and elect another in their place?"

[20]Even Simon (1971), a forceful early critic of economists' notion of rationality, regarded it as an appropriate standard of decisionmaking, though he believed that it was unattainable for most people for various cognitive and other reasons. To underscore this view, he coined the term "bounded rationality" to refer to departures from the supposedly normative benchmark.

to a single mechanical forecasting strategy at all times and in all circumstances. Thus, contrary to widespread belief, in the context of real-world markets, the Rational Expectations Hypothesis has no connection to how even minimally reasonable profit-seeking individuals forecast the future in real-world markets. When new relationships begin driving asset prices, they supposedly look the other way, and thus either abjure profit-seeking behavior altogether or forgo profit opportunities that are in plain sight.

THE DISTORTED LANGUAGE OF ECONOMIC DISCOURSE

It is often remarked that the problem with economics is its reliance on mathematical apparatus. But our criticism is not focused on economists' use of mathematics. Instead, we criticize contemporary portrayal of the market economy as a mechanical system. Its scientific pretense and the claim that its conclusions follow as a matter of straightforward logic have made informed public discussion of various policy options almost impossible. Doubters have often been made to seem as unreasonable as those who deny the theory of evolution or that the earth is round.

Indeed, public debate is further distorted by the fact that economists formalize notions like "rationality" or "rational markets" in ways that have little or no connection to how noneconomists understand these terms. When economists invoke rationality to present or legitimize their public-policy recommendations, noneconomists interpret such statements as implying reasonable behavior by real people. In fact, as we discuss extensively in this book, economists' formalization of rationality portrays obviously irrational behavior in the context of real-world markets.

Such inversions of meaning have had a profound impact on the development of economics itself. For example, having embraced the fully predetermined notion of rationality, behavioral economists proceeded to search for reasons, mostly in psychological research and brain studies, to explain why individual behavior is so grossly inconsistent with that notion—a notion that had no connection with reasonable real-world behavior in the first place. Moreover, as we shall see, the idea that economists can provide an overarching account of markets, which has given rise to fully predetermined rationality, misses what markets really do.

2

The Folly of Fully Predetermined History

In MODERN ECONOMIES, individuals and companies engage in innovative activities, discovering new ways to use existing physical and human capital, and new technologies in which to invest. The institutional and broader social context within which this entrepreneurial activity takes place also changes in novel ways. And innovation itself influences the future returns from economic activity in ways that no one can fully foresee. Thus, change in capitalist economies is to a significant extent nonroutine, for it cannot be adequately captured in advance with mechanical rules and procedures.

Because nonroutine activities are an important component of change, investment decisions in modern economies are themselves inherently nonroutine. In the vast majority of cases, the prospects of investment projects—the stream of future returns —cannot be understood in standard probabilistic terms.[1] It is impossible to know all potential outcomes, let alone the probabilities with which they might occur.

This is obviously true for investments in innovative products and processes for which estimates of returns cannot be based

---

[1]Frydman and Goldberg (2007, chapter 3) propose a way to use probabilistic descriptions in the context of mathematical models that do not assume away nonroutine change.

solely on the profit history of existing products and processes. Even if an investment decision involves a much simpler choice, such as in our example (in the Introduction) of fisherman's switch to a well-known technology, future changes in a variety of factors that cannot be fully foreseen might have a significant impact on the return. Describing the consequences of nonroutine activities with a single probabilistic rule ignores the fact that nonroutine change, by its very nature, alters the set of possible future outcomes and their associated probabilities.

Capitalist economies' key institutions—particularly private ownership of capital and the financial markets that allocate claims to it—enable them to stimulate and foster innovative activities and cope with nonroutine change. Although Karl Marx recognized that private ownership and financial markets play key roles in stimulating capitalism's inherent dynamism, he regarded them as the ultimate source of the system's egregious social and economic problems.[2] Private ownership fueled gross injustice, including exploitation and alienation of labor, while the financial system's endemic and unavoidable instability was one of the principal causes of recurrent economic crises.[3] These arguments laid the foundation for the belief that state control and allocation of society's capital were necessary to avoid crises and achieve social justice.

This economic model was forcibly implemented in the Soviet Union in 1917 and exported by Soviet "liberators" to Eastern Europe after World War II. The results fell far short of the vision: the Soviet experiment ended in 1989 with the reintroduc-

---

[2]For econometric evidence on the central importance of private ownership for economic performance in the context of post-communist transition economies, see Frydman et al. (1999).

[3]See Marx (1981). For an overview of Marxian analysis of the connection between the financial system and the broader economy, see Crotty (1986) and references therein. For influential non-Marxian arguments that financial markets misallocate capital and are prone to instability, see Keynes (1936) and Minsky (2008). We reconsider Keynes's arguments in Chapters 7 and 8 in light of the financial crisis that started in 2007.

tion of basic capitalist institutions, having produced neither well-functioning economies nor improved social justice.

The Soviet-style command economies sought to use centrally controlled allocations of capital to mimic what capitalist financial markets do. Ironically, while that experiment was heading inexorably to its demise, the vast majority of Western macro- and financial economists were embracing an approach that bears an uncanny resemblance to the planners' futile ambition.

THE FATAL CONCEIT REVISITED

The Soviet blueprint for communist societies was supposed to replace private property and markets with a comprehensive system of central planning.[4] In theory, centrally performed calculations would determine the full gamut of final and intermediate products over the planning horizon. The planners would also decide how much of society's output should be divided between consumption and investment, and how investment should be allocated to meet production targets.

In practice, five-year plans were based on a wish list and the notorious input-output tables (used to compute the material balances needed to produce planned quantities). When confronted with reality, these plans had to be adjusted every year to reflect new realities and political bargains between the party and state enterprises.[5] As one of the best-informed observers of the Soviet system noted, "In view of the changing and often ephemeral nature of the plans, . . . [t]he existence of . . . a central national plan, coherent and perfect, to be subdivided and implemented at all levels, is only a *myth*" (Zaleski, 1980, p. 484, emphasis in the original).

[4]This section draws on Frydman and Rapaczynski (1993).
[5]The input-output tables were central indicators specifying proportions of raw materials and intermediate products for any given finished good (see Hare, 1981a). For analyses of the investment process in Czechoslovakia, Hungary, and Poland during the post-World War II period and for further references, see Montias (1962), Hare (1981b), and Vajna (1982).

The Soviet system not only failed to create incentives for lower-level decisionmakers to transmit relevant local information to planners; it generated powerful incentives to distort and hide potentially useful information. Such informational distortions facilitated corruption and other activities that diverted resources from the state to private uses.

But the ultimate reason that central planning was impossible is that it supposed that a group of individuals—the planners—could predict and shape the future. To the extent that planning would require predicting future prospects of alternative investments of society's capital and their economy-wide consequences, planners could not, in principle, replicate the way financial markets in capitalist economies allocate society's savings.

Indeed, in modern capitalist economies, allocating scarce capital involves decisions by many market participants, who use a wide variety of informal and formal procedures. The way in which financial markets aggregate these decisions to allocate society's savings to alternative investment projects is fundamentally different from the attempts by a single individual to maximize her well-being:

> The economic problem of society is . . . not merely a problem of how to allocate "given" resources—if "given" is taken to mean given to a single mind which deliberately solves the [resource-allocation] problem. . . . It is rather a problem of how to secure the best use of resources known to any of the members of society, for ends whose relative importance only these individuals know. Or, to put it briefly, it is a problem of the utilization of knowledge which is *not given to anyone in its totality.* [Hayek, 1945, pp. 519–20, emphasis added]

This problem of inherently imperfect knowledge was particularly daunting to the Soviet-style command economies when it came to investment decisions, which, in the absence of financial markets, were largely controlled by the state. For example, even in Hungary, which moved very far in the direction of decentralization and socialist market reforms after 1956, the state retained crucial control over investments in new areas and the creation of new firms.

Faced with the problems that nonroutine change posed for their assessments of returns and the consequences of alternative investment projects, one solution that central planners attempted was to discourage innovation. They were discouraged even if the innovations were in principle desirable and even if they were based on relatively simple ideas. For example, finding a way to produce bus seats using less costly materials would conflict with planned investment and production targets. Procuring the new materials, increasing their production, or taking them away from other uses would create such problems that the innovation was not worth the trouble.

Even after successive waves of reform, the communist economies innovated at a very low rate, operated with largely obsolete capital stock, and produced a small assortment of shabby products. To the extent that larger scale changes were introduced, they were for the most part based on preexisting technologies imported from the capitalist countries. But even then, the socialist economies could not produce replacement parts.[6] The new technology was simply too much to handle for an economic system focused on routine processes.[7]

[6]For example, Poland imported preexisting technologies, such as cars, on a large scale in the 1970s. But when petrodollar financing dried up at the end of the decade, Poland had to produce its own replacement parts. Unable to manufacture a capitalist car even with imported technology, Poland could not repay the debt. In fact, it had to borrow more to import replacement parts. Arguably, the weight of Poland's crushing debt burden, which was rooted in its inability to innovate, accelerated the collapse of the communist system.

[7]The effects of the communist system's focus on routine processes lasted beyond its collapse in 1989. To survive in the new environment of capitalist competition, state-owned enterprises had to cut costs or innovate. For the more routine process of cutting costs, they performed as well as privatized companies. But when it came to innovation, the performance of state-owned enterprises was far inferior to those operated by new private owners. For analysis and empirical evidence, see Frydman et al. (1999, 2000, 2006).

THE PRETENSE OF EXACT KNOWLEDGE

Far from attempting to minimize nonroutine activities, capitalist economies thrive on them. Yet Western economists seemed undeterred by the failure of central planners to comprehend and shape the future as if history unfolded according to fully predetermined mechanical rules. They set out to construct mathematical models that accurately capture how financial markets assess the prospects of alternative investment projects and companies not only today but for all past and future periods as well. Such fully predetermined models and the sharp predictions they produce are the hallmark of the contemporary approach to macroeconomics and finance

Individuals as Robots, Markets as Machines

To account for market outcomes, such as asset prices, economists relate them to the decisions of individual market participants.[8] There are two main approaches to modeling individuals' decisions. Nearly all economists appeal to a set of a priori assumptions that they use to characterize how rational individuals should act across all contexts and time periods.[9]

In contrast, behavioral economists appeal to considerable evidence that they have uncovered indicating that individuals make decisions in a manner inconsistent with the conventional standard of rationality. Their research has been fundamentally important in opening economics to alternative explanations of individual decisionmaking and market outcomes. It has led to new

---

[8]This section draws on Frydman and Goldberg (2007, 2010a), who present the contemporary approach to modeling individual decisionmaking and market outcomes in the context of a simple algebraic model.

[9]For an exposition of these assumptions, see Gollier (2001) and Sargent (1987).

models in which some or all a priori assumptions have been replaced with formalizations of empirical findings.

But, as different as their explanations are, behavioral economists, especially those involved in mathematically modeling financial markets, have followed their conventional colleagues in the belief that models must generate sharp predictions to qualify as scientific.[10] Consequently, behavioral finance modelers also formalize individual decisionmaking and market outcomes with mechanical rules that they specify in advance. Whether based on the conventional standard of rationality or on behavioral considerations, the contemporary approach to macroeconomic and financial modeling is thus much like engineering the movements of "interacting robots."

But if individuals really did behave like robots, the task of predicting future market outcomes would be relatively easy. It would involve mere routine calculation based on the mechanical rules governing decisions. In such a world, institutions and economic policy would unfold in entirely foreseeable ways. New information about variables deemed relevant for forecasting would not really be news. Economists would know all possible values that news could take on for each point in the future, as well as the correct probability of each value occurring. They would also know when and how their robots might revise their forecasting strategies. As a result, economists could calculate every possible future price and its associated probability. These imagined probabilities, conditional on current information, constitute their supposedly sharp predictions of market outcomes.

THE ECONOMIST AS ENGINEER

Following a research program that views capitalist economies as "a mechanical artificial world populated by interacting ro-

---

[10]See Rabin (2002) and Barberis and Thaler (2003). We return to this point in Chapter 6.

bots" (Lucas, 2001, p. 21), a contemporary economist looks for ways to represent every component of his model of a financial market with mechanical rules. By sketching how he does it, we can see why this approach is always likely to be as futile for seeking adequate explanations of price movements as central planning was in trying to do away with the market altogether.

In modeling an individual's decisionmaking, an economist makes assumptions about which factors influence her well-being. For example, individuals are often thought to care about the expected return on buying, say, a specific combination of stocks, and about the risk that the actual return might differ from her expectation. Diverse combinations lead to different expectations of return and risk. In characterizing an individual's preferences for alternative portfolios, economists usually assume that her well-being (or utility) increases with expected return and decreases with risk. They also attribute to her a decision rule that picks the best portfolio that is within her means to buy.

But to determine which portfolio this might be, the economist must characterize how an individual forecasts the future return and risk on alternative portfolios. So he attributes a forecasting strategy to the individual that relates future returns and risk to a set of causal variables, for example, current and past corporate earnings and inflation rates.

In real-world markets, however, individuals' preferences concerning expected return and risk differ; for example, some investors are less tolerant of risk than others. Moreover, individuals form their forecasts on the basis of different strategies, which reflect their diverse understandings about the process driving asset prices.

Economists sometimes recognize the importance of this diversity by attributing different preferences, decision rules, and forecasting strategies to different groups of market participants. To determine the price of an asset at some point in time, the economist tallies individuals' buy and sell decisions in his model and assumes that the equilibrium price—the value at which total demand equals total supply—is quickly reached. Because these buy and sell decisions depend on causal variables, the model implies a relationship between these variables and the price. In this way, economists' models provide an account of the causal process underpinning asset prices.

The problem for these models is that, over time, individuals alter the way that they make decisions. It may be reasonable to assume that preferences and decision rules are fairly stable for extended periods. But it is simply far-fetched to assume that participants in asset markets never change their forecasting strategies.

There are many reasons why market participants not only revise their strategies, but also often do so in ways that they themselves, let alone economists, could not adequately capture in advance with mechanical rules. Economic policies, technology, and other aspects of the social context change in novel ways and alter how the causal variables unfold over time, influencing how individuals predict future returns and risk. And even in the absence of novel changes in the social context, the very process by which financial markets allocate society's capital makes forecasting their outcomes an essentially nonroutine activity.

Financial markets translate participants' decisions to buy and sell assets into changes in prices. This process leads to alternative allocations of capital, which change the prospects of the underlying projects and companies. In attempting to forecast these ever-changing prospects, financial market participants search for new ways to use the same causal variables, or for potentially more relevant variables on which to base their strategies. If, for example, many market players (or large ones) decided that federal budget deficits in the United States were to become important for forecasting, the set of causal variables itself could change.

Such changes in the causal process driving asset prices can never be fully foreseen. Even if an economist were to attempt to portray the future in probabilistic terms, changes in the economy in general would alter the set of prices and probabilities that might be relevant in characterizing outcomes at each future date. Thus, to generate their supposedly sharp predictions—a single set of prices and probabilities for each future date—contemporary macroeconomic models must fully prespecify all possible changes in the economy.

Remarkably, nearly all economists construct models that allow for absolutely no change in the process generating economic outcomes. These models portray individuals not just as robots, but as robots that obey only one set of prespecified rules that apply at every point in time. They also presume that the tendency of policy variables, such as interest rates and money supply, to take on particular values never changes. As such news becomes available, market participants supposedly update their forecasts of future returns in exactly the same way at every point in time. Likewise, their preferences and decision rules are assumed to remain forever constant. Markets function like machines; the routine appearance of news causes prices to adjust mechanically, in ways that can be specified in advance.

Sometimes contemporary economists do recognize that the social context or individual decisionmaking changes. But they still insist on building models that generate sharp predictions, thereby assuming that economists can do what market participants themselves cannot: specify in advance exactly how the social context will change and how individuals will alter their understanding of markets and their forecasting behaviors.[11] These models, too, can be put on a computer and run, because they view individuals as robots and markets as machines.

Staying the Course in the Face of Reason

It would take us too far afield to compare the "voluntary" social process through which Western economists attained and maintained faith in their core assumptions with the coercive orga-

---

[11]Sometimes economists model this change as probabilistic. When they do, they assume one set of potential changes and attach one set of probabilities to these possible changes. For further remarks and references on this point, see Chapter 3, footnote 1.

nization of the society according to the overarching idea that the
state could ignore imperfect knowledge and repress nonroutine
change. Nevertheless, one point in particular merits notice: although there are undoubtedly many fundamental differences between these belief systems, they both entail steadfast refusal to
reconsider one's conception of economic and social development
in the face of its obvious epistemological flaws and empirical failures. In this respect, contemporary economists' research bears a
striking resemblance to the attempts by Soviet and Eastern European rulers to reform their failing economies while preserving the
system's irreparably flawed foundations.[12]

Redefining Empirical Success

Nothing illustrates contemporary economists' refusal to
reconsider the relevance of fully predetermined models more vividly than their continued reliance on the Rational Expectations
Hypothesis as the way to model rational forecasting in the face of
its repeated empirical failures. Even prior to the crisis that began
in 2007, the sharp predictions of Rational Expectations models
have time and again turned out to be grossly inconsistent with
actual movements of asset prices and risk. Frydman and Goldberg (2007, chapters 7 and 8) provide an overview of dozens of
studies—many carried out by REH economists—that document
empirical failures in the currency markets alone. Studies of other
markets, such as those for equities, have also uncovered gross empirical failures.[13]

---

[12]Our arguments in this section build on Popper (1946, 1992), who analyzed similarities between the dangers posed by limits on critical discourse in
science and the disastrous effects of attempts to impose on society overarching
ideological projects, such as the Soviet system and central planning.

[13]In a pathbreaking paper, Shiller (1981) showed that conventional models of stock prices are grossly inconsistent with their actual movement. Mehra
and Prescott (1985) provided a seminal analysis of the failure of conventional
models to account for equity risk premiums.

Faced with the failure of Rational Expectations models, economists have typically responded in two ways. Nearly all have engaged in an intensive search for fully predetermined models that, while maintaining the Rational Expectations Hypothesis to capture market participants' forecasting behavior, rely on modifications of assumptions about preferences, economic policy, and other aspects of the social context to remedy empirical failures.

An important part of this effort to save the Rational Expectations Hypothesis has involved redefinition of the notion of empirical failure itself. Before the ascendancy of the conventional approach, economists, like all scientists, relied primarily on standard methods of statistical inference to confront their models with empirical data. In contrast, promoters of Rational Expectations have decided that these methods are too stringent for judging the adequacy of their models. As Thomas J. Sargent, one of the leading proponents of the Rational Expectations Hypothesis, recounted, "after about five years of doing [standard statistical tests] on rational expectations models, I recall Bob Lucas and Ed Prescott both telling me that those tests were rejecting *too many good models*" (Evans and Honkapohja, 2005, p. 568, emphasis added).

Not wanting to reject "too many good" Rational Expectations models, conventional economists jettisoned standard statistical tests and developed an alternative methodology that abandoned attempts to explain the actual time paths of economic outcomes.[14] As intended, lowering the standards for what constitutes an adequate model has obscured many of the inconsistencies between Rational Expectations models and the empirical data, inevitably increasing the number of such models that are supposedly adequate (for further discussion, see Frydman and Goldberg, 2007, chapter 2).

---

[14]This alternative methodology has been called "calibration," a term that suggests fine-tuning a machine rather than testing economic models. For an overview and trenchant critique, see Kydland and Prescott (1996) and Sims (1996), respectively.

Misinterpreting Empirical Failure

Behavioral economists, for their part, offered a more radical response to the failure of conventional models. They pointed out that conventional formalization of preferences and forecasting strategies lacks psychological realism: individuals act in ways that are grossly inconsistent with these models' assumptions.

Many economists have found behavioral insights persuasive, and the relatively quick success of behavioral economists in eroding the near monopoly of the conventional approach is remarkable. After all, the behavioral critique has focused on the realism of the assumptions underpinning conventional models, an aspect of model building to which macroeconomists and finance theorists have traditionally paid very little attention.

Arguably, however, the most important aspect of the behavioral approach—and one that may explain the relatively muted resistance to it by many economists—is that its theorists have emphasized that their mathematical models preserve the core assumptions of the contemporary approach (Camerer et al., 2004, p. 3). Thus, behavioral finance economists formalize empirical findings about how individuals behave with mechanical rules, and they continue to subscribe to the belief that the Rational Expectations Hypothesis provides an adequate model of rational forecasting behavior.[15]

To be sure, not all behavioral economists have embraced fully predetermined models. Indeed, some of the leaders of behavioral finance and macroeconomics continue to rely on a largely narrative mode of analysis, enabling richer descriptions of fluctuations and risk in asset markets than fully predetermined models of

---

[15] As with conventional models, the potential empirical difficulties of fully predetermined accounts of irrational decisionmaking have been obscured by the abandonment of standard statistical methods when testing behavioral finance models. For a survey of behavioral finance models, see Shleifer (2000) and Barberis and Thaler (2003).

rational or irrational behavior can deliver.[16] But they, too, read irrationality into their findings: individuals in real-world settings act
in ways that are inconsistent with the conventional standard of
rationality.

There is, of course, an alternative interpretation of the failure of the conventional standard of rationality to explain economic outcomes: purposeful decisionmaking in capitalist economies
cannot be adequately portrayed with an economist's fully prespecified mechanical rules. The history of the Soviet-bloc economies
did not unfold mechanically from the past. And their very collapse, although foretold by thinkers like Friedrich Hayek, was
largely unexpected. The same fundamental unpredictability is cer-
tainly true of history in modern capitalist economies.

The belief that this basic fact can be safely ignored is not
only unscientific, it is also likely to continue to derail economists'
efforts to understand real-world markets and provide useful guidance for policymaking and public debate. The attempts by contemporary economists to justify the foundations of their fully predetermined models by arguing that they adequately capture how
rational individuals think about the future and make decisions
turns on its head the very notion of what most people would consider even minimally reasonable behavior in the real world.

[16]Shiller's (2000) book on irrational exuberance in stock prices has become a classic work of this kind. For a recent narrative account of behavioral
macroeconomics, see Akerlof and Shiller (2009).

3

The Orwellian World of
"Rational Expectations"

THE SEARCH FOR fully predetermined accounts of individual decisionmaking and market outcomes actually predates economists' embrace of the Rational Expectations Hypothesis as the way to characterize rational forecasting behavior. Prior to this hypothesis, economists portrayed market participants' forecasting strategies with mechanical rules that made no explicit reference to how they reason about the way the economy works or how the causal process underpinning outcomes might change over time. John Muth proposed the Rational Expectations Hypothesis as a way to incorporate such considerations into models of forecasting. Criticizing pre-REH forecasting rules, he argued that

> the character of dynamic processes is typically very sensitive to the way expectations are influenced by the actual course of events. Furthermore, it is often necessary to make sensible predictions about the way expectations would change when either the amount of available information or the structure of the system is changed. [Muth, 1961, pp. 315–16]

Muth's idea was that by relating participants' forecasting strategies to an economic model that purportedly captured the structure of the economy, economists would be able to make such sensible predictions over time. Consequently, he formulated the

Rational Expectations Hypothesis as a hypothesis that market participants' forecasts "are essentially the same as the predictions of the relevant economic theory" (Muth, 1961, p. 316).

Muth was well aware that the term "rational expectations" suggests some notion of rationality. Indeed, he explicitly recognized the possibility that the name he picked for his hypothesis would create confusion He warned that the Rational Expectations Hypothesis should not be viewed as a normative hypothesis about how rational individuals should forecast the future. As he put it, "At the risk of confusing this *purely descriptive* hypothesis with a pronouncement as to what firms *ought to do,* we call such expectations 'rational'" (Muth, 1961, p. 316, emphasis added).

Even viewed as a purely descriptive hypothesis, it is far from clear how the Rational Expectations Hypothesis should be used to describe forecasting strategies. To implement it, economists had to take a stand on the question of the relevant economic theory to which the hypothesis refers.

Muth did not discuss the difficulties inherent in selecting the relevant theory that should be used in implementing the Rational Expectations Hypothesis. In a fateful decision that triggered the Rational Expectations Revolution in macroeconomics and finance roughly a decade later, he embedded the hypothesis in a simple model of the agricultural market with a production lag. The model portrayed the price of produce at each point in time, t, as being dependent on farmers' expectations formed at some earlier time, $t - 1$, when they had to decide what crop size to aim for. The implementation of the Rational Expectations Hypothesis in this model is particularly straightforward: farmers' expectations regarding the market price at t are set equal to the prediction of that price, implied by an economist's model, at $t - 1$.

By using his own model as the relevant economic theory, Muth in effect ignored many other potentially relevant theories on offer. Indeed, not only do market participants have diverse views, but economists themselves are notorious for their disagreements about what underpins outcomes, particularly in financial markets and the macroeconomy. Thus, even if the relevant theory is a model based on economic theory, which is how economists have interpreted the Rational Expectations Hypothesis, each of their many extant models, as well as any combination of them, is in principle available to individuals forming their forecasts about the future. Moreover, as time passes, profit-seeking individuals and career-minded economists discover inadequacies in old models and attempt to formulate new ones, thereby expanding or contracting the set of relevant theories that market participants might use when forecasting the future.

Muth's idea that market participants pay attention to changes in the structure of the economy when forming their forecasts is compelling. However, the hypothesis that the relevant theory that captures how they use this information to think about the future is one particular economist's model is farfetched. Nevertheless, economists have used the Rational Expectations Hypothesis in exactly the way that Muth did: when an economist devises a model that relates market outcomes to participants' forecasts of these outcomes, he implements the hypothesis by equating these forecasts with the predictions generated by his own model.

In viewing the Rational Expectations Hypothesis as a description of how market participants forecast, disregarding the plurality of extant economic models and forecasting strategies is not the only serious shortcoming. An even more fundamental problem is that for contemporary economists, the relevant theory is a fully predetermined model. Indeed, the agricultural market model that Muth used to introduce the Rational Expectations Hypothesis is fully predetermined. Thus, like the pre-REH forecasting rules, the hypothesis excludes, by design, the possibility that individuals revise their forecasting strategies in nonroutine ways. Because a fully predetermined model implies an overarching forecasting strategy, the Rational Expectations Hypothesis amounts to assuming that one strategy specified in advance adequately characterizes how market participants will think about the future at every point in time.[1]

By following the contemporary practice of modeling outcomes with fully predetermined models, Muth subverted his own insight. His idea that changes in the structure of the economy would generally alter market forecasting strategies merely morphed into another mechanical rule that presumed that participants never revise their forecasting strategies in ways that they, or an economist's Rational Expectations model, has not foreseen.[2]

Early criticism of the Rational Expectations Hypothesis focused on its epistemological flaws as a model of rational forecasting. In doing so, the critics also pointed out its behavioral implausibility as the purely descriptive hypothesis that Muth envisaged. The crux of the matter was shown in Frydman (1982): there is an inherent conflict between its presumption that people's beliefs can be adequately represented as one outcome of an economist's theorizing and the premise that market participants are motivated by self-interest. Simply put, profit-seeking individuals would not, in general, adhere to a single forecasting strategy.

Thomas Sargent, one of the most forceful early advocates of the Rational Expectations Hypothesis, acknowledged these critical arguments and recognized that treating the hypothesis as a (plausible) description of how market participants forecast the future is misleading:

---

[1]Economists model this strategy with a single probability distribution. Frydman and Goldberg (2007, chapter 6) show rigorously that even if an economist allows for changes in forecasting strategies, as Hamilton (1988) does, he fully prespecifies such revisions, and thus in effect portrays forecasting with a single overarching strategy—a single probability distribution—that characterizes forecasting for all times: past, present, and future.

[2]For an alternative way to formalize the idea that economists' models might be useful in modeling market forecasting, see the Theories–Consistent Expectations Hypothesis in Frydman and Phelps (1990). Frydman and Goldberg (2007, chapters 10 and 15) show how this hypothesis can be used to examine empirically the movements of exchange rates using models that place imperfect knowledge at the center of the analysis.

The idea of rational expectations is sometimes explained informally by saying that it reflects a process in which individuals are inspecting and altering their forecasting records.... It is also sometimes said that [the Rational Expectations Hypothesis embodies] the idea that economists and the agents they are modeling should be placed on equal footing: the agents in the model should be able to forecast and profit-maximize and utility-maximize as well as ... the econometrician who constructed the model.

[T]hese ways of explaining things are *suggestive, but misleading,* because they make [the Rational Expectations Hypothesis] sound less restrictive and more behavioral than it really is. [Sargent, 1993, p. 21, emphasis added]

The implausibility of the Rational Expectations Hypothesis as a descriptive hypothesis undermines Muth's hope that it would enable economists to make sensible predictions about the way expectations change in response to changes in policy or any other change in their context.[3] However, somewhat paradoxically, the implausibility of this hypothesis as a description of forecasting in real-world markets is entirely consistent with his warning that it should not be viewed as a hypothesis about what firms ought to do.

Muth's Warning Ignored

Lacking a normative or other justification for using the Rational Expectations Hypothesis to represent individual forecasting, macroeconomists working in the 1960s largely ignored it in model-

---

[3]Central banks around the world, spurred by widespread acceptance of Lucas's (1976) arguments that Rational Expectations models, unlike the traditional pre-REH Keynesian econometric models, offer the means to examine the effects of changes in economic policy on market forecasting strategies, adopted the idea that Rational Expectations models provide an adequate description of forecasting behavior. See Frydman and Goldberg (2008) for a discussion of this milestone in macroeconomic policy analysis.

ing forecasting behavior. Indeed, when Edmund Phelps organized a milestone conference in 1969 on the role of expectations in modeling the microfoundations of macroeconomic theories, the papers collected in the conference volume (Phelps et al., 1970) made no use of the hypothesis, and it is not even listed in the index.

Lucas set out to justify the use of the Rational Expectations Hypothesis as *the* way to portray rational forecasting.[4] His justification was based on the core belief that underpins the contemporary approach to macroeconomic theory and finance: fully predetermined models can provide adequate accounts of market outcomes.

Lucas observed that when an economist formulates a theoretical account of market prices, he, like every scientist, hypothesizes that his account adequately portrays how these outcomes unfold over time. Were an economist to impute to a representative agent forecasts that differed from the predictions of his own fully predetermined model, he would in effect be assuming that the agent is obviously irrational: she steadfastly adheres to a forecasting rule that generates forecasts that systematically differ from the model's hypothesized market prices.

Because Lucas took for granted the premise that a fully predetermined model could provide an adequate account of how actual prices evolve over time, he presumed that the ostensibly easily detectable forecast errors implied by such a model with a non-REH portrayal of forecasting pointed to obvious, yet unrealized, profit opportunities in real world markets. As he later emphatically put it, "if your theory reveals profit opportunities, you have the wrong theory" (Lucas, 2001, p. 13) of "actual prices."

In a leap of faith that would change macroeconomics and finance for generations, Lucas brushed aside Muth's warning[5] and

[4]Lucas (1995, 2001) provides a fascinating account of the way he arrived at this justification and its importance for subsequent developments in macroeconomics and policymaking.

[5]For an extensive discussion and a formal exposition of the reasons behind Lucas's normative interpretation of the Rational Expectations Hypothesis

presumed that the "right theory" is a fully predetermined model in which the Rational Expectations Hypothesis is used to characterize how individuals forecast future market outcomes. Lucas's odd claim gained wide acceptance among macroeconomists and finance theorists. The hypothesis was embraced by economists, spanning the Chicago free-market and the Massachusetts Institute of Technology (MIT) New Keynesian schools. Remarkably, the vast majority of economists came to believe that the Rational Expectations Hypothesis could finally turn macroeconomics and finance into an exact science.

THE RATIONAL EXPECTATIONS REVOLUTION: MODEL CONSISTENCY AS A STANDARD OF RATIONALITY

The imposition by the Rational Expectations Hypothesis of exact consistency between the predictions of market outcomes implied by an economist's own fully predetermined model and individuals' forecasting strategies quickly became the standard way to represent how rational individuals think about the future.

Because it could be applied in every fully predetermined model, the REH-based standard had much to recommend it to economists who believe that fully predetermined accounts of market outcomes are within reach of economic analysis. Faith in the divine apotheosis of economic theory led economists to hypothesize that every time one of them formulates his fully predetermined model, he has discovered such an account of market outcomes. Once an economist entertained such a fanciful hypothesis, it seemed reasonable to presume that profit-seeking would compel market participants to search for such a model, which they should do be able to discover, because, after all, an economist already had.

---

and the striking difference between his position and Muth's (1961, p. 316) warning that it should not be confused with "a pronouncement as to what firms ought to do," see Frydman and Goldberg (2010a).

THE SPURIOUS NARRATIVE OF
RATIONAL EXPECTATIONS

Seeking to justify the Rational Expectations Hypothesis as a characterization of how profit-seeking market participants forecast the future, economists have assumed the existence of a fanciful World of Rational Expectations. In this world, a rational individual is supposed to believe at each point in time that she has found a true account of how market outcomes unfold into the indefinite future.

But nonroutine change and imperfect knowledge are not the only problems plaguing attempts to justify the Rational Expectations Hypothesis as a standard of rational forecasting. In contexts like financial markets, there is a two-way interdependence between how outcomes unfold over time and how market participants in the aggregate forecast. Consequently, it makes sense for rational individuals to incorporate into their forecasting strategies their views about how others are forecasting.

Additional assumptions that underpin a World of Rational Expectations, however, ensure that a rational individual does not need to worry about the forecasts of other participants. She is assumed to believe that all other rational individuals populating a World of Rational Expectations have discovered the same true process driving market outcomes over time.[6] And, because an economist imputes his Rational Expectations model to every rational individual, he presumes that his model adequately captures the truth that they all have discovered. In a glaring example of how far research may be led astray by a logic based on fanciful assumptions, a World of Rational Expectations is constructed on the prem-

---

[6]Economists sometimes construct Rational Expectations models that do not make this so-called "common knowledge" assumption. However, dropping this assumption leaves unexplained why, even in the context of a fanciful World of Rational Expectations, an economist's model characterizes how profit-seeking individuals forecast the future.

ise that if other participants are rational, their forecasting strategy will be identical to one's own.

In a World of Rational Expectations, the standard of rational forecasting purportedly provided by the Rational Expectations Hypothesis turns the very notion of rationality on its head. What economists imagine to be rational forecasting in this world would be considered blatantly irrational by anyone in the real world who is minimally rational. After all, a rational, profit-seeking individual understands that the world around her will change in nonroutine ways. She simply cannot afford to believe that, contrary to her experience, she has found a true overarching forecasting strategy, let alone that others have found it as well. Instead, she will look for new ways to forecast, which cannot be fully foreseen.

A WORLD OF STASIS AND THOUGHT UNIFORMITY

What would a place look like in which economists, policy-makers, or social planners (let alone profit-seeking market participants) could safely ignore nonroutine changes, imperfect knowledge, and diversity of views?[7] Consider equity markets. Like all other asset prices, equity prices in the real world depend on the market's forecast, which is based on market participants' forecasting strategies and the causal variables—such as interest rates, inflation rates, and gross domestic product growth rates—that they believe are relevant. Moreover, some or all causal variables may impact prices directly, that is, independently of how they influence individuals' forecasts.

Most economists who rely on the Rational Expectations Hypothesis presume that both the impact of the market's forecast

---

[7]This section and the following one build on arguments in Frydman (1982, 1983).

on prices and the direct effects of casual variables undergo absolutely no change.[8] They also suppose that the social context, including technology, managerial practices, institutions, and economic policies, remains static. In this world, the processes governing the causal variables are constant over time, and news about them unfolds in a strictly routine way.

But even with the underlying structure of the market and economy irrevocably fixed, the process relating equity prices to a set of causal variables would, in general, still undergo change. Every time a significant number of participants altered their forecasting strategies, the causal process underpinning price movements would change. So to rule out nonroutine change, one would have to construct a world in which not only the social context is irrevocably fixed, but also profit-seeking participants adhere to one forecasting strategy endlessly.

A self-interested, rational individual would remain faithful to one forecasting strategy only if she believed that a better strategy was forever beyond her reach. A rational individual could believe this if she were persuaded that she had discovered a model that accurately captured the true unchanging structure of the economy. But, even believing that, she might not stick to one strategy, because what matters for prices is not the forecast of any particular individual, but the market's forecast.

To square this circle, every market participant in a World of Rational Expectations must not only believe that she knows the true underlying structure of the economy; she must also know that everyone else has this knowledge.[9] Moreover, each participant must believe that everyone else bases their forecast-

---

[8]Some Rational Expectations theorists contemplate a world in which such change does occur but is strictly mechanical. For this reason, the main thrust of our argument would not be affected by considering this slightly more complicated setup.

[9]On strictly logical grounds, it would be sufficient to attribute to an individual in a World of Rational Expectations the belief that only the average, rather than each, of the other participants' forecasting strategies is consistent with the supposedly true process driving outcomes. However, as we show in Chapter 4, this seemingly weaker assumption requires an economist to impose much stronger

ing strategy on this knowledge. Only if an individual believes that she lives in a world populated by others who think exactly as she does about the process driving market prices and risk—and who forecast these outcomes according to that knowledge—would it be rational for her to use a fixed forecasting strategy based on her knowledge.[10]

The Rational Expectations Hypothesis thus leads economists to imagine a world of perfect knowledge and universal thought uniformity. In a World of Rational Expectations, individuals are able to predict perfectly the future prospects of all companies and investment projects, except for random forecasting errors that cancel each other out over time. And, because all rational individuals base their forecasts of prices and risk on these predictions and think alike, the market's forecast is also omniscient. Moreover, in a World of Rational Expectations, the market itself is nearly perfect: it sets prices equal to the true discounted values of the prospects of underlying assets, save for random errors that average to zero.[11]

Imagining a world of thought uniformity and omniscience transports the economist quite far from the real world. But it still does not tell him how a rational individual would forecast. He must cross yet another ocean of epistemic turbulence before he reaches the untroubled shores of a World of Rational Expectations. He must disregard economists' lack of consensus

---

restrictions in defining a World of Rational Expectations: rigid, fully predetermined connections between the forecasts of the other participants.

[10]Despite their empirical findings, some seminal behavioral models continue to use the Rational Expectations Hypothesis in modeling forecasting behavior (DeLong et al., 1990a, 1990b). In these models, there is a subset of market participants who are uninformed and base their forecasts on erroneous considerations. The "smart" or rational individuals are assumed to have a full understanding of how the uninformed participants forecast. As we discuss in Chapter 6, this mixing of rational and irrational participants is even more incoherent than a World of Rational Expectations.

[11]In a World of Rational Expectations, participants may fall prey to self-fulfilling price movements away from what they know are true fundamental values. We return to this possibility in Chapter 6.

concerning the relative validity of their existing theories and presume that his own Rational Expectations model, which he hypothesizes to be true, is in fact the model that everyone else believes to be true. Like the rational individuals in his imagined world, the economist believes that he, too, has "solved [his] 'scientific problem'" (Sargent, 1993, p. 23): he has found the model that sharply predicts all possible future contingencies and their associated probabilities. The economist presumes that his model correctly predicts true fundamental values, as well as prices and risk at each future date.

This approach to modeling individual forecasting behavior assumes what any market participant would consider as simply unreasonable in the real world. No one in her right mind would think that she has discovered the true causal process behind market and economic outcomes, and that everyone thinks exactly as she does.[12] If thought uniformity and omniscience prevailed, there would be no need for markets to set prices and assess the prospects of companies and projects. All economists and each rational market participant would be capable of accomplishing this feat entirely on their own.

Economists' Rationality and Socialist Planning

Economists believed that their presumption of thought uniformity in a World of Rational Expectations enabled them to model market outcomes that result from the decisions of many individuals by studying the decisions of one representative citi-

---

[12]Even in a static world, there are potentially many causal variables that might be relevant for explaining outcomes. But convergence of market participants' learning to one "true" set of such variables requires even stronger assumptions about thought uniformity than those that define a World of Rational Expectations. See Frydman (1982), Frydman and Phelps (1983), Phelps (1983), and Frydman and Goldberg (2010a).

zen. And, having confused this world with the real world, it was only a short step for economists to think that their fictitious citizen's objectives—self-interest or maximization of well-being—could be imputed to the market and society as a whole. Banishing nonroutine change from his model, an economist could simply prespecify all change and impute to society his own fixed understanding of the future. All he had to do was to solve the maximization problem of the representative individual, whose preferences and Rational Expectations forecasting strategy would become those of everyone.

Like a socialist planner, an economist thus believes that he can accomplish great feats, because he supposes that he has finally uncovered the fully predetermined mechanism that drives market outcomes and that his model adequately captures how market participants think about the future. He generally believes that his theory enables him to ascertain whether state intervention is warranted to, say, correct market failures or deal with swings in asset prices. He also uses his theory to prescribe how government should conduct macroeconomic policies and to study the consequences of those policies on society's welfare.

The problem that haunts the Rational Expectations Hypothesis is the same one that doomed socialist planning: no fully predetermined mechanism that drives market outcomes can, in principle, be uncovered. Basing the explanation of market outcomes on the decisionmaking of one individual who forecasts according to an economist's Rational Expectations model ignores the division of knowledge, which, as Hayek (1945) pointed out, is what distinguishes resource allocation by decentralized markets from a so-called "optimal" deployment of resources by a single individual.[13] Indeed, Lucas's (1995, 2001) account of how the Rational Expecta-

---

[13]This section builds on Frydman (1983), who shows that they apply directly to a large class of Rational Expectations models with decentralized information developed by Lucas (1973), which are fundamentally flawed for some of the same reasons that Hayek used to show that socialist planning is impossible in principle.

tions Hypothesis led him to embrace the representative-agent construct stands in stark contrast to Hayek's position.

In discussing market outcomes for a competitive industry, Lucas (2001, p. 13) argues that "one can show that an industry over time will operate so as to maximize a discounted, consumer surplus integral—a problem that is mathematically no harder than the present value maximizing problem faced by a single firm." He then asks, "[W]ho, exactly, is solving this planning problem?" As Hayek did, he recognizes that the answer is "Adam Smith's 'invisible hand', of course, *not any actual person*" (Lucas, 2001, p. 13, emphasis added). Nevertheless, in a striking leap of faith, Lucas claims that an economist—that is, an actual person—can adequately represent what the invisible hand of the market does by solving the value-maximizing problem faced by a single firm.

For Hayek (1945, p. 520), the division of "knowledge which is not given to anyone in its totality" was the key to his argument that central planners could not, in principle, substitute for markets. In contrast, Lucas believes that because Rational Expectations models rule out nonroutine change and the division of knowledge, they enable an economist to make use of single-agent optimization techniques, and thus are the right tools to comprehend market outcomes: "[T]he mathematics of planning problems turned out to be just the *right equipment* needed to understand the decentralized interactions of a large number of producers" (Lucas, 2001, p. 14, emphasis added).

In effect, Lucas posits that Smith's invisible hand could be made visible and intelligible, after all. To understand markets, economists need only learn how to solve optimal allocation problems that a fictitious central planner confronts, but which actual planners could never solve. Indeed, graduate students in economics are instructed to devote most of their time to solving just such problems.

Lucas, of course, is not the first economist to ignore Hayek's arguments that thinking of society's resource-allocation problem as maximization by a single individual—an economist, a planner, or a policy official—is not "the right equipment" to analyze market outcomes. Oskar Lange considered markets to be ill equipped to solve the resource-allocation problem and thus advocated socialist planning (ultimately leaving the University of Chicago to become a senior official in Poland's Communist government). Having focused on the insufficiency of market prices for longer-term decisions, Lange argued, in ways reminiscent of Rational Expectations theorists, that planners' mathematical modeling and computers could do a better job than markets in allocating capital to longer-term projects:

> After setting up an objective function . . . and certain constraints, future . . . prices can be calculated. These . . . prices serve as an instrument of economic accounting in long-term development plans. Actual market equilibrium prices do not suffice here, knowledge of preprogrammed future . . . prices is needed. . . . Mathematical programming turns out to be an essential instrument of *optimal* economic planning. Here the electronic computer does not replace the market. It fulfills a function which the market *never was able* to perform. [Lange, 1967, p. 161, emphasis in the original]

As we have seen, Rational Expectations models similarly presume that markets do not play an essential role in allocating society's resources. Thus, it stands to reason that Lange thought that planners could use what later became the single-individual mathematics of Rational Expectations models of markets to abolish markets and fully predetermine the future.

4

The Figment of the "Rational Market"

IN PROPOSING the Rational Expectations Hypothesis, Muth did not think of it as a normative hypothesis that individuals were omniscient or that they all thought alike. He also did not claim that the hypothesis presumes that every market participant must forecast according to the relevant economic theory: the Rational Expectations Hypothesis "does not assert that the scratch work of entrepreneurs resembles the system of equations [in an economist's model] in any way" (Muth, 1961, p. 317). Moreover, it does not imply "that predictions of [individuals] are perfect or that their expectations are all the same" (Muth, 1961, p. 317).

However, Muth held out the promise that one day economists would formulate a fully predetermined model that would adequately portray how the market—its participants in the aggregate—forecasts the future. Indeed, he viewed the Rational Expectations Hypothesis as if an economist's fully predetermined model could provide an adequate portrayal of both the market's forecasting strategy and the process driving market outcomes. The Rational Expectations Hypothesis supposes that both are "essentially the same":[1]

---

[1]By "essentially the same," Muth meant that, when an economist imposes the Rational Expectations Hypothesis in his fully predetermined model, he hypothesizes that the causal factors and weights that he selects adequately capture a combination of market participants' forecasting strategies—each with potentially different causal factors and different weights attached to them.

The hypothesis can be rephrased a little more precisely as follows:
... expectations of [participants] (or, more generally, the subjective probability distribution of outcomes) tend to be distributed, for the same information set, about the prediction of the theory (or the "objective" probability distributions of outcomes). [Muth, 1961, p. 316]

Muth appealed to the notion of an objective distribution to clarify what one might mean by "the relevant economic theory." Moreover, his restatement of the Rational Expectations Hypothesis embodies its key presumption: it is reasonable to hypothesize that a particular economist's fully predetermined model is the relevant theory and delivers the unique objective (supposedly true) probability distribution of market prices and risk: the set of all possible future outcomes and their likelihoods. Indeed, this is how many, if not most, macroeconomists and finance theorists interpret the Rational Expectations Hypothesis: only the market, not any individual participant, is omniscient and gets prices right.

But hypothesizing the adequacy of a fully predetermined model is nothing short of supposing that the way markets set prices can be understood as if nothing genuinely new ever happens, either on the individual or aggregate level. Muth's version of the Rational Expectations Hypothesis, which supposes that a fully predetermined model could portray how the market forecasts the future is just as bogus as the presumption that such a model could adequately portray how each of its profit-seeking participant forecasts the future.

In economists' discourse, "the market" is a metaphor that summarizes the behavior of all participants. As such, the notion of the "rational market" presumes a somewhat different imaginary place than a World of Rational Expectations.[2] But the use of Rational Expectations models to analyze outcomes in real-world markets, or to design government policies, involves building pro-

---

[2]In Chapter 5, we extensively discuss the market metaphor and how economists formalize it in modeling outcomes.

verbial castles in the air. The foundation of the "rational market" is the weightless belief that every time an economist devises a Rational Expectations model, he has discovered the way to capture, in an exact representation, what Hayek (1945) referred to as the use of knowledge in society and how its division unfolds over time.

Pseudo-Diversity in the "Rational Market"

In real-world markets, participants must rely on their own imperfect understanding of which variables are important for forecasting and how those variables are related to future outcomes. No participant, let alone an economist, knows in advance how she will revise her forecasting strategies, or how the social context will change as the future unfolds. Myriad possible changes may lead to a rise or decline in an asset price. At each point in time, it is reasonable for some participants to expect the price to rise, and for others to expect that it will fall. It may even be reasonable for some individuals to remain consistently bullish or bearish during a period in which the asset price moves steadily against them. Indeed, an individual might reasonably decide to increase the size of her long or short position precisely because the price has moved farther away from her expected level.

Muth sidestepped this diversity and formulated the Rational Expectations Hypothesis as a hypothesis about the market's forecasting strategy.[3] He did, however, believe that this hypothesis

[3]Because Rational Expectations models produce a single overarching forecasting strategy, they cannot by design explicitly represent the diversity of these strategies in real-world markets. However, these models have been used to model heterogeneity of market participants' forecasts. Such representations suppose that every participant forecasts according to the Rational Expectations Hypothesis and that differences in their forecasts arise solely from participants' access to, or their choosing to rely on, different information. Such formulations include Lucas's (1973) model with decentralized information and Stiglitz's (2001) models with asymmetric information. As Frydman (1982, 1983) showed rigorously and we discuss in Chapter 1, our critique of the standard Rational Expectations models that ignore decentralized information also applies to models that

is compatible with it. This belief seems to be widely shared. Many economists view the Rational Expectations Hypothesis as an approximation that enables them to capture in a parsimonious way the diversity and market participants' revisions of their forecasting strategies.[4]

What Muth and others have overlooked, however, is that the Rational Expectations Hypothesis requires that the micro-level diversity—the proportions of participants' holding particular views of the future and their forecasting strategies—must unfold over time in a fully predetermined way.[5] The same mechanical rules are presumed to characterize this pseudo-diversity of participants' forecasting strategies at all times. Indeed, any change in the proportion of bulls and bears in the market or revisions to their views must be mechanically tied to each other to ensure that, in the aggregate, the expectations of market participants remain essentially the same as the predictions of an economist's fully predetermined model.

To see these REH castles in the air, consider a particularly simple example of diversity in the so-called "rational market": two groups of participants—say, bulls and bears in an equity market—whose forecasting strategies are portrayed in accordance with the contemporary approach by two distinct, fully predetermined forecasting rules. An economist typically assumes that an aggregate of bulls' and bears' forecasts of future outcomes determines stock prices and risk at each point in time, t, in a fully predeter-

---

allow for heterogeneity of information used by market participants in forming their forecasts.

[4]Despite the importance that macroeconomists ascribe to basing accounts of market outcomes on individual foundations and the central role that the Rational Expectations Hypothesis plays in modeling these microfoundations, there has been surprisingly little discussion in macroeconomics about viewing this hypothesis as applicable only to the market. See Frydman and Goldberg (2007, chapter 3; 2010a) for a rigorous analysis of the inherent conflict between contemporary economists' program of relating market outcomes to individual foundations and their insistence on modeling these foundations in fully predetermined ways.

[5]For a rigorous demonstration of the claims made in this section, see Frydman and Goldberg (2010a).

mined way.[6] Moreover, he supposes that his Rational Expectations model describes the aggregate of these forecasting strategies.

Suppose, further, that at some point in time, some individuals revise their forecasting strategies and switch from being bulls to being bears or vice versa. In real-world markets, such revisions occur at moments that, in principle, none of the participants, let alone an economist, can fully foresee. Moreover, none of the participants can foresee the myriad alternative strategies to which they will switch. To be compatible with the Rational Expectations Hypothesis, the resulting diversity would have to unfold in a fully predetermined, mechanical way that bears no resemblance, even in the most abstract, rudimentary sense, to the way that diversity arises in real-world markets.

To illustrate this point, we simplify matters and assume that bulls follow a common forecasting strategy, as do the bears. Consider a situation in which some of the bulls come to think that the bearish strategy is more appropriate and decide to become bears instead. In the absence of any change in the bears' or bulls' forecasting strategies, the greater proportion of bears would, of course, influence the aggregate (i.e., market) forecast. But a Rational Expectations model attributes the same fully predetermined forecasting strategy to the market at every point in time. Thus, to describe adequately the market's forecast at every moment, shifts in the proportion of bulls and bears would have to be accompanied in the model by particular revisions of, say, the bears' forecasting strategy. The Rational Expectations Hypothesis determines these revisions mechanically: given the greater proportion of bears in the market and the way the other group (the bulls) forecasts the future, those who switch from bull to bear, as well as those who were already bears, must all adopt the same revised strategy. Even if the former bulls switch to a different bearish strategy, the three strategies that would emerge must be tied to one another in a mechanical way to ensure compatibility with a fully predetermined model based on the Rational Expectations Hypothesis.

[6]In Chapter 5, we discuss a typical formulation of such a model.

By focusing on the market, the Rational Expectations Hypothesis does abstract from differences between bulls and bears' forecasting strategies. But in presuming that an economist's fully predetermined model adequately approximates the aggregate forecast, the hypothesis does not approximate the diversity underpinning outcomes in real-world markets, as is commonly believed; it accomplishes this only in economists' imaginary rational market. In this fanciful world, abstraction is built upon abstraction: each Rational Expectations model abstracts from an already constructed pseudo-diversity that unfolds according to rigid, prespecified mechanical rules and has no connection with how differences of views in real-world markets unfold over time.[7]

THE IRRELEVANCE OF THE "RATIONAL MARKET"

Beyond its inherent incompatibility with how participants revise their diverse forecasting strategies in real-world markets, the widespread belief that the Rational Expectations Hypothesis approximates this diversity on the micro-level renders incoherent the very notion of the rational market. If this rational market were populated by participants who make use of different forecasting strategies, every one of them would always ignore systematic forecast errors and thereby endlessly forgo profit opportunities.[8]

Recognizing diversity reveals that even if REH models were to apply only to the market, they could hardly be considered a statement about its rationality. On the contrary, the REH's socalled "rational markets" are populated by irrational individuals.

To avoid this incoherence, economists would have to return to a World of Rational Expectations. But in this world, diver-

[7]Some contemporary economists interpret Muth's version of the Rational Expectations Hypothesis as hypothesizing that market participants' forecasting strategies differ from some aggregate—the "market's" strategy—by a random error term that averages to zero. Then the law of large numbers is supposed to ensure the hypothesis. However, this definition of diversity is just another, slightly weaker, version of the assumption of unanimity: on average, each market participant's forecasting strategy conforms to the same mechanical rule.

[8]See Frydman and Goldberg (2010a) for a rigorous demonstration.

sity is replaced by thought uniformity: each participant thinks alike, and forecasting by one of them—a representative agent—captures both forecasting on the individual and aggregate levels. But even if one views the Rational Expectations Hypothesis as being about a representative agent who thinks like all others and is "the market," assuming that market participants ignore non-routine change severs any connection between its portrayals of the supposedly rational market and what real-world markets and their participants actually do.

The importance of nonroutine change in driving outcomes implies that even if a Rational Expectations model were to adequately capture the past relationship between causal variables and aggregate outcomes in a selected historical period, it would cease to be relevant at moments that cannot be fully foreseen by anyone.[9] Profit-seeking participants understand that change in markets and the economy cannot be boiled down to a model that, by assuming away the importance of nonroutine change, mechanically connects the future to the past. Indeed, as we discuss more fully in Chapter 11, an important source of profits in financial markets arises from activities devoted to spotting and responding to nonroutine change.

Beware of Rational Expectations Models

Unsurprisingly, imposing consistency within economic models did not deliver what its promoters promised: a miraculously simple solution to the daunting problem of modeling how rational

---

[9]As we discuss in the next section, Rational Expectations models are not only fully predetermined but also constitute a particularly restrictive version of such models. Beyond implying a set of causal factors, they require the weights on those factors to satisfy stringent constraints (so-called "cross-equations restrictions") that have repeatedly failed empirically on the basis of time-series data. Although fully predetermined models that do not impose such constraints—for example, the traditional pre-REH Keynesian models—may be useful for describing particular episodes, this is unlikely to be true of Rational Expectations models even over limited periods of time.

individuals think about the future. Instead, it constrained economists to search for explanations of market outcomes that assume
that market participants' forecasting does not play an autonomous
role in driving these outcomes. Once an economist decides how to
model market participants' preferences and the context within
which they make decisions at all times, he no longer needs to worry
about how they interpret the process driving outcomes and forecast
the future. His model tells him how they think: "In rational expectations models, people's beliefs are among the outcomes of our theorizing. They are not inputs."[10]

In Rational Expectations models, the causal variables that
enter a market participant's forecasting strategy are those that an
economist chooses to represent her preferences and constraints.
Moreover, to impose the Rational Expectations Hypothesis—to
render the model's predictions on the aggregate and individual
levels identical—an economist must set the weights attached to
the model's causal variables to be exactly related to the parameters
of the model's other components.[11] In this way, the Rational Expectations Hypothesis bars an economist from exploring explanations
of forecasting that consider factors and parameters other than
those appearing in his specifications of the other nonexpectational
components of his model.

This lack of an autonomous role for market participants'
forecasting in Rational Expectations models has been viewed as
their principal virtue, because it disciplines economic analysis in a
way that was absent in previous models. Indeed, Lucas's stricture,
"beware of theorists bearing free parameters [and causal factors
arising from autonomous forecasting]"[12] had a profound impact
on the evolution of economics. But as we have pointed out, economists and the public alike should beware of Rational Expectations
models: they have absolutely no connection to real-world fore-

[10]Thomas J. Sargent, in an interview with Evans and Honkapohja (2005, p. 566).

[11]For a simple algebraic example of this point, see Frydman and Gold-berg (2007, chapter 3).

[12]Attributed to Lucas by Sargent (2001, p. 73).

casting and thus cannot serve as a foundation for thinking about markets and public policy.

The Fatal Conceit of the Rational Expectations Hypothesis

Although some economists may steadfastly maintain that building Rational Expectations models offers a way to advance economic science, it is simply unreasonable to presume that a world in which these models could adequately capture the way market outcomes unfold over time could ever become a reality. Even communist authorities, backed up by considerable state power, could not create such a world. They not only failed to banish change that they could not fully foresee, but, as we have seen, they also failed to coerce, let alone persuade, the aggregate of society to conform to one view—their view—of the future.

In an interview with Thomas Sargent, one of the pioneers of the Rational Expectations approach to macroeconomics, George Evans and Seppo Honkapohja asked: "Do you think differences among people's models are important aspects of macroeconomic policy debates?" Sargent replied:

> The fact is that you simply cannot talk about those differences within the typical rational expectations model. There is a communism of models. All agents inside the model, the econometrician, and God share the same model. The powerful and *useful* empirical implications of rational expectations . . . derive from that communism of models. [Evans and Honkapohja, 2005, p. 566, emphasis added]

But the reason that markets play an essential role in modern economies is precisely that nonroutine change is important, and knowledge is imperfect, giving rise to diverse views. Thus, any societal design or scientific program based on a "communism" of ideas—such that everyone believes in the same view of the future, or that market participants, economists, social planners, or policy officials can fully foresee or determine the future—cannot in principle deliver what it promises.

The fundamental flaws of the Rational Expectations Hypothesis will continue to impede economists' search for useful accounts of market outcomes. The time to consider jettisoning it is thus long overdue. Its implications concerning the role of markets, and its assessments of the consequences of various government policies, have no scientific underpinning. As history has shown, such fundamentally flawed theories, when implemented in practice, are likely to produce economically disastrous and socially dangerous consequences.

5

Castles in the Air:

The Efficient Market Hypothesis

T HE THEORY OF the rational market arose as an attempt to provide a scientific underpinning to the Efficient Market Hypothesis, which serves as the cornerstone of financial economics. According to the hypothesis, asset "prices always 'fully reflect' available information" (Fama, 1970, p. 383).

As it stands, the Efficient Market Hypothesis says very little about how prices unfold over time, or whether markets allocate capital well. There is an abundance of publicly available information about economic, political, and social factors and events that is quickly disseminated to individuals around the world. Participants select from this flow of information when forming their forecasts of future prices and risk. These forecasts underpin their decisions to buy and sell, which the market aggregates in setting prices. In this way, prices fully reflect the information that participants deem relevant in forecasting.

If by "available information," one means the particular information chosen by participants in thinking about the future, then the Efficient Market Hypothesis is merely a descriptive hypothesis about markets. To turn it into a theory of asset prices, economists have had to take a stand on what is meant by "all available information" and how it gets "fully reflected in asset prices."

By presuming that the Rational Expectations Hypothesis adequately captures how intelligent, rational participants forecast future prices and the prospects of assets, the Efficient Market Hypothesis was transformed into the hypothesis that markets allocate society's scarce capital almost perfectly by setting prices to fluctuate randomly around their "true" fundamental values. This claim is supposed to apply to an individual investment, a sector, an asset class, or a market as a whole. As a result, the Efficient Market Hypothesis also implies that using available information in an attempt to earn excess returns after taking risk into account is bound to fail.

When these striking claims entered the public debate, the assumptions that underpinned them were left behind in the academic literature. But, as we have shown in Chapter 3, the conclusions that follow in a World of Rational Expectations have no connection to what real-world markets do and how their participants behave. The transformation of economists' descriptive account of financial markets into a fully predetermined theory of efficient, rational markets provides a striking demonstration of how fanciful assumptions have led economists to build castles in the air.

The Market Metaphor

When economists speak about the "market," they do so "metaphorically . . . [as] a convenient way of summarizing the decisions of individual investors and the way these decisions interact to determine prices" (Fama, 1976, p. 135). The assumptions that they use to formalize this metaphor are often expressed using sophisticated mathematics. However, when the mathematics is stripped away, these assumptions, far from being merely convenient, are revealed to disregard essential features of individual decisionmaking in financial markets.

In these markets, participants' trading decisions depend on their forecasts of future returns and the risk or chance that returns might be different than predicted.[1] In the equity market, for

[1]In standard models, risk is related to cross-correlations between assets' returns.

example, the return on buying shares in a company today depends on the future price at which they can be sold; any dividends that the company pays over the holding period; and the cost of capital, usually measured by a prevailing interest rate. To forecast prices, dividends, and risk, participants must choose from a large set of potentially relevant factors, ranging from company-specific variables (such as corporate earnings and industry trends) to economy-wide variables (such as announcements by the central bank, inflation rates, and overall economic activity). Each participant formulates a forecasting strategy, which reflects her own knowledge and intuition about which factors are relevant and how each one should be interpreted when thinking about the future.

At each moment in time, participants' forecasts differ. As of this writing (summer 2010), for example, overall economic activity in the U.S. economy had increased over the past two quarters, suggesting that the two-year downturn that began at the end of 2007 had already ended. Corporate earnings, overall employment, and exports had also been rising, and the Federal Reserve announced plans to keep short-term interest rates at very low levels for some time to come. Such news is often interpreted bullishly for stocks, which may lead participants to forecast higher future prices and dividends.

However, there was also a great deal of news pointing in the opposite direction. Much of the increase in overall economic activity so far had come from companies restocking their inventories. Consumer spending and business expenditures on new plant(s) and equipment showed no real sign of rising from historic lows. The muddle over financial reform, health care, and the environment created considerable uncertainty about how the legal and regulatory frameworks undergirding private enterprise might change. And the stock market had risen above historical levels, based on earnings and dividends—news that is thought to lead some participants to forecast lower prices and dividends.

At each point in time, participants may revise their forecasts of returns and/or risk because of new information or new ways of thinking about the future. If an individual's forecast of returns rises relative to the compensation that she requires for taking on the risk that actual returns might differ from her forecast, she buys stock, whereas if it falls, she sells.[2] Prices move to the value that leads to a balance between total supply and demand for a given stock, thereby reflecting an invisible weighting of bullish and bearish views about the future.

To model this process, economists typically suppose that the excess of total buying over total selling of a stock at each point in time is related to an average of participants' forecasts of returns and that of their premiums. If those averages imply a market forecast greater than the market premium, total buying will exceed total selling. To balance total buying and selling, prices must move in ways that they equate the market's forecast of returns with its premium after accounting for the cost of capital.

In the aggregate, the market's forecasting strategy depends on an invisible weighting of current and past information on the variables that its participants consider relevant in forming their forecasts of returns and risk. As the market's forecast of prices and dividends changes, so do prices. In formalizing these changes, economists usually focus on new information about the relevant variables. But movements of forecasts—and thus of prices—result not only from new information but also from revisions of the market's forecasting strategy. Until an economist takes a stand on change stemming from both sources, his market metaphor says very little about how stock prices will unfold over time.

IMAGINING MARKETS IN A FULLY PREDETERMINED WORLD

Fully Predetermined "Uncertainty"

Contemporary economists typically model economic outcomes and forecasting behavior with fully predetermined proba-

---

[2] Economists refer to such compensation as a "risk premium." They often relate this premium to standard statistical measures, such as the standard deviation of returns and an individual's distaste for taking on risk.

bilistic models. They understand that many changes cannot be anticipated. No one can be sure how a company's earnings prospects and dividends will unfold over the next year, let alone over ten or twenty years. The values of such outcomes will depend on many changes, including yet-to-be-invented technologies, new ways of organizing human and physical capital within organizations, and unforeseeable changes in institutions and economic policies worldwide. Economists attempt to capture this unpredictable change by adding "stochastic shocks," or error terms, to their models. As Paul Samuelson (1965a, p. 147) put it:

> Just as Ehrenfest and other physicists had to add probability to the causal systems of physics in order to get around the time-irreversibility feature of classical mechanics that was so inconsistent with the second law of thermodynamics, so we must, in the interests of realism, add stochastic probability distributions to our economic and biological causal systems.

Economists' probabilistic models suppose that the impact of change on economic outcomes can be captured with two components: one involving a fully predetermined expected future value that is conditional on available information and the other being stochastic news that is uncorrelated with available information.

To render their probabilistic descriptions of outcomes fully predetermined, economists specify in advance the probability distribution governing news—the set of possible future values and their associated probabilities of the stochastic component of outcomes. Over time, the stochastic news shocks are assumed to average to zero.

To see what this argument entails, consider the problem of modeling the future dividend stream of a company. The fully predetermined component of the specification would consist of a mechanical rule that attempts to capture all future change that can be anticipated on the basis of current and past information. This rule might relate future dividends to the values of other causal variables, such as industry trends and overall economic activity. But a particularly simple rule that is common in the economics literature would suppose that a company's dividend tends to grow at a constant rate, say, 1% per year. So if this year's dividend is $1.00, next year's will be $1.01.

Adding stochastic news shocks to the description of the dividend process implies that the actual dividend value observed in each period depends on a fully predetermined change from the previous year and the value (realization) of the news term in the current year. Next year's dividend is then described by a probability distribution, conditional on its current value. If the same conditional probability distribution were to apply over time, the stochastic shocks would cancel one another out, and dividends would on average follow their fully predetermined time path involving 1% annual growth. In this way, the description severely restricts unpredictable change to a random deviation from a fully predetermined path.

Economists use such conditional probability distributions to portray participants' forecasting strategies at each point in time. Using our example, a participant's forecast today of next year's dividend would be the average of the possible values, which, with a random error term, is just 1% higher than this year's dividend. Next year's dividend, of course, will differ from this year's forecast because of a stochastic shock. And, because this shock can take on one of many values, the forecast error could be large or small.

Manufacturing Random Price Fluctuations

In a seminal paper, Samuelson (1965b) constructed a fully predetermined probabilistic model of the market. His formalization implied that, barring some "inefficiency," movements of an asset price were best described by flipping a coin.

To transform the market metaphor into a mathematical model of the market, an economist must specify how the market forecasts the return on holding the stock between today and some future period. The expected return today depends on the market's forecasts of both next period's price and next period's dividend. In turn, price movements between today and next period depend on how the market's forecast of future prices and dividends changes over this period.

To see how Samuelson formalized these movements in the so-called "present-value model," suppose that today the market's forecasts of next year's stock price and dividend are $100 and $1, respectively. The price that the market would be willing to pay today for this expected future payoff depends on its value in today's dollars, or what economists call its "present discounted value." If we assume that the cost of capital is 1% per year, $101 received next year would be worth $100 today. In bidding for shares, then, participants in the aggregate would push today's stock price to $100. At this value, the expected dividend would just offset the cost of capital, and the market would expect no change in price over the coming year.

Whether the price in one year is $100 or some other value depends on the market's expectation of price and dividend next year for the following year. To derive implications for actual price movements in the model, therefore, Samuelson had to characterize how the market's thinking about the future in one year's time would differ from its thinking today.

By insisting on fully predetermining their models, economists ignore any revisions to forecasting strategies that they cannot prespecify. Samuelson did so by assuming no change at all; he used the same conditional probability distribution to characterize the market's forecasting strategy at every point in time into the indefinite future. With the market's forecasting strategy for price and dividend assumed to be forever fixed, Samuelson could relate the market's expectation today of next year's price to its expectation of price and dividend in two years. Samuelson carried this forward iteration into the indefinite future, showing that the market would push today's price to equal its estimate of what economists call the "intrinsic" value: the present discounted value of all dividends that the market expects to receive in all future periods under the assumption that the future follows mechanically from the past.

For example, suppose that an economist assumes that the market's forecasts of dividends follow a simple mechanical rule: they are expected to grow by 1% per year. In this case, a simple calculation implies that the intrinsic value each year would be a fixed multiple of that year's dividend. If the interest rate were, say, 6% per year, this fixed multiple would be about 20.[3] With a stock's intrinsic value equal to a fixed multiple of the current dividend, it would grow on average at the same 1% annual rate at which dividends are assumed to grow.

Whether the present-value model implies that the price will actually tend to grow at 1% per year depends on whether the market is presumed to forecast accurately the way that dividends unfold over time. As with the forecasting of price movements, Samuelson ignored all change and assumed that the same conditional probability distribution characterized dividends at every point in time. He also assumed that the market knows exactly, up to the fully predetermined stochastic error term, how dividends actually unfold over time. Thus, he set the market's forecasting strategy for dividends and the actual development of dividends to be one and the same. With its forecasts of all future dividends supposedly correct on average, the market's estimate of a company's intrinsic value would deviate from the true value only by a random forecast error that is uncorrelated with available information.

The so-called "martingale property" of stock prices—that the actual price fluctuates randomly around its expected fully predetermined time path and that available information cannot be used to earn above-average returns consistently over time— follows as a matter of straightforward logic. In a world in which the market is presumed to assess nearly perfectly the future prospects

---

[3]The constant multiple of dividends in this case equals the ratio of one plus the dividend growth rate to the difference between the interest rate and the dividend growth rate, that is, $(1.0 + 0.01)/(0.06 - 0.01)$.

of projects and companies and to forecast accurately dividend payouts, a stock's price equals the market's supposedly true estimate of the company's intrinsic value. This estimate takes into account all available information (the current dividend) and the fully predetermined change that is assumed to occur (the assumed tendency for dividends and price to grow at 1% per year).

The actual change in price in each period is presumed to differ from the market's expectation of a 1% annual growth rate only because new information—a stochastic shock—arrives and affects dividends. These shocks are assumed to be random and thus uncorrelated with prior information. As such, there is no possibility of using available information to predict when price changes will differ from their 1% growth path—and thus no possibility of earning consistently above-average returns over time.

Samuelson's martingale result had a seminal impact on financial economics. It provided a theoretical connection between the observation that participants use available information and the belief that asset prices reflect their supposedly true fundamental values. Moreover, the martingale result was believed to demonstrate rigorously that no one could use available information to beat the market consistently in the real world.

SAMUELSON'S DOUBTS

Samuelson himself was quite dubious of the relevance of his analysis for modeling real-world markets, publishing his result more than 10 years after arriving at it. In that publication, he "confess[ed] to having oscillated over the years . . . between regarding it as trivially obvious (and almost trivially vacuous) and regarding it as remarkably sweeping." He pointed out that "the applicability of the . . . model to economic reality must be kept distinct from the *logical* problem of what is the model's implied content" (Samuelson, 1965b, p. 45, emphasis added). He cautioned his readers against attaching too much importance to his result, emphasizing that

[i]t does not prove that actual competitive markets work well . . . or that speculation is a good thing or that randomness of price changes would be a good thing . . . or that anyone who makes money in speculation . . . has accomplished something good for society or for anyone but himself. All or none of these may be true, but that would require a different investigation. [Samuelson, 1965b, p. 48]

Samuelson's doubts anticipated many of the difficulties inherent in characterizing economic outcomes with an overarching model. His list of qualms begins with the observation that he has "not here discussed where the basic probability distributions are supposed to come from" (Samuelson, 1965b, p. 48). He likely felt uneasy that his basic distributions presume that no change ever happens. In the world of his model, individuals never change the ways that they think about the future, and companies' earnings prospects unfold in the same way for all time—past, present, and future.

It might be reasonable in some time periods to suppose that over the short term, market participants' forecasting strategies (at least in the aggregate) and the process underpinning the causal variables do not change very much. But, sooner or later, profit-seeking individuals revise their forecasting strategies, and the causal variables move in ways that are not mechanical—and thus cannot be fully prespecified. Despite the presence of random error terms, a single conditional probability distribution is simply unable to capture such change.

Suppose, for example, that a conditional probability distribution that related a company's stock price to, say, its earnings in the previous year and the current interest rate adequately describe the market's forecasting strategy over the recent past. If a sizable number of market participants today decided that the economy's inflation rate was also relevant for forecasting future prices, the original stochastic specification would cease to provide an adequate characterization of the market's forecasting strategy.

The problem is that no participant, let alone an economist, can fully foresee how she might revise her forecasting strategy in one year, let alone for longer time horizons. Paraphrasing Karl Popper (1957, p. xii): "no society [or group of people, such as market participants] can predict the future states of knowledge."

Samuelson showed that strong conclusions follow from assuming that one overarching distribution can adequately capture outcomes at all times.[4] But he was the first to warn that such an approach has no connection to what individuals and markets really do. Indeed, he questioned the foundations of his own market model:

> [A]re [the basic probability distributions] ... supposed to belong to the market as a whole? And what does that mean? Are they supposed to belong to the "representative individual," and who is he? Are they some defensible or necessitous compromise of divergent expectation patterns? [Samuelson, 1965b, p. 48]

The answer, which Friedrich Hayek so clearly understood, is that they are in no one's mind. Participants in financial markets simply cannot afford to adhere to one forecasting strategy endlessly. Change, and the imperfect knowledge that it engenders and reflects, leads to diversity among participants concerning how they think about the future. As Hayek (1945, p. 519) put it, "the fact [is] that knowledge of the circumstances of which we must make use never exists in concentrated or integrated form but solely as the dispersed bits of incomplete and frequently contradictory knowledge which all the separate individuals possess."

In deriving his martingale result, Samuelson assumed that the market "knows" the truth about how prices and dividends un-

---

[4]Sometimes economists allow for different characterizations of forecasting at different points in time. However, such models of fully predetermined change imply a characterization of outcomes with a single overarching distribution. See footnote 1 in Chapter 3 for further discussion and references.

fold over time. Participants, of course, do not have this knowledge, and Samuelson wondered "in whose minds [the basic probability distributions] are ex ante," and whether there is "any ex post validation" (Samuelson, 1965b, p. 48) of their forecasting strategies.

However, once the assumption that the market is omniscient is dropped, the model no longer implies that a stock's price would provide the correct estimate of its supposed actual intrinsic value—or, thus, that the martingale property applies. Consider a simple case: suppose that the market expects dividends to grow by 1% in every period, while the actual growth rate is 2%. Each period, the market would push the stock's price to the value at which, after accounting for a 1% growth rate in dividends, it expected prices to rise 1% over the coming period. However, this price is lower than its intrinsic value, which is based on the higher dividend growth rate. Each period, dividends would tend to be higher than expected, and thus prices would also tend to rise faster than expected. Such price increases would clearly be correlated with available information, thereby violating the martingale property.

Samuelson himself did not attempt to "pronounce on these interesting questions" (Samuelson, 1965b, p. 49), either in his initial publication in 1965 or in his follow-up article on the stock market (Samuelson, 1973). However, Fama and other financial economists thought that they had found the right answers in the Rational Expectations Hypothesis.

The Illusory Stability of the "Rational Market"

Proponents of the Efficient Market Hypothesis often view it as simply implying that profit-seeking participants will quickly spot systematic behavior in prices. In attempting to exploit such behavior, they will cause prices to fluctuate randomly around intrinsic values.

Prior to the Rational Expectations revolution, economists argued informally for this claim. Milton Friedman, for example, believed that speculation in currency markets would work to stabilize prices around fundamental values, because otherwise "speculators [would] lose money ... on the average [and] sell when the currency is low in price and buy when it is high" (Friedman, 1953, p. 175).

Fama believed that in an efficient market "the actual price of a security will be a good estimate of its intrinsic value." He did point out, however, that

> intrinsic values can themselves change across time ... [because of] such things as the success of a current research and development project, a change in management, a tariff imposed on the industry's product by a foreign country, an increase in individual production or any other *actual or anticipated* change in a factor which is likely to affect a company's prospects. [Fama, 1965, p. 56]

Consequently, Fama (1965, p. 56) acknowledged that "in an uncertain world the intrinsic value of a security can never be determined exactly." Indeed, even if one could estimate with a reasonable degree of confidence a company's earnings in the near term, coming up with estimates, let alone a probability distribution, that would adequately describe these prospects in ten or twenty years is beyond the reach of anyone. Once one acknowledges change and imperfect knowledge,

> there is always room for disagreement among market participants concerning just what the intrinsic value of an individual security is, and such disagreement will give rise to discrepancies between actual prices and intrinsic values. [Fama, 1965, p. 56]

Nonetheless, Fama (1965, p. 56) believed that if such discrepancies were "systematic rather than random, participants ... [would] attempt to take advantage of this knowledge ... [and] neutralize [it] in price series."

By Fama's own account, there is no true intrinsic value that competition among intelligent participants could establish. Thus, even if all participants base their trading decisions on estimates of intrinsic values, the market price will reflect some weighted average of these estimates. Participants do indeed speculate based on their own thinking and views, but no one can determine intrinsic values exactly. The idea that individuals act as if they can arbitrage away discrepancies between actual prices and intrinsic values simply has no meaning.

Acknowledging nonroutine change and ever-imperfect knowledge, as Fama does, implies that financial markets are imperfect assessors of asset values. However, by embracing the Rational Expectations Hypothesis and Samuelson's martingale result, Fama himself, as well as other financial economists, reached a sharply different conclusion.

The Rational Expectations Hypothesis transformed the Efficient Market Hypothesis statement that asset "prices always 'fully reflect' available information" from a descriptive hypothesis about markets into a supposedly normative theory of asset markets with a central implication: barring informational asymmetries and other market failures, markets populated by "rational individuals" are stable, in the sense that they set prices to fluctuate randomly around intrinsic values.

The stability of rational markets has two implications. First, prices on average are correctly connected to companies' short- and long-term earnings capacities. They, therefore, exactly reveal which companies have the best chance of using society's capital productively. As a company's future prospects improve, its stock price rises and enables it to raise greater capital through issuance of new shares. In a World of Rational Expectations, price signals generated in financial markets enable society to allocate capital nearly perfectly. Second, the stability of rational markets implies that available information is always properly reflected in prices. Returns, then, unfold randomly over time, so that available information cannot be used to earn above-average returns consistently.

The Rational Expectations Hypothesis seemed to offer the missing justification for the assumptions behind Samuelson's martingale result. However, it does so only in a World of Rational Expectations. In that castle in the air, price movements occur only

because of new information about the relevant fundamental variables. When new information becomes available, all investors
properly interpret it in estimating a stock's intrinsic value. If their
estimate of this value were to rise, for example, they would all
wager large amounts of capital on the expectation that the stock's
price would rise to equal its new estimated intrinsic value. Investors' attempts to speculate would immediately push up the stock's
price to the new estimate of its intrinsic value.

Fama (1976, p. 167) recognized that tying the Efficient
Market Hypothesis to the Rational Expectations Hypothesis does
not provide "a completely accurate view of the world ... but formal tests require formal models." By the late 1970s, the hypothesis
that markets are efficient had become synonymous with the conjecture that "asset prices [were] being determined by the interaction of rational agents" (LeRoy, 1989, p. 1584).

As with the confusion between the Rational Expectations
Hypothesis and how profit-seeking individuals actually forecast in
financial markets, the implication that rational markets set prices
to fluctuate randomly around true values has been conflated with
the claim that real-world markets are stable, allocate capital nearly
perfectly, and thus cannot be beaten on average.

But, with the Rational Expectations Hypothesis having no
connection to the decisionmaking of profit-seeking participants,
financial economists are left exactly where they were prior to the
Rational Expectations revolution: clinging to informal arguments
without any rationale, let alone scientific underpinning, for the
strong claims by the Efficient Market Hypothesis about market
stability and perfection.

Fama (1976, p. 168) argues that "what we really have in
mind ... is a market where there is disagreement among investors but where the force of common judgments is sufficient to
produce an orderly adjustment of prices to new information."
But what, exactly, "common judgments" and "orderly adjustment"
are supposed to mean, and how such phenomena might lead to
prices that fluctuate randomly around mythical values, are left
unanswered.

EFFICIENT MARKET HYPOTHESIS
AND ASSET-PRICE SWINGS

The global crisis that started in 2007 seriously undermined the view that asset markets set prices nearly perfectly. The crisis was triggered and fueled by long and sharp downswings in housing and equity prices that began in 2006, which were preceded by long upswings that had pushed prices to very high levels compared to most estimates of common benchmark levels. Such excessive fluctuations are difficult to fathom in the context of the Efficient Market Hypothesis.

Even before the crisis, however, economists understood that all asset prices that are freely determined by the forces of supply and demand have a tendency to undergo persistent swings away from and toward benchmark levels. Figures 5.1 and 5.2 provide just two examples. They plot the price of the S&P 500 relative to a trailing 10-year average of earnings and the German mark–U.S. dollar exchange rate, respectively, along with estimates of a typical benchmark level.

Economists have uncovered much evidence that such benchmark levels act as a sort of anchor for asset-price swings.[5] Eventually, price swings that rise far above or fall well below most estimates of benchmark levels are judged by the market to be excessive; such swings are followed by sustained movements back toward those levels. As John Cochrane put it in a recent interview, "when stock prices are high relative to earnings—that seems to signal a period of low returns. . . . [w]e all agree on [that] fact" (Cassidy, 2010b, p. 1).

But in defending the Efficient Market Hypothesis, proponents point out that such "volatility of stock prices alone [does not] disprove market efficiency" (Cochrane, 2009, p. 2). After all, news about dividends or other informational variables and changes in discount rates are supposed to lead to variation in true intrinsic

---

[5]We discuss this evidence in Chapter 11.

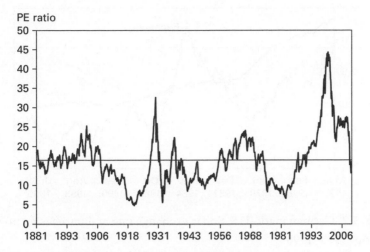

Fig. 5.1. S&P 500 price-earnings ratio, 1881–2009

Notes: The monthly price-earnings ratio is based on a 10-year trailing moving average of earnings and makes use of data from Shiller (2000), which are updated on his website. The horizontal line in the figure is the historical average of the price-earnings ratio over the 128 years of the sample, which equals 16.4.

values. Efficient markets imply stable prices, not in the conventional sense of being nearly "fixed" but in the sense of fluctuating randomly around intrinsic values.

In their attempt to reconcile the long swings that are evident in Figures 5.1 and 5.2 with such supposed stability, financial economists have suggested that the intrinsic values of assets themselves undergo long swings away from and toward estimates of common benchmark levels. According to this view, such persistent movements in true fundamental values arise because of the swings in the discount rate on which they are based.

In the present-value model, the discount rate depends inversely not only on the interest rate, but also on how individuals in the aggregate assess the riskiness of holding an asset and the degree to which they dislike risk. For example, if individuals' assessment of risk or degree of risk aversion were to fall, they would lower the extra return—the premium—that they expect to earn over and above the sure returns on safe assets, which compensates

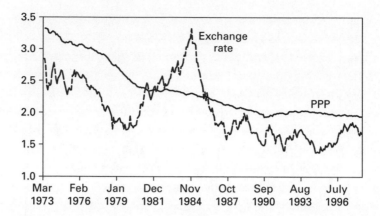

Fig. 5.2. German mark–U.S. dollar exchange rate and purchasing power parity, 1973–1998

Notes: The monthly German mark–U.S. dollar rate is plotted along with its purchasing power parity value, which implies that a dollar spent in either New York or Frankfurt will have the same purchasing power. Purchasing power parity exchange rates are widely used by academics, policymakers, and market participants as a simple way to determine whether exchange rates are overvalued or undervalued.

them for taking on risky speculative positions in stocks. As individuals' risk premiums (and thus discount rates) fall, they become more willing to buy claims to the uncertain future cash flows generated by the asset. Consequently, its intrinsic value rises.

As with forecasts of future prices, Rational Expectations models presume that individuals can on average correctly forecast the riskiness of assets—typically portrayed with standard measures of volatility. However, ever since Mehra and Prescott (1985), economists have known that REH-based risk-premium models are grossly inconsistent with the time-series behavior of the market's risk premium. Even if cyclical variation in attitudes toward risk is incorporated into these models, they simply are unable to account for the basic features of the data in equity and other asset markets. As two leading financial economists put it, "the traditional [rational] framework is appealingly simple ... [but] after years of effort, it has become clear that basic facts about the aggregate stock market, the cross-section of average returns and individual trading behavior are not easily understood in this framework" (Barberis and Thaler, 2003, p. 1053).

Despite this evidence, proponents of the Efficient Market Hypothesis continue to invoke imaginary movements in the market risk premium to square the theory with long-swing fluctuations in asset markets. In equity markets, they conjecture that individuals' dislike of risk might vary inversely with the business cycle: "people's willingness to take on risk . . . is lower in bad economic times" (Cochrane, 2009, p. 2). So the long upswing in U.S. equity prices in the 1990s, for example, came about because the economic boom at the time supposedly increased rational market participants' willingness to bear risk, which in turn led to steadily rising intrinsic values. By the same token, the recession that began in the second quarter of 2001 supposedly depressed participants' appetite for risk, causing intrinsic values to fall during that time.

Although this story has an air of plausibility, it is largely inconsistent with empirical evidence. This is unsurprising, given that, when confronted with time-series evidence, REH-based risk-premium models have been rejected in study after study. Financial economists do point to a few empirical studies reporting that estimates of the risk premium in the U.S. equity market moves inversely with the business cycle, while the price-earnings ratio and other valuation measures move pro-cyclically (see Fama and French, 1989).

However, the timing of the swings in asset prices and the economy simply do not line up in a way that is consistent with conventional economists' risk-premium story. For example, the long upswing in U.S. equity prices began well before the 1990s and proceeded largely unabated through the recession of 1991. Moreover, the long downswing in equity prices that began in mid-2000 preceded by one year the downturn in the U.S. economy and employment. Had a countercyclical risk premium been driving price fluctuations during these periods, we should have seen a significant downswing in stock prices in 1991, and the downswing that began in mid-2000 should not have started until mid-2001.

There is another problem with the statistical research used to support the Efficient Market Hypothesis view of long swings: it is based on estimating models that presume unchanging patterns in the data over samples of up to six decades. Over such long stretches of time, the relationships describing how participants forecast risk and correlations in the data are bound to change. Imposing stability on a statistical model merely mixes data from different periods with different relationships and is likely to mask the underlying patterns.[6]

Zheng (2009) and Mangee (2011) provide empirical evidence suggesting that this is indeed the case. Using monthly data, they find instability in the relationship driving the market risk premium for stocks. Once Zheng (2009) allows for this instability, she obtains results that differ markedly from those of earlier studies. Figure 5.3 is taken from her study, which focuses on the period from mid-1997 to late 2008. The figure suggests that the estimated risk premium tends to rise and fall in concert with swings in the price-earnings ratio relative to the benchmark—the gap—rather than inversely to them.

A positive relationship between the market risk premium and the gap between the asset price and estimates of its benchmark level is also found in Frydman and Goldberg (2003, 2007), Cavusoglu et al. (2009), and Stillwagon (2010), which together examine fourteen currency markets in developed and developing countries. Figure 5.4 plots the monthly risk premium along with the gap between the British pound–dollar exchange rate and purchasing power parity. The tendency for the currency risk premium to move positively with the swing in the exchange rate relative to the purchasing power parity benchmark is striking.

This evidence on the comovements of the premium with asset prices is grossly inconsistent with attempts by the advocates of the Efficient Market Hypothesis to treat long swings in equity

---

[6]We return to this problem, which plagues most statistical research in macroeconomics, in Chapter 11, where we discuss the empirical evidence that the proponents of the Efficient Market Hypothesis have interpreted as strongly supportive of their theory.

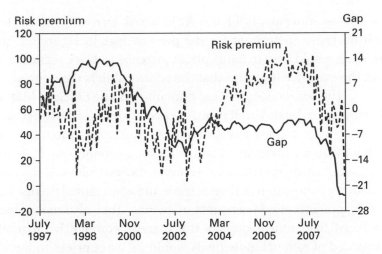

Fig. 5.3. Stock market risk premium and the gap, 1997–2008
Source: Zheng (2009).
Notes: The market risk premium is proxied by regressing actual future excess stock returns on interest rates and Shiller's (2000) price-earnings ratio. The gap variable is based on deviations of this ratio from its historical average of 16.4.

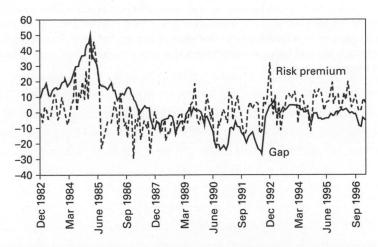

Fig. 5.4. British pound–U.S. dollar risk premium and the gap, 1982–1997
Source: Frydman and Goldberg (2007).
Notes: The market risk premium is proxied using survey data from Money Market Services International, which conducted weekly surveys of market participants' one-month-ahead exchange-rate forecasts. For more details, see Frydman and Goldberg (2007, chapter 12).

markets as movements of the REH-based intrinsic values. For
their narrative to account for the price swings in Figure 5.1, the
premium would have to fall as prices increase and vice versa. However, the evidence indicates that the relationship is the opposite.[7]

The widely documented difficulties of the Efficient Market
Hypothesis and standard Rational Expectations models to account
for asset-price swings has sparked an enormous amount of research by both conventional and behavioral economists. In developing alternative models, most economists have followed the contemporary conception of their science and constrained themselves
to fully predetermined accounts of swings. They also maintained
the belief that informationally transparent, competitive markets
composed of rational individuals would set asset prices to fluctuate randomly around their intrinsic values. These beliefs led both
conventional and behavioral economists to view price swings as
bubbles, which they portrayed as departures from these supposedly true fundamental values.

[7]These empirical results suggest that the key factor characterizing how
participants assess the riskiness of speculative positions lies not in standard measures of volatility but in participants' perceptions of the departure of asset prices
from common benchmark levels. This observation has led us to develop an IKE
model of bulls' and bears' risk premiums that captures this behavior. We sketch
this model in Chapter 10.

6

The Fable of Price Swings as Bubbles

 T HE GLOBAL FINANCIAL CRISIS that began in 2007 has led many observers to question the relevance of contemporary macroeconomic and finance theory for understanding outcomes and guiding policy. Many economists have also recognized that their portrayals of individual behavior and markets are deficient. But they have remained steadfast in their belief that they should continue to search for better, and even more complete, fully predetermined accounts of outcomes.[1]

To be sure, swings in housing, equity, and other markets, which are often blamed for the crisis, substantially eroded faith in the ability of financial markets populated by rational participants to allocate society's capital nearly perfectly. Nevertheless, Rational Expectations accounts of the intrinsic values of assets have continued to serve as the foundation for modeling swings in prices and risk. For example, in modeling asset-price swings, economists portray them as mechanical departures from REH-based, supposedly true values of prospects and companies.

---

[1]For example, Krugman (2009) overlooked the possibility that economists' insistence on fully predetermined accounts of market outcomes should be reconsidered. Echoing a widely held belief, Krugman suggested that adding a mechanistic account of the financial sector to Rational Expectations macroeconomic models, as Bernanke et al. (1999) had done, would render such models relevant for understanding outcomes and guiding policy. For further remarks on this point, see footnote 17 in Chapter 1.

Thus, as different as the "rational market" and bubble views may appear to be, they share the core assumptions of contemporary macroeconomic and finance theory. They both portray true intrinsic values with the Rational Expectations Hypothesis and characterize asset-price movements with fully predetermined models. As a result, both approaches—rational market models, with their stable prices around supposedly "true" fundamental values, and bubble models, with their portrayals of swings as departures from these values—yield distorted accounts of asset-price and risk movements in real-world markets.

REINVENTING IRRATIONALITY

A modern macroeconomic model's predictions concerning an asset price depend on its assumptions about the forecasting behavior of individual investors. As we have seen, Rational Expectations models assume that individuals act as if they all forecast according to the economist's own overarching model, whose predictions concerning the market price and those that it attributes to individuals are constrained to be one and the same. In contrast, mathematical behavioral finance models explore the implications of not imposing such model consistency and thus are widely interpreted as capturing departures from full rationality. But all overarching models, as Lucas (2001, p. 21) memorably put it, can be "put on a computer and run." Thus, even as crude approximations, they are simply false explanations of economic outcomes, which are driven by nonroutine change.

Nowhere is such change more important than in financial markets. Thus, consistency between individual and aggregate levels in a fully predetermined model has no connection to rationality in real-world markets, and inconsistency within these models is not a symptom of departures from full rationality in those markets. The consistency of participants' fully prespecified forecasting strategies with an economist's representation of aggregate outcomes is, to put it bluntly, beside the point. Imputing such strategies to market participants merely presumes that everyone gives up looking for new profit opportunities.

To be sure, psychology and emotions are important for understanding how individuals make decisions, and behavioral economists have contributed important insights about such behavior. But because they formalize these insights with overarching mechanical rules, their models do not characterize departures from full rationality but are merely alternative portrayals of obviously irrational behavior.

BUBBLES IN A WORLD OF RATIONAL EXPECTATIONS: MECHANIZING CROWD PSYCHOLOGY

The notion that market participants may sometimes bid up an asset price far away from valuations based on fundamentals because crowd psychology and mania lead them to expect ever-rising prices has a long history in economics and the popular press.[2] The so-called "tulip mania" in Holland in the 1600s and the South Sea bubble of the 1700s, which involved speculation in exotic types of bulbs and government debt, respectively, are often viewed as two of the best examples of a purely speculative bubble.

These episodes suggest that crowd psychology and manias may play a role in some markets now and then. But appealing to manias to explain price fluctuations in major asset markets, such as those for stocks, bonds, and currencies, suggests that long upswings are an aberration from otherwise normal times, during which the market sets asset prices at their supposedly true fundamental values. In fact, the long swings shown in Figures 5.1 and 5.2 are the norm, not the exception.

[2]For an excellent history of financial crises from this point of view, see Kindleberger (1996).

"Rational bubble" models ignore this observation and attempt to account for the dramatic upswings that sometimes characterize asset prices while preserving the Rational Expectations Hypothesis. In these models, crowd psychology can lead putatively rational individuals to downplay the importance of an asset's intrinsic value when forecasting future prices, even though they are assumed to have access to the supposedly true process governing this value.

In the simplest models, all investors sometimes come to believe that everyone else expects that, over successive periods, the asset's price will rise increasingly above what they all believe to be its intrinsic value. Partly because all market participants' forecasts embody this belief, it becomes self-fulfilling: the price moves steadily on average away from the hypothesized fundamental value. The Rational Expectations Hypothesis amounts to presuming that individuals act as if they possess an overarching model not only of an asset's intrinsic value but also of how crowd psychology actually develops when it takes over the market.

What might trigger individuals to think that crowd psychology has begun to influence an asset's price is left unspecified in the model. Presumably, a few successive price increases can lead to excitement and a sort of mania about the possibility that the price will continue to rise over an extended period of time.

All such bubble movements are assumed to end eventually. What triggers their collapse, as with what triggers their start, is usually not specified. The model merely presumes that some extraneous event causes the mania to dissipate. When it does, it is assumed to dissipate completely, thereby implying that the asset price immediately falls all the way back to its pseudo-intrinsic value implied by the Rational Expectations Hypothesis. Once a bubble bursts, then, the market is supposed to revert to setting asset prices nearly perfectly at their supposedly true values.

The validity of our argument that Rational Expectations models characterize grossly irrational behavior is not diminished when crowd psychology is incorporated into the analysis. On the contrary, it is difficult to fathom how anyone might forecast such an ephemeral phenomenon, let alone come to believe that it develops over time according to an overarching mechanical rule.

Like all REH-based models, the Rational Expectations bubble models also suffer from empirical difficulties. During a bubble, prices are supposed to rise steadily, save for a few random movements in the opposite direction. However, the dramatic upswings shown in Figures 5.1 and 5.2 all involve extended periods in which the asset price undergoes a persistent but partial movement back toward its benchmark value.

Consider the long upswing in the German mark–U.S. dollar exchange rate that occurred in the first half of the 1980s. By January 1983, the price of the dollar had begun to rise well above most estimates of its benchmark value. Over the ensuing two years, the exchange rate rose from 2.37 to 3.40, implying a further dollar appreciation of 44%. At its height, the dollar was overvalued relative to purchasing power parity by roughly 60%. Like most such dramatic upswings, economists and others referred to the dollar's rise as a bubble (see, e.g., Frankel, 1985; Krugman, 1986).

Figure 6.1 plots the daily German mark–U.S. dollar exchange rate during this supposed bubble, showing several periods in which the exchange rate moves persistently but partially back toward purchasing power parity. On January 9, 1984, for example, the market entered a nine-week period during which the dollar fell steadily, from 2.84 to 2.55 (points A and B in the figure). In fact, the dollar fell in eight of the nine weeks during this period. If the long upswing really had been due to crowd psychology and mania, it had surely dissipated by the beginning of 1984. But according to the Rational Expectations bubble model, the dollar should have immediately crashed to its fundamental value. No such crash occurred, and by mid-March 1984, the dollar had resumed its long upward climb.

Rational Expectations bubble models also fail to explain the long downswings that sometimes characterize asset prices. To begin with, while the downturns that follow the collapse of bubbles are supposed to involve a crash back to pseudo-intrinsic values implied by the Rational Expectations Hypothesis, these bubble

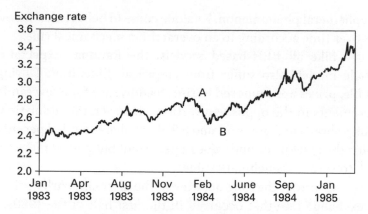

Fig. 6.1. Swing in the German mark–U.S. dollar exchange rate, 1983–1985

models do not generate protracted movements below the pseudo-intrinsic values.[3] There are, of course, episodes when prices fall by large magnitudes in the course of a single day—for example, the dramatic declines of U.S. equity prices on October 24, 1929 ("Black Thursday"), and on October 19, 1987 ("Black Monday"). But the long upswings depicted in Figures 5.1 and 5.2 are mostly followed by protracted downswings that last for years. For example, after U.S. equity prices reached their highs in September 1929 and March 2000 and began falling, they did not reach their lows until roughly three years later in both cases.[4]

The frequency, duration, and unevenness that characterizes the upswings and downswings that we actually observe in asset prices indicates that Rational Expectations bubble models do not provide even an approximate description of fluctuations in these markets.

[3]Declining Rational Expectations bubbles are ruled out, because they have the potential to push prices to zero, which implies that such downswings could never get started.

[4]For an econometric analysis of the inability of Rational Expectations bubble models to account for price swings in currency markets, see Frydman et al. (2010b).

A Seductive Narrative of Behavioral Bubbles

Behavioral economists attempt to incorporate observation of how market participants actually behave into their models. They have recognized that, although collective manias may occur from time to time, price swings are an inherent feature of asset markets and thus cannot be explained on the basis of exceptional displays of crowd psychology. This observation has led them to seek less unusual patterns in decisionmaking to account for long swings.

One of the key findings emphasized in the literature comes from surveys of professional market participants concerning their trading strategies. These surveys reveal that the use of technical trading strategies is widespread, with many participants relying on them, at least in part, to make their trading decisions. Many of these so-called "chartist" strategies entail nothing more than extrapolating past price trends in one way or another (see Schulmeister, 2003, 2006). Consequently, formalizing the use of such strategies seemed like a particularly useful avenue for modeling asset-price swings.

Behavioral models also draw from the results of many controlled experiments in which payoff-relevant outcomes are uncertain. The results reveal that individuals' decisionmaking tends to deviate from what would be expected on the basis of standard probabilistic rules. These deviations often exhibit patterns. For example, when given new information, individuals tend to revise their beliefs about the likelihood of the uncertain outcomes slowly relative to what the laws of probability would imply, a phenomenon cognitive psychologists call "conservatism" (see Edwards, 1968; Shleifer, 2000). Psychologists interpret such patterns as suggesting that individuals rely on useful heuristics to aid them in making decisions in an uncertain world. In real-world markets, the tendency for a market participant to revise her forecasting strategy piecewise and moderately makes sense, given that which new strategy she should adopt is never clear.

And yet, while behavioral economists and psychologists have accumulated a massive amount of evidence showing that individuals do not act according to contemporary economists' standard of rationality, many of the behavioral bubble models use the Rational Expectations Hypothesis to portray the decisionmaking of a group of so-called "smart" or "informed" investors.[5] By doing so, these models embody the same basic narrative that underlies the Efficient Market Hypothesis: if the market were populated solely by "intelligent investors" (Fama, 1965, p. 56), the price of the asset would roughly equal its "true" intrinsic value.

To generate bubble movements away from a model's pseudo-intrinsic values, an economist assumes the presence of so-called "irrational" or "uninformed" speculators. These individuals are "subject to animal spirits, fads and fashions, overconfidence and related psychological biases that might lead to momentum trading" (Abreu and Brunnermeier, 2003, p. 173). The forecasting behavior of the uninformed is often portrayed with one or more technical trading rules, which these participants use in a mechanical way and which extrapolate past price trends. This leads the uninformed to bid up prices, even though they may already be above the "smart" investors' assessment of intrinsic values.

By portraying the use of chartist rules as purely mechanical, behavioral economists transform what is a reasonable heuristic, which may supplement assessments based on inherently imperfect knowledge, into a strategy that is obviously incompatible with what anyone in real-world markets would consider even minimally reasonable behavior: participants supposedly never look for nonroutine change and remain forever faithful to their mechanical technical trading strategy.

[5]Seminal behavioral bubble models include Frankel and Froot (1987) and DeLong et al. (1990b). For more recent models, see Abreu and Brunnermeier (2003) and De Grauwe and Grimaldi (2006). Frankel and Froot (1987) and De Grauwe and Grimaldi (2006) assume that all traders have access to what would be the true overarching model relating asset price to fundamentals in the absence of their use of chartist rules.

LIMITS TO ARBITRAGE: AN ARTIFACT OF MECHANISTIC THEORY

The insistence on overarching models leads to another difficulty. If it were really the case that smart investors roughly knew the "true" fundamental values of assets, they should be willing to wager large amounts of capital on any departures from these values. But if they did, they would bid prices to fluctuate randomly around their supposedly true values, implying that bubbles would not occur, despite the presence of uninformed or "less-intelligent" traders.

This difficulty has led to much research attempting to explain why smart investors do not always arbitrage away departures from the supposedly true intrinsic values. The literature on modeling so-called "limits to arbitrage" in a fully predetermined world has shown that if economists' smart individuals are risk-averse, they will voluntarily limit the amount of capital that they wager on the return of prices to their supposedly true intrinsic values.[6] The smart investors are assumed to know about the presence of the uninformed speculators, whose trading behavior increases the riskiness of investors' arbitrage positions. This risk further limits the size of these positions and enables the trading behavior of the momentum speculators to create a bubble.[7]

Economists have also looked at several institutional features of trading in real-world markets when modeling limits to arbitrage. For example, they have emphasized that all market participants face various capital constraints, which limit the size of both their long and short positions. Abreu and Brunnermeier (2003) assume such constraints as well as asymmetric information among their "rational" investors. In their model, momentum traders can create a bubble. The assumed information problem creates

---

[6]See Gromb and Vayanos (2010) for a review of this literature.

[7]For empirical evidence that the importance of chartist rules and momentum trading is not nearly as great as is often believed and actually diminishes during the excessive phase of swings, see Chapter 7.

two types of smart investors: those who know that a bubble has formed and those who do not. Eventually, however, the price inflates so much that a sufficient number of smart investors become aware of the bubble, at which point the bubble bursts and the smart investors bid the price all the way back to its pseudo-intrinsic value. There is a possibility in the model that the smart investors who learn about a bubble early may not arbitrage a price's departure from its supposedly true fundamental value. Instead, they may initially bet on a continuation of the upswing in order to "ride the bubble though they know that the bubble will [eventually] burst" (Abreu and Brunnermeier, 2003, p. 175).[8]

The Trouble with Behavioral Bubbles

Of course, the need to model limits to arbitrage arises only because economists presume that asset prices unfold according to overarching mechanical rules, and that rational individuals somehow know the true process driving market outcomes. This core premise has led to an intensive search not only for institutional and other features of trading that motivate limited arbitrage but also for supposedly irrational heuristics and psychological biases that might justify the presence of mechanical momentum traders in bubble models.

There is no doubt that participants face capital constraints, and that some rely on technical trading and other heuristics. But by focusing on these issues, economists have missed the key problem facing market participants: the importance of nonroutine change and imperfect knowledge, which implies that even supposedly irrational behavior cannot be adequately modeled with fully predetermined mechanical rules.

---

[8]Allen and Gorton (1993) show that agency problems and compensation structures based on short-term (quarterly or annual) performance also can lead portfolio managers, who supposedly know an asset's true value, to bet on a movement away from this level.

Beyond their flawed foundations, it is difficult to reconcile behavioral bubble models with the long swings that we actually observe in asset markets. For one thing, the many models, such as that of Abreu and Brunnermeier (2003), that rely on asymmetrically informed smart investors to generate bubbles, are simply not credible explanations of outcomes in major asset markets, such as those for stocks and currencies. In these markets, a plethora of publicly available information is quickly disseminated around the world. Of course, company insiders have private information, and there may be isolated cases in which trading on such information influences a stock's price. But this scenario would not explain swings in broad stock-price indexes or currencies, such as those captured in Figures 5.1 and 5.2.

The Abreu and Brunnermeier (2003) model and many other Rational Expectations bubble accounts imply that once a bubble bursts, the asset price returns immediately to its supposedly true intrinsic value. But, as we have already seen, such an account does not provide even an approximate description of the downswings in financial markets.

Some behavioral bubble models do generate long-lived downswings. For example, in Frankel and Froot (1987) and De Grauwe and Grimaldi (2006), long swings away from pseudo-intrinsic values occur because all traders gradually switch over time between forecasting on the basis of an REH-based fundamental model and chartist rules. A long upswing in price occurs because market participants slowly abandon their fundamental model in favor of a chartist rule, whereas a long downswing arises because this process is eventually reversed.

Behavioral bubble models suggest that there is a relatively straightforward policy by which officials could deflate bubbles as soon as they begin. Instead of taking on the formidable task of fighting crowd psychology and manias, policy officials need only start a short-term price trend back toward the putative true fundamental value. According to behavioral models, this action would lead both chartists and smart investors to respond mechanically to the new trend, thereby reinforcing and sustaining it.

But this implication is contradicted by experience. One well-known example of the difficulty that policy officials face in engendering sustained countermovements in asset prices is provided by former Federal Reserve Chairman Alan Greenspan's attempt to warn U.S. stock markets on December 5, 1996, of "irrational exuberance."[9] Initially, this pronouncement led to a sharp drop in equity prices. But if behavioral bubble models really captured the process driving equity values, this change in trend would have been more than sufficient to trigger a sustained reversal. Instead, U.S. stock prices resumed their upward trend, which lasted another four years.[10]

FORGOTTEN FUNDAMENTALS

Despite their apparent differences, the basic mechanism that underpins Rational Expectations and behavioral bubble models is essentially the same: upswings away from pseudo-intrinsic values arise because participants in the aggregate, for various reasons, increasingly downplay the importance of fundamental factors. Supposedly, then, fluctuations in asset markets are disconnected from movements of fundamental factors for long periods, implying that markets often grossly misallocate society's scarce capital. As we discuss in the next chapter and Chapter 11, this prediction is grossly inconsistent with the empirical record on asset-price fluctuations.

[9]Greenspan (2007) recounts the time leading up to and following his famous warning to the markets.

[10]Research on the efficacy of official intervention in currency markets also shows that policy officials face difficulties in influencing asset prices in any sustained way. Researchers have generally found that, although official intervention is effective in the near term at moving exchange rates in the desired direction, it does not usually lead to a sustained countermovement. For example, see Dominguez and Frankel (1993) and Fatum and Hutchison (2003, 2006).

PART II

An Alternative

It is better to be roughly right than precisely wrong.
—Attributed to John Maynard Keynes,
The Economist, January 19, 2006

7

Keynes and Fundamentals

T HE RUN-UPS IN housing, equity, and other asset markets and the subsequent sharp reversals that were among the proximate causes of the financial crisis that began in 2007 solidified the belief that asset-price swings are largely unrelated to fundamental considerations. Instead, price bubbles supposedly form and collapse as a result of the trading decisions of market participants who are irrational, prone to emotions and other psychological factors, or engage in momentum trading.

Many observers point to the long upswing in U.S. equity prices during the 1990s as a prime example of such behavior and widely refer to this upswing as the "dot.com or internet bubble." During this period, there was indeed much confidence, optimism, and even a sense of euphoria about internet stocks, with initial public offerings for many companies witnessing remarkable price increases. Globe.com and eToys, just to name two, saw price rises on the first day of trading of 606% and 280%, respectively. During October 1999, the six largest technology-related companies— Microsoft, Intel, IBM, Cisco, Lucent, and Dell—had a combined market value of $1.65 trillion, or nearly 20% of U.S. gross domestic product. At its height in August 2000, the broader S&P 500 price index had climbed to roughly 43 times its underlying earnings (Figure 7.1).[1] This number eclipsed the market's valuation in Octo-

---

[1]The use of a 10-year trailing moving average to construct the price-earnings ratio in the figure addresses the problems that the current level of re-

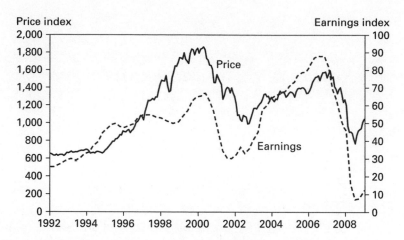

Fig. 7.1. S&P 500 stock price and current earnings, 1992–2009
Source: Data are from Robert Shiller's website: www.econ.yale.edu/~shiller/.

ber 1929 of 33 times earnings, which had stood as the market's all-time high until the 1990s.

To be sure, psychological factors played a role in leading participants in the aggregate to bid up stock prices in the 1990s. Technical trading can also contribute to price trends. But the bubble notion's assumption that such considerations alone could *sustain* an upswing lasting an entire decade is implausible. Technical trading mostly takes place over minutes or hours. Schulmeister (2003) points out that the technical rules differ in terms of how quickly they generate a buy or sell signal once a price trend has already started. This difference can lead speculators to prolong an initial price trend.[2] However, the trigger times of most technical strategies differ only in

---

ported earnings can be quite volatile from month to month and can be negative in a month if companies' losses are large enough. Using a moving average of earnings also leads to a better measure of the benchmark level around which stock prices fluctuate. See Campbell and Shiller (1988, 1998). Of course, alternative measures of earnings (for example, operating earnings) or a longer or shorter moving average would lead to different price-earnings valuations. However, these alternative valuations would also indicate historically very high stock prices relative to underlying earnings in 1999 and 2000.

[2] See also Schulmeister (2003, 2006) for an analysis of such scenarios.

terms of hours or days. Such speculation simply cannot account for long swings lasting many months or years.

To account for the asset-price swings actually observed in markets, therefore, we must look beyond both psychological and technical trading considerations. Indeed, the purely psychological accounts of asset markets overlook the possibility that to forecast price movements, participants look to fundamental factors that they think will move the market over whatever horizon, short or long, they are interested in for the purpose of assessing investment returns. Any confidence and optimism that might exist in the market would quickly evaporate if, say, earnings and overall economic activity consistently moved in the opposite direction.

During much of the 1990s, for example, corporate earnings, gross domestic product, employment, exports, productivity levels, and other economic indicators were rising strongly, while inflation rates were declining or holding at benign levels. Free-trade agreements and other political and institutional changes, together with loose monetary policy, were also conducive to growth. As these developments unfolded, they no doubt reinforced confidence and optimism in the widespread view that the U.S. and other economies were in the midst of an information-technology revolution. The bullish trends in fundamental factors and the increased confidence that they engendered led many market participants, including those with shorter- and longer-term horizons, to raise their forecasts of stock returns, thereby bidding up prices.

The importance of fundamental factors in driving asset prices is easily seen in Figure 7.1, which plots the S&P 500 price index along with the basket's underlying earnings. The comovement of the two series is striking. Not only do the broad swings in the series rise and fall together, but their major turning points in 2000, 2003, and 2007 are also closely synchronized. The figure belies the bubble view that long upswings in stock prices are unrelated to fundamental factors and concerns about future prospects.

To be sure, the upswing in broad stock market indexes in the 1990s did reach levels that history and the subsequent long downswings tell us were excessive. But, as later chapters show, such excessive fluctuations result not because market participants' trading decisions ignore fundamental factors, but because, in forecasting future outcomes, participants must cope with ever-imperfect knowledge about how to interpret trends in fundamental factors.

In fact, even if an individual is interested only in short-term returns—a feature of trading in many markets—the use of historical data and news on fundamental factors to forecast these returns is extremely valuable. Formal and informal evidence that trends in a wide array of fundamentals play a key role in driving asset-price swings is overwhelming.

Was Keynes a Behavioral Economist?

John Maynard Keynes is often invoked to support the argument that asset prices are driven by purely psychological considerations. This reading of Keynes, however, seems to overlook the role played by fundamentals in his account of asset markets.

In a widely quoted passage, Keynes (1936, p. 156) likened the problem facing professional investors and speculators in asset markets to

> those newspaper competitions in which the competitors have to pick out the six prettiest faces from a hundred photographs, the prize being awarded to the competitor whose choice most nearly corresponds to the average preferences of the competitors as a whole; so that each competitor has to pick, not those faces which he himself finds prettiest, but those which he thinks likeliest to catch the fancy of the other competitors, all of whom are looking at the problem from the same point of view. It is not a case of choosing those which, to the best of one's judgment, are really the prettiest, nor even those which average opinion genuinely thinks the prettiest. We have reached the third degree where we devote our intelligences to anticipating what average opinion expects the average opinion to be. And there are some, I believe, who practice the fourth, fifth and higher degrees.

Behavioral economists and many other observers often invoke Keynes's (1936) beauty-contest metaphor as a rationale for their bubble view of swings (see Akerlof and Shiller, 2009, p. 133). Faced with having to guess "what average opinion expects the average opinion to be," market participants supposedly ignore fundamental factors in forecasting and fall prey to crowd psychology, emotions, psychological biases, and momentum trading.[3] Indeed, throughout chapter 12, Keynes makes repeated reference to psychological considerations in describing speculation and investment, such as *"confidence* with which we ... forecast" (p. 148), "mass psychology" (p. 154), "spontaneous optimism" (p. 161), and "animal spirits" (p. 162). At one point, he even compares short-term speculation in asset markets with "the activities of a casino" (p. 159), suggesting, as many observers do nowadays, that markets may allocate society's capital haphazardly.

There are crucial differences, however, between Keynes's (1936) account of asset markets and bubble accounts. The most important is that he placed unforeseeable change and imperfect knowledge at the center of his analysis of financial markets.[4] Thus, he surely would have viewed fully predetermined behavioral finance models, which portray swings as mechanical departures from the supposedly true fundamental values based on the Rational Expectations Hypothesis, as utter nonsense. Although psychological factors undoubtedly played a role in his thinking about financial markets, there is much in Keynes (1936, chapter 12) that suggests that fundamental considerations are important to his view of asset-price fluctuations.[5]

Keynes (1936) is fairly explicit about the role of fundamentals in forecasting average opinion and how fundamentals are related

[3]See, for example, Shiller (2000), Brunnermeier (2001), and Akerloff and Shiller (2009) and references therein.
[4]His life-long emphasis on the inadequacy of standard probabilistic portrayals of uncertainty is also seen in Keynes (1921).
[5]We develop a mathematical model of asset-price swings that places imperfect knowledge about how fundamentals influence outcomes at the center of the analysis, and that also incorporates behavioral insights, in Frydman and Goldberg (2007, chapter 14; 2010b). For a nontechnical discussion, see Chapter 9.

to psychological considerations. To forecast what average opinion thinks the average opinion will be over the short term, one would look for factors that underpinned the average opinion. Even if one believed that the level of confidence, optimism, and animal spirits were the main considerations, these psychological factors are difficult to measure and observe directly. Moreover, as Keynes himself argues, they depend on a wide array of fundamental factors. In fact, when one contemplates the beauty-contest problem, fundamental considerations are, for the most part, the only tangible factors one could use to guess how the mood of the market might change.

IMPERFECT KNOWLEDGE AND FUNDAMENTALS

The number of scholarly journal articles and books about Keynes; *The General Theory* (Keynes 1936); his ideas about financial markets; and his other economic, political, and social writings is sufficient to fill an entire library.[6] More than 50 years after his death, there continues to be much debate about the meaning of his writings and their implications for public policy.

Scholars, for example, disagree over what Keynes really meant by the term "animal spirits" and how important they are for his thinking about asset markets. The term is used by behavioral economists and many other observers to suggest that decisionmaking is primarily driven by psychological factors or is irrational and contrary to reason and forethought. However, some scholars have argued that the notion of animal spirits "is wholly rational, as is the use of direct knowledge" (Dow and Dow, 1985, p. 52). Melberg (2010, p. 4) points out that Keynes introduces the term only toward the end of chapter 12 of *The General Theory*, and, after reviewing the literature, concludes that "the attempt to use Keynes's idea about animal spirits to provide a behavioral foundation for a theory about economic fluctuation does not seem very promising."

---

[6]For the authoritative account of Keynes and his ideas, see Skidelsky (1983, 1992, 2000, 2009).

It is uncontroversial to point out, however, that Keynes thought that asset markets are imperfect assessors of values. The short-term nature of professional speculation and psychological considerations were important for his understanding of the problem. But the underlying reason for the imperfection of markets was the inherent imperfection or uncertainty of knowledge with which we must all cope. At the beginning of Chapter 12, he writes:

> The outstanding fact is the extreme precariousness of the basis of knowledge on which our estimates of prospective yield have to be made. [Keynes, 1936, p. 149]

No one, therefore, can attach a precise probability distribution to future outcomes:

> By uncertain knowledge, let me explain, I do not mean merely to distinguish what is known for certain from what is only probable. The game of roulette is not subject in this sense to uncertainty.... The sense in which I am using the term is that in which the prospect of a European war is uncertain, or the price of copper and the rate of interest 20 years hence, or the obsolescence of a new invention, or the position of private wealth owners in the social system in 1970. About these matters there is no scientific basis on which to form any calculable probability whatever. We simply do not know. [Keynes 1971–1989, vol. XIV, pp. 113–14]

Keynes recognized that the imperfection of knowledge opens the door for psychological considerations, such as confidence and optimism, to play a role in market participants' decisionmaking. But he begins his analysis of asset markets by discussing how "expectations of prospective yields" are, in the first place, rooted in individuals' understanding of fundamentals or "facts." Participants "fall back on what is, in truth, a convention . . . [which] lies in assuming that the existing state of affairs will continue indefinitely, except in so far as we have specific reasons to expect a change" (Keynes, 1936, p. 152). The existing state of affairs entails "knowledge of the facts which will influence the yield of the investment," and the "existing market valuation ... will only change in proportion to changes in this knowledge" (p. 152).

Keynes discusses the short-term nature of speculation and psychological considerations not because he thinks participants' forecasts are unrelated to knowledge of the facts, but because these considerations help us to understand why this "conventional valuation" is at times subject to so much variation. He presents his beauty-contest metaphor in a section devoted to elaborating "some of the factors which accentuate this precariousness" (Keynes, 1936, p. 153). Animal spirits are introduced in the penultimate section of chapter 12 as another reason for "instability due to the characteristic of human nature" (p. 161). But, at the end of that section, Keynes warns:

> We should *not* conclude from this that everything depends on *waves* of irrational psychology. We are merely reminding ourselves that ... our *rational selves* [are] choosing between alternatives as best as we are able, calculating where we can, but often falling back for our motive on whim or sentiment or chance. [Keynes, 1936, pp. 163–63, emphasis added]

For Keynes, unlike for behavioral economists, reliance on psychological factors in decisionmaking is not a symptom of irrationality. He emphasizes that while rational individuals in the real world use knowledge of facts, knowledge is imperfect and thus calculation alone is insufficient for decisionmaking. Although psychological considerations play a role in individual decisionmaking, by themselves "waves of irrational psychology" could not sustain recurrent long swings in asset prices. Indeed, comprehending changes in fundamental factors is crucial for understanding how confidence and other sentiments are influenced over time.

ARE FUNDAMENTALS REALLY IRRELEVANT IN THE BEAUTY CONTEST?

No matter how many "higher degrees" a judge might contemplate in guessing what others think, in the end he must choose some criteria on which to base his decision. In doing so, he would rely on his understanding of the factors on which he thought the other judges were likely to base their decisions.

One of these factors might be the beauty of the contestants. Beauty, of course, is in the eye of the beholder. So if a judge thought that others were basing their guesses on this criterion, he would want to know the cultural background according to which beauty was being judged. A group of judges from the U.S. Midwest, he might believe, would assess beauty differently from a group from New York City or from the Niger delta.

Factors other than beauty also might be important for guessing the winners. Judges may fall back on sentiments concerning the particular socioeconomic backgrounds of the contestants in making their final selections. It is difficult to know which factors other judges will rely on, or how they will weight them in their decisionmaking. Although psychological considerations play a role, in the end, what others think is not purely random; they must also choose a set of factors on which to guess the guessing strategies of others.

In attempting to forecast average opinion in financial markets, short-term speculators pay close attention to news about fundamentals. Indeed, there are many participants who comb through company reports, study industry developments, and examine trends in a wide array of fundamental factors to find companies whose future prospects they believe are likely undervalued by the market. The idea is that sooner or later the market will discover the undervaluation and bid up prices. Warren Buffet of Berkshire Hathaway and Seth Klarman of The Baupost Group are just two well-known examples of such value speculators.

As industry developments and trends in other fundamentals unfold over the short term, value speculators alter their thinking about future prospects. Their trading, in turn, influences prices. To forecast average opinion even over a few hours or days, then, one would need to anticipate news about fundamental factors and how this news might be interpreted not just by value speculators but also by other short-term speculators.

To be sure, psychological and other considerations, which are not directly related to an asset's prospective yield, enter into investors' assessments regarding where average opinion might be moving. Indeed, Keynes (1936, p. 148) invoked the beauty contest to emphasize such considerations. He attached particular importance to the "*state of confidence* . . . [as a factor to which] practical men always pay the closest and most anxious attention."

An investor's confidence, of course, depends in part on purely psychological elements, and it is impossible for anyone to look directly into the psyches of other investors. How, then, might an investor pay the closest attention to the state of confidence in the market, let alone forecast its future unfolding? As with the newspaper beauty contest, she must choose factors that are observable to others and on which she thinks confidence and other psychological considerations depend.

Keynes is rather explicit that these factors are largely related to fundamental considerations. In fact, for him, psychological considerations, such as confidence, exert their impact through the manner in which investors use and alter their knowledge of the facts. To clarify the role of the "state of confidence," he writes that speculation does not

> solely depend . . . on the most probable forecast . . . [but] on the confidence with which we make this forecast—on how highly we rate the likelihood of our best forecast turning out quite wrong. If we expect large changes but are very uncertain as to what precise form these changes will take, then our confidence will be weak. [Keynes, 1936, p. 148]

By "large changes," Keynes is referring to movements in both fundamentals and their interpretations.

Relating the state of confidence to the uncertainty of knowledge suggests that it is connected to the fundamental factors that participants use to forecast future prospects. Indeed, five lines after Keynes points out that speculation entails forecasting "what the market will value [an asset] at, under the influence of mass psychology, three months or a year hence," he reveals how to pay attention to the state of confidence and play the beauty contest: "Thus, the professional investor is forced to concern himself with the anticipation of impending changes, in the *news* ... of the kind by which *experience* shows that the mass psychology of the market is most influenced" (Keynes, 1936, p. 155, emphasis added).

Later in the chapter, Keynes adds "spontaneous optimism" and "animal spirits" to his list of psychological factors. But here, too, he suggests that these sentiments, which underpin decisions to invest in new capital, have a basis in fundamental considerations. The impact of optimism and animal spirits imply "not only that slumps and depressions are exaggerated in degree, but that economic prosperity is excessively dependent on a political and social atmosphere which is congenial to the average business man" (Keynes, 1936, p. 162).

Keynes (1936, p. 162) points out that confidence and optimism might also depend on "nerves and hysteria." But in the end, short-term speculators need observable factors on which these sentiments depend if they are going to anticipate their influence on average opinion. As we will see in the next section, "experience shows" that confidence, optimism, and other psychological considerations depend on news concerning a wide range of fundamental factors, including company earnings, interest rates, and reports on the political and social context in which participants make decisions.

It is, of course, difficult to anticipate which pieces of news will impact the market, let alone the nature and size of their separate influences. No one would expect confidence and optimism to be connected to fundamental considerations in any mechanical way. And the unfolding of news and sentiment will influence in nonroutine ways individuals' use of fundamentals to forecast both the average opinion and the future prospects of assets. Likewise, the timing and nature of revisions of forecasting strategies, as well as policy and institutional changes, cannot be fully foreseen.

In financial markets, then, we would expect that fundamental factors underpin prices, but in different ways during different time periods that inherently cannot be "put on a computer and run" (Lucas, 2001, p. 21). Keynes's insights about uncertain knowledge, the short-term nature of speculation and the "beauty contest," and the role of the state of confidence and other psychological considerations, far from implying that fundamentals are unimportant, actually suggest that fundamentals are the central drivers of asset-price movements.

FUNDAMENTALS AND EQUITY-PRICE MOVEMENTS: EVIDENCE FROM BLOOMBERG'S MARKET STORIES

Psychological considerations, such as confidence and optimism, are difficult to measure and incorporate into formal statistical analysis of the determinants of price fluctuations in asset markets. But to the extent that these sentiments depend on fundamental considerations, empirical researchers and market participants alike perceive their effects by examining the relationships between fundamentals and asset prices.

The importance of psychological considerations and imperfect knowledge, however, implies that these relationships change at times and in ways that no one can fully specify in advance. So to examine the relationship between asset prices and fundamentals, empirical researchers need to allow for such contingent change. In Chapter 11, we discuss formal statistical studies that do so. As we would expect from considering the beauty-contest metaphor, these studies find clear evidence not only of a changing relationship, but also of different fundamentals mattering during different time periods.[7]

Moreover, whereas statistical analysis is important for testing the implications of competing economic theories, there is an abundance of less formal evidence showing the central role that fundamental factors play in asset markets. Indeed, one only has to

---

[7]Nearly all empirical studies of asset markets, however, disregard change altogether. Not surprisingly, they report little or no evidence that fundamentals matter. See Chapter 11.

watch Bloomberg Television or CNBC for a week or two to realize that news on a wide range of fundamental factors drives prices in major asset markets. As earnings announcements are made or policy developments in Washington, D.C., become known, one sees the markets react. One also sees that the fundamentals that matter change over time.

Bloomberg News as a Window into Markets

Each day, business journalists keep track of which pieces of news have moved asset prices. They also survey market participants about their views of the day's developments and the factors that drove their trading. The information contained in these business reports provides a record of the key factors that move asset prices from day to day.[8]

Mangee (2011) extracts this information from the Bloomberg News daily market-wrap (end-of-day) stories on the U.S. stock market for January 4, 1993 (Bloomberg's first report) through December 31, 2009.[9] Bloomberg News is a subsidiary of Bloomberg LP, the largest financial news and analysis company in the world. It caters to professional players at major financial institutions around the globe, although policymakers and academics also are among its more than 250,000 clients, as are roughly 450 newspapers and magazines worldwide. Its news and analysis is a bellwether for the professional investor.

In writing market-wrap stories, Bloomberg's journalists rely on contacts with one hundred to two hundred fund managers and other actors directly involved in the markets. Every one of their wrap stories includes at least one direct quote from one or more of these individuals concerning their views about the key factors driving the market. These stories thus provide a window

---

[8]Our discussion in this and the remaining sections of this chapter draws on Mangee's (2011) data and analysis.

[9]Bloomberg Finance LP has generously allowed us access to Bloomberg Professional, which archives Bloomberg's wrap stories.

into the decisionmaking of the professional players whose trading determines prices.

Bloomberg's wrap stories show that a wide array of fundamental factors influences market participants' trading decisions. The categories and specific types of fundamental news that underpin Mangee's (2011) textual data are listed in Table 7.1. His data track the proportion of days over the sample in each month that a particular category or piece of fundamental news was reported to have moved stock prices.

Unlike the quantitative data typically used by researchers in carrying out formal statistical analysis, the textual data contained in Bloomberg's wrap stories are not constrained to track the importance of only fundamental considerations. Bloomberg journalists indicate in their reports that psychological considerations (such as confidence, optimism, and fear) as well as technical considerations (such as momentum trading, profit taking, and the January effect) also play roles in the day-to-day trading decisions of professional players. Tables 7.2 and 7.3 list the specific types of psychological and technical considerations, respectively, picked up by Mangee's (2011) analysis.

Mangee scores each day's wrap story in terms of the fundamental, psychological, and/or technical factors that it reports to have been important in driving prices that day. For example, if a story reports that only news about earnings and interest rates moved the market on a particular day, then these factors each receive a score of 1 on that day, while all the other factors in Tables 7.1–7.3 receive a score of 0.[10] In all, Mangee scores 4,206 separate wrap stories.

One might expect that Bloomberg journalists would be predisposed to report the importance of psychological and technical factors over fundamental factors. After all, optimism, euphoria, fear, and momentum are more sensational—and thus demand

---

[10]Mangee's data also record the qualitative relationships between movements of the factors in Tables 7.1 and 7.2 and stock prices. For example, he finds that when company earnings are reported to have mattered, their rise or fall always influences prices in the same direction. See Mangee (2011) for more details about his scoring and findings.

TABLE 7.1
Fundamental Factors Influencing Daily Stock Prices

Category	News topic	Category	News topic
Economy	GDP	Housing	Housing starts
	GDP growth rate		Home sales
	Index of leading economic indicators		Foreclosures
	Industrial production		Housing slump
	Productivity		Real estate prices
	Consumer income		Mortgage rates
	Service sector		Commercial property value
	Employment (nonfarm)		
	Unemployment rate		
	Jobless claims		
	Job creation		
	Manufacturing index		
	Factory orders		
	Durables		
	Nondurables		
Interest rates	Fed funds	Oil	Crude oil prices
	Discount rate		OPEC oil supply
	Treasury notes yield		
	Treasury bills yield		
	Treasury bonds yield		

(continued)

TABLE 7.1 (*cont.*)

Category	News topic	Category	News topic
Inflation	Producer price index	Currency markets	Value of dollar
	Consumer price index		Value of foreign currency
	Manufacturing price index		Introduction of euro
	Wages		
Earnings	Earnings and profits	Sales	Revenues
			Retail sales
			Auto sales
Gap/valuation	Distance from historical levels	Trade	Agreements (NAFTA, GATT)
	Overvalued		Tariffs
	Undervalued		Quotas
			Subsidies
			Current account deficit
			Current account surplus
Company variables	Bankruptcy	Government	Fiscal policy
	CEO or CFO leaves		Administrative comments
	Malpractice, legal, or accounting issues		Taxes and rules on CEO bonuses
	Firm added to index		Credit worthiness
	Firm market value		Stimulus plan
	Dividends		Bailout
	Mergers and acquisitions		Nationalization of banks or healthcare

Category	Type
	Book-to-bill ratio
	Firm layoffs or labor strike
	Stock split
	Share buyback
	Large stake in firm
	IPOs
	Business spending or investment
Central bank	Monetary policy
	Minutes or comments
	Bailouts
Terrorism	General terrorism or attacks
ROW	All of the above factors as they pertain to rest of world
	Budget surplus
	Budget deficit
	Political event or election
	Political conflicts, instability, or corruption
	Armed conflicts or nuclear testing
	FDIC/SEC restructuring; regulations stress tests
	Treasury secretary leaves
Consumption	Consumer spending or demand
	Consumer confidence
Financial/credit markets	Financial markets or sector
	Weakness in credit markets
	Credit ratings
	Lack of capital funding
	Credit card defaults
	Restructuring or regulation

Notes: See Mangee (2011) for descriptions of the categories and types of fundamentals. CEO, chief executive officer; CFO, chief financial officer; FDIC, Federal Deposit Insurance Corporation; GATT, General Agreement on Tariffs and Trade; GDP, gross domestic product; IPO, initial public offering; NAFTA, North American Free Trade Agreement; OPEC, Organization of Petroleum Exporting Countries; ROW, rest of world; SEC, Securities and Exchange Commission.

TABLE 7.2

Psychological Factors Influencing Stock Prices

Optimism	Concern
Pessimism	Euphoria
Confidence	Crowd psychology
Sentiment	Exuberance
Greed	Worry
Fear	

Note: See Mangee (2011) for descriptions of the types of psychological considerations.

TABLE 7.3

Technical Trading: Factors Influencing Stock Prices

Non-momentum	Momentum
Profit taking	Market rally
Firm added to index	Market momentum
Holiday effect	Momentum traders
January effect	Bandwagon
End-of-month effect	Price-to-price loop
End-of-quarter effect	Moving average
Friday effect	Chartism
End of the year effect	
Giving-back effect	
Triple witching	
Santa Claus effect	

Note: See Mangee (2011) for descriptions of the types of technical considerations.

greater attention from news outlets like Bloomberg—than earnings and interest rates as drivers of the market.

However, Mangee's data show that at least one fundamental factor in Table 7.1 was mentioned as a driver of stock prices on virtually every day in his sample. At least one psychological factor was mentioned on 55% of the days over the sample, suggesting that they, too, play an important role in underpinning price fluctuations in equity markets. In contrast, technical factors were mentioned as important price drivers roughly one day on average in each month of 20 trading days (6%). Table 7.4 lists all categories of fundamental, psychological, and technical factors tracked in Mangee's analysis, along with the proportion of days in the sample that each was mentioned as having driven the market.

TABLE 7.4
Factor Frequencies over Entire Sample

Factor	Factor frequency (%)
Fundamentals	99
Earnings	65
Psychological considerations	55
Psychology with fundamentals	54
Economy	47
Interest rates	38
Sales	23
Company variables	23
Inflation	20
Oil prices	19
ROW	14
Gap/valuation	12
Government	12
Consumption	12
Central bank	11
Housing	8
Technical trading	6
Currency markets	6
Financial or credit markets	6
Uncertainty	6
Technical non-momentum	5
Bubble considerations	3
Technical momentum	2
Terrorism	2
Trade	1
Pure psychology	1

Notes: Factor frequencies denote the percentage of days over the sample that each factor was mentioned in driving the aggregate market from January 4, 1993, to December 31, 2009. ROW, rest of world.

The Nonroutine Importance of Fundamentals

Over 16 years of reporting, Bloomberg's journalists tell a consistently clear story: fundamental considerations are the central drivers of day-to-day price fluctuations in stock markets. Three excerpts illustrate how the importance of these factors was reported.

> U.S. stocks rose, sending the Dow Jones Industrial Average to its first gain in six days, after General Electric Co., the second-biggest U.S. company by market value, said 1999 earnings will meet expectation. [December 15, 1998]

> U.S. stocks rallied after the Federal Reserve surprised investors by cutting interest rates for the fourth time this year. The Nasdaq Composite Index soared to its fourth biggest gain. [April 18, 2001]

> "The environment is pretty doggone good for stocks," said Robert Phillip, chairman of Walnut Asset Management LLC, which oversees $725 million in Philadelphia. "Earnings appear to be stronger than anticipated." [March 1, 2004]

As we would expect, given the close co-movement of stock prices and earnings in Figure 7.1, Bloomberg's stories show that earnings considerations—mentioned as a main driver of prices on 65% of the days in the sample (Table 7.4)—are the most important category of fundamentals.[11] But even the relationship between earn-

[11]This measure of the frequency with which earnings are mentioned by Bloomberg's wrap stories includes company announcements of earnings and earnings forecasts. It also includes mentions of stock-price movements that are reported to have arisen because other informational variables, for example interest rates or sales, led participants to revise their earnings predictions. Mangee (2011) provides an alternative measure that tracks the frequency of company announcements of earnings and earnings forecasts alone; he finds that these announcements are mentioned as a main driver of stock prices on 45 % of the days on average. This frequency may seem surprisingly high, given that many companies generally announce earnings over a roughly two-week period each quarter.

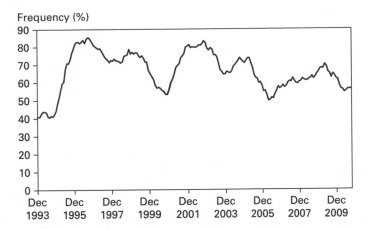

Fig. 7.2. Average monthly frequency of mentions in wrap reports: Earnings
Source: Mangee (2011).

ings and stock prices is not a mechanical one. To see how the importance of earnings varies over time, Figure 7.2 plots a 12-month moving average of the proportion of days in each month that these considerations were mentioned as having influenced the market. The figure shows that, for the most part, the importance of this category varies over a fairly wide range of 50–80%.

Although the importance of earnings exhibits substantial variation over the sample, such nonroutine change is much more pronounced with other fundamentals. Consider, for example, the price of oil, inflation, and interest rates, whose monthly moving averages we plot in Figures 7.3, 7.4, and 7.5, respectively.

Figure 7.3 shows that the market did not pay much attention to oil prices until the end of 2003, when its importance began rising dramatically. By the end of 2004, 60% of each month's wraps mentioned this factor as a driver of the market. As for inflation (Figure 7.4), its importance varies considerably over the sample. In 2002 and 2003, inflation reports were given little notice. But beginning in 2004, investors started to focus on them increasingly.

However, it is not uncommon for companies to make earnings announcements outside of the earnings seasons.

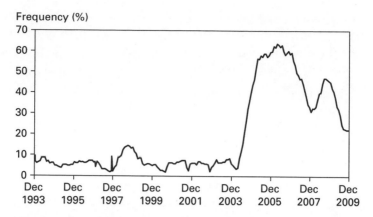

Fig. 7.3. Average monthly frequency of mentions in wrap reports: Oil prices
Source: Mangee (2011).

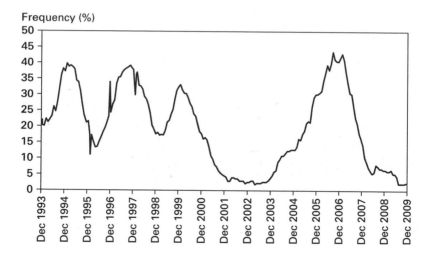

Fig. 7.4. Average monthly frequency of mentions in wrap reports: Inflation rate
Source: Mangee (2011).

The most likely explanation is that inflation provided clues about the future course of monetary policy at a time when short-term interest rates began rising. This interpretation is consistent with Figure 7.5, which shows that the market considered movements in interest rates to be of increasing importance beginning in 2004. By the end of 2006, this factor was mentioned in 60% of each month's wraps as a major driver of prices.

Another indication of the nonroutine relationship between stock prices and fundamentals is provided by tracking the average number of individual fundamentals that were mentioned as drivers in each month's wraps. This average is plotted in Figure 7.6, which shows that in some periods (for example, 2000 and 2001), three fundamental factors mattered on average, whereas in other periods (for example, 2005 and 2006), the number was five. Of course, given ever-imperfect knowledge, no one can fully foresee which fundamental factors might matter, the scope of their influence on prices, or when relevant fundamentals and their influence will change.

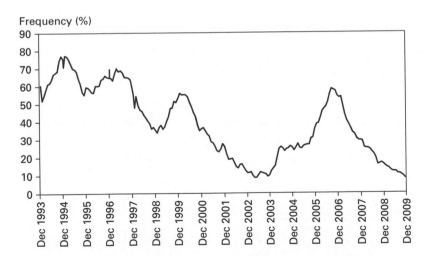

Fig. 7.5. Average monthly frequency of mentions in wrap reports: Interest rates
Source: Mangee (2011).

Number of fundamentals

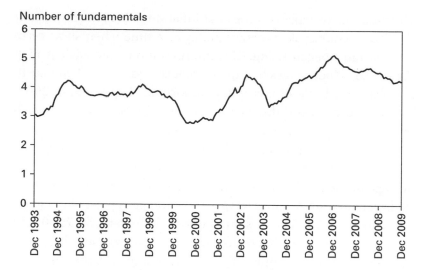

Fig. 7.6. Average monthly frequency of mentions in wrap reports:
Number of fundamentals
Source: Mangee (2011).

Rationalizing Psychological Factors with
News about Fundamentals

Mangee's (2011) textual data show that psychological considerations are mentioned quite frequently in the market-wrap stories (Figure 7.7). But the most striking finding is that Bloomberg's journalists, as well the market participants they talk to, rationalize their role almost entirely in terms of news about fundamentals and participants' interpretations of the impact of fundamentals on asset-price movements. Two of Bloomberg's wrap stories illustrate this close connection. Consider the report on April 21, 2009, titled "U.S. Stocks Rise as Qualcomm Earnings Boost Nasdaq Composite":

> "IBM earnings are extremely positive," said Howard Cornblue, a money manager for Pilgrim Investments, which oversees $7 billion. "This will give confidence and stability to the market."

Frequency (%)

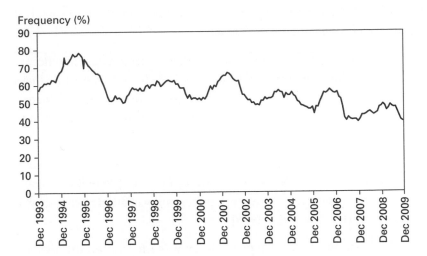

Fig. 7.7. Average monthly frequency of mentions in wrap reports:
Psychological considerations
Source: Mangee (2011).

Likewise, the report on March 2, 2009, titled "U.S. Stocks Tumble,
Trimming Gains at End of Three Week Rally," included the following account:

> "You have got a lot of fear going into earnings," said John Nichol,
> who manages $1 billion in Pittsburgh, including the Federated
> Equity Income Fund, which has beaten 74 percent of its peers
> over the past five years.

Table 7.4 shows that the proportion of days that a psychological consideration was mentioned in connection with a fundamental factor over the entire sample is 54%, whereas this proportion, as we saw, is 55% for psychological considerations in total.
The difference does not quite capture the influence of pure psychology (psychological factors mentioned separately from fundamentals), because on some days psychology with fundamentals
and pure psychology are both mentioned, and the overall category
for psychology tracks the proportion of days on which at least one
psychological factor was mentioned. The following two excerpts

illustrate how Bloomberg's journalists reported on the impact of pure psychological considerations:

> "I do think it's mania," said Ned Riley, chief investment officer at BankBoston Corp., which oversees $26 billion. "Any time stocks appreciate 30 to 50 percent in a day, it's the greater fool theory. People think there will always be someone who will pay a higher price." [April 21, 1998]

> "The selling is feeding on itself," said Ned Riley, chief investment officer at BankBoston Corp., which oversees $30 billion. "People are indifferent about stock prices and valuations. Now they're fearful." [August 4, 1998]

Table 7.4 shows that pure psychology was mentioned on only 1% of the days over the sample.

As with oil prices and inflation, the proportion of days over the sample that a factor was mentioned could mask its importance during specific stretches of time in the sample. Indeed, the

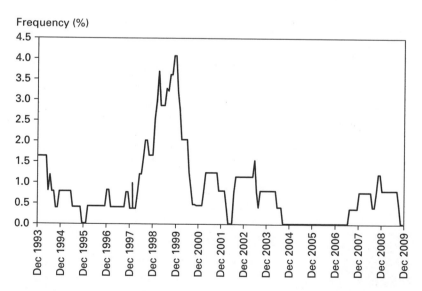

Fig. 7.8. Average monthly frequency of mentions in wrap reports: Pure psychology
Source: Mangee (2011).

bubble models claim that crowd psychology and mania have their main impact during the long upswings that characterize asset-price fluctuations.

As shown in Figure 7.8, the importance of pure psychological considerations does rise sharply at the end of 1997, but at its height, in November 1999, such factors are mentioned less than once a month on average (4%). This observation, together with the evidence on fundamentals, suggests that pure psychological considerations had only a marginal impact on stock prices. Moreover, much of the upswing in stock prices relative to underlying earnings (see Figure 5.1) occurred prior to 1997, when pure psychological factors were hardly mentioned at all. And there is no evidence that these factors played any role in the long upswing in stock prices that occurred in the 2000s.

What Role, If Any, for Momentum Trading in Upswings?

Behavioral bubble models rely on momentum trading—due either to psychological considerations or to reliance on technical trading—to account for the long upswings that characterize asset-price fluctuations. However, even if we combine pure psychological and technical considerations, there is little support in Bloomberg's wrap stories for this bubble view.

Figure 7.9 plots the 12-month moving average of the proportion of days each month that a technical consideration was mentioned at least once in Bloomberg's stories as having influenced the market. Figure 7.10 provides a similar plot for the subcategory of momentum-related technical factors, which include technical trading and other considerations that indicate that feedback effects from past price trends are influencing prices.

Three excerpts from Bloomberg's market-wraps illustrate these factors:

> International Business Machines Corp. led the Dow average's drop after falling below its 50-day moving average. . . . accounting for all of the Dow average's decline. [August 2, 1999]

Frequency (%)

Fig. 7.9. Average monthly frequency of mentions in wrap reports:
Technical considerations
Source: Mangee (2011).

The Nasdaq extended gains after 1 pm surging more than 2 percentage points in an hour, as "momentum" investors, or those
who make short term bets on a stock's direction, rushed to buy
shares, traders said. [January 11, 2001]

So-called momentum investors have been buying technology
shares because "they have to get their foot back in the door and not
get left behind," Rittenhouse's Waterman said. [October 4, 2001]

The other subcategory of technical considerations entails
factors, such as profit taking and the Monday effect, that are unlikely to sustain momentum trading.[12] Two excerpts from Bloomberg's wrap stories illustrate these factors:

U.S. stocks closed broadly lower after a sell-off triggered by today's quarterly expiration of stock options and stock-index op-

---

[12]Profit taking entails the decision to reduce or eliminate a profitable
position to realize some or all of its gains. The Monday effect refers to the tendency of stock returns to be lower on Mondays than on other days. See Mangee
(2011) for discussion on these and other effects.

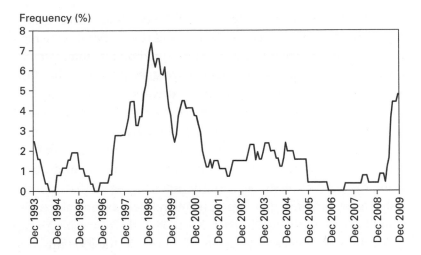

Fig. 7.10. Average monthly frequency of mentions in wrap reports: Momentum-related technical considerations
Source: Mangee (2011).

tions and futures sent the market reeling in the final hour. [June 18, 1993]

U.S. stocks declined today, breaking a string of record highs in 1994, as investors cashed in gains before tomorrow's crucial report on wholesale prices. "It's a predictable backlash," said Jim Benning, a trader at BT Brokerage. "We were up so much in the past few days." [January 11, 1994]

Figures 7.9 and 7.10 show that the importance of technical considerations and momentum-related technical factors varies considerably over the sample. Their greatest impact occurred in the second half of the 1990s, suggesting perhaps some support for the behavioral bubble view of long upswings. Moreover, the average proportion of days per month that such factors were reported to have influenced prices rose sharply in 1996 from roughly 0% to a high in February 1999 of roughly 7%.

However, Figure 7.10 shows that there is little evidence for the behavioral bubble view. For one thing, momentum-related technical factors, as with pure psychological considerations, were hardly mentioned at all during much of the 1990s upswing in stock prices. The importance of these factors did rise in 1999. But a high mark of 7% means that they were mentioned on less than two out of twenty trading days per month on average. Whatever their impact on prices, they were not the main drivers of the upswing.

Another problematic feature of the data for the behavioral bubble view is that the importance of momentum-related technical factors began falling rapidly in February 1999. This fall occurred a year prior to the sharp equity-price reversal in mid-2000, during the most excessive part of the upswing—exactly when the bubble view implies that momentum-related technical factors should have their greatest impact. Moreover, the Bloomberg wrap stories show that these factors played no role in the long upswing in stock prices that began in 2003. If anything, Figure 7.10 shows that these factors had some impact during the second phase of the downswing that began in 2007. Even if we combine pure psychological and momentum-related technical factors to obtain an

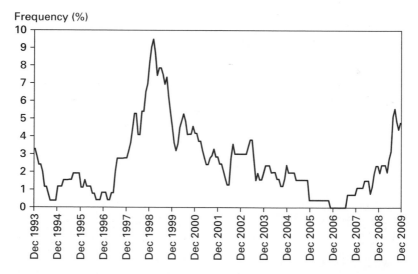

Fig. 7.11. Average monthly frequency of mentions in wrap reports: Bubble considerations
Source: Mangee (2011).

overall measure of the potential impact of bubble-related considerations, we end up with much the same story (see Figure 7.11).

Bloomberg's market-wrap stories yield an exceptionally
strong conclusion: in virtually no cases do psychological or technical considerations alone move the market. Moreover, the role of
bubble considerations in accelerating the swing seems marginal.
Even if one were to view this striking evidence that psychology and
technical considerations alone do not drive asset-price movements as too soft to constitute a formal rejection of the bubble
view, Bloomberg news stories point unambiguously to the importance of fundamentals in sustaining swings.

However, these stories also show that fundamentals matter in nonroutine ways, a conclusion that is supported by much
formal statistical analysis, which we discuss in Chapter 11. To account for asset prices and risk on the basis of fundamental considerations, and yet accord psychological factors a role in their movements over time (without presuming obvious irrationality on the
part of market participants), we need to jettison fully predetermined models and the mechanistic notion of rationality. In chapters 8–10, we discuss how this can be done.

8

Speculation and the Allocative Performance of Financial Markets

FINANCIAL MARKETS provide assessments of the relative prospects of companies' assets. They set prices to reflect the stream of expected future returns on past investments, as well as that of new investment projects for which financing is being sought. Markets allocate capital based on these price signals: the higher the price of a company's assets, the easier it is for it to attract financial capital, whereas lower prices make financing more difficult. For markets to perform this allocative function well, participants' decisions to, say, buy and sell shares of particular companies should reflect changes in the relative prospects of companies or projects and the risks associated with investing in them.

As trading decisions in financial markets are based on assessments of future returns and risk, they are inherently speculative. Thus, reliance on financial markets to allocate society's capital presumes that speculation leads to an allocation that on the whole generates better longer-term returns to investors and society than an alternative arrangement might deliver. The experience of successful capitalist economies, particularly compared to the Soviet experiment in capital allocation without reliance on financial markets, attests to the soundness of this presumption.

However, the success of economies with highly developed financial markets should not be construed as evidence that these markets can somehow fully foresee the longer-term prospects of alternative investment projects. Yet this is precisely what happens in the Rational Expectations portrayal of financial markets: the behavior of so-called "rational" speculators is assumed to ensure that asset prices reflect nearly perfectly their mythical true longer-term values, thereby ensuring nearly perfect allocation of society's capital.

For various reasons discussed throughout this book, contemporary finance theory has also been led to the other extreme and simplistic account of the process through which financial markets allocate capital across alternative projects. Fully predetermined behavioral finance models portray asset prices as being driven primarily by psychological factors, resulting in a largely haphazard allocation of capital.

The latter view—that financial markets are best thought of as speculative casinos—is often traced to Keynes. Given the weight attached to his views, especially in the aftermath of the global financial crisis, this interpretation of Keynes's position has obscured the public debate about the necessary reforms. The debate has largely failed to recognize that speculation is inherent to how financial markets perform their essential role in modern economies, which would imply the need to focus on harnessing speculation to improve capital allocation and curbing excesses that might cause a future crisis. Instead, the premise of the debate is that many or all speculators are irrational, prone to emotions, and susceptible to waves of mass psychology, and that their activities are largely harmful to modern economies, or at best socially useless.

Keynes recognized the role of market psychology, and indeed, some of his arguments can be interpreted as suggesting that short-term speculation may impair financial markets' allocative performance. But he did recognize the importance of fundamental considerations in sustaining market psychology. In fact, he ultimately concluded unequivocally that, on balance, it would be difficult to improve on the way that markets allocate resources across economic activities. In particular, he was adamant that the state could not deliver a better allocation.

Most importantly, Keynes's primary concern was not whether the strength of psychological factors might grossly impair financial markets' ability to allocate capital among available investment projects. Instead, he focused his analysis on the role played by professional speculators in depressing the overall volume of investment projects that entrepreneurs are willing to undertake.

As Keynes saw it, the primary problem with short-term speculation, even if it is based on fundamental considerations, is that it could lead to "precariousness" or unstable markets, "which creates no small part of our contemporary problem of securing sufficient investment" (Keynes, 1936, p. 153) to achieve full employment. "[I]f effective demand is deficient, not only is the public scandal of wasted resources intolerable, but the individual enterpriser who seeks to bring these resources into action is operating with the odds loaded against him" (Keynes, 1936, pp. 379–81). To reduce the influence of short-term speculation, and thus the precariousness of markets, Keynes advocated the "introduction of a substantial Government transfer tax on all [asset-market] transactions" (Keynes, 1936, p. 160), a measure that nowadays is referred to as a "Tobin tax."

Keynes advocated lowering the rate of interest to stimulate investment and consumption spending to levels consistent with full employment. As long as "the state is able to determine the aggregate amount of resources devoted to [investment] and the basic rate of reward to those who own [capital] . . . it will have accomplished all that is necessary" (Keynes, 1936, p. 378).

Keynes suspected that interest-rate policy alone might be insufficient, and that "a somewhat comprehensive socialization will prove the only means of securing an approximation to full employment." But he wanted "public authority . . . [to] co-operate with private initiative" (Keynes, 1936, p. 378), not replace it. As Keynes's greatest biographer put it: "The public was never to substitute the private, but merely to complement it" (Skidelsky, 2010, p. 1).

To be sure, in his analysis of financial markets in chapter 12 of *The General Theory*, Keynes suggested that short-term speculation, beyond engendering instability that might depress overall investment, moves prices in response to factors that have little or no connection to changes in assets' longer-term prospects:

> Day-to-day fluctuations in the profits of existing investments, which are obviously of an ephemeral and non-significant character, tend to have altogether excessive, and even an absurd, influence on the market. It is said, for example, that the shares of American companies which manufacture ice tend to sell at a higher price in summer when their profits are seasonally high than in winter when no one wants ice. [Keynes, 1936, pp. 154–55]

Even in the absence of such effects, Keynes believed that psychological factors drive a wedge between asset-price movements and changes in longer-term prospects. But he did recognize that there were "serious-minded individuals" who "purchase investments on the best genuine long-term expectations [they] can frame . . . and that it makes a vast difference to an investment market whether or not they predominate in their influence over the game-players" (Keynes, 1936, p. 156). Nevertheless, there are several reasons why the "game-players" might dominate:

> Investment based on genuine long-term expectation is so difficult today as to be scarcely practicable . . . [it] is intolerably boring and over-exacting . . . [those who] ignore near-term market fluctuations [need] greater resources for safety and must not operate on so large a scale, if at all, with borrowed money. [Keynes, 1936, p. 158]

But Keynes never believed that the state should take over the role of private capital markets. On the contrary, he argued forcefully at the end of *The General Theory* for the "advantages of individualism" and private initiative. "They are," he wrote,

> partly advantages of efficiency, the advantages of decentralization and of the play of self-interest, [which are] even greater, perhaps, than the nineteenth century supposed. . . . [T]he reac-

tion against the appeal to self-interest may have gone too far [and]. . . . if [individualism] can be purged of its defects and its abuses, [it] is the best safeguard of personal liberty . . . of the variety of life. . . . [It] preserves the traditions which embody the most secure and successful choices of former generations; it colors the present with the diversification of its fancy; and, being the handmaid of experiment as well as of tradition and of fancy, it is the most powerful instrument to better the future. [Keynes, 1936, p. 380]

By "defects," Keynes was referring to the "failure" of "economic society . . . to provide for full employment and its arbitrary and inequitable distribution of wealth and incomes" (Keynes, 1936, p. 372). But in discussing the role of government in lifting the economy back to full employment, he emphasized his commitment to the allocative superiority of private markets. Indeed, despite remarks in chapter 12 suggesting that market-based allocations are haphazard, Keynes claimed in the concluding chapter of *The General Theory* that he saw

> *no reason* to suppose that the existing system seriously misemploys the factors of production which are in use. There are, of course, errors of foresight; but these would *not* be avoided by centralizing decisions. When 9,000,000 men are employed out of 10,000,000 willing and able to work, there is no evidence that the labor of these 9,000,000 men is misdirected. The complaint against the present system is not that these 9,000,000 men ought to be employed on different tasks, but that tasks should be available for the remaining 1,000,000 men. It is in determining the volume, *not the direction,* of actual employment that the existing system has broken down. [Keynes, 1936, p. 379, emphasis added]

Keynes developed *The General Theory* to explain how such a breakdown could occur, and what policies the state might pursue to redress it. But he never explained the inherent tension between his belief that short-term speculation impairs the performance of financial markets in allocating resources and his categorical claim that there is "no reason to suppose that the existing system mis-employs the factors of production which are in use."

Keynes never explored how imperfect knowledge and the importance of fundamentals in driving outcomes—either directly or indirectly (by underpinning psychological considerations)—could rationalize his claim of good allocative performance of private markets. Had he done so, he would likely have been led to reconsider his view that short-term speculation plays virtually no role in helping financial markets set asset prices to reflect longer-term prospects.

Short-Term and Value Speculators

Keynes's argument that game-players tend to dominate trading in financial markets is persuasive. As these short-term speculators are largely focused on near-term returns, they base their trading decisions primarily on news about short-term trends in a wide array of fundamental factors. Much of this information is easily obtainable at no or little cost from a plethora of reliable news sources, such as Bloomberg, the *Wall Street Journal,* or the *Financial Times.*

Many short-term speculators digest this basic information for clues about returns on companies' shares—such as their earnings, sales, and costs—over the coming months or quarters, as well as about future interest rates, inflation, and other fundamental factors that influence companies' short-term prospects. Some speculators rely on technical trading strategies to some extent. But Mangee's (2011) Bloomberg data and the close comovement of stock prices and corporate earnings (see Figure 7.1) suggest that reliance on fundamental considerations to anticipate short-term prospects and returns is widespread.

There are also participants who try to anticipate companies' prospects and returns beyond the next year. For example, many mutual funds pursue a so-called "growth-income" strategy of picking stocks whose longer-term earnings will enable them to pay a steady stream of dividends over the coming years, as well as provide potential for capital gains. Warren Buffet of Berkshire Hathaway, Seth Klarman of the Baupost Group, and many others also speculate over the longer term in the hope of gaining a better return (net of risk and information costs) than short-term speculators could earn over the equivalent period.

These "value speculators," as we call them, often expend considerable resources to gather additional detailed information on companies' structure and activities, such as their management and control, research and development projects, and evolving product lines and production processes. By doing so, they can identify companies whose strong longer-term prospects are more difficult to spot by market participants who trade on the basis of information on short-term trends alone.

However, although information on such developments as new research projects may improve forecasts of companies' longer-term prospects, such information is necessarily fuzzy, adding uncertainty to forecasts that take it into account. Thus, when forming their forecasts of longer-term prospects, value speculators also rely on their interpretation of the effect of news on short-term changes in the same set of more readily quantifiable fundamentals as that taken into account by short-term speculators:

> It would be foolish, in forming our expectations, to attach great weight to matters which are very uncertain. It is reasonable, therefore, to be guided to a considerable degree by the facts about which we feel somewhat confident, even though they may be less decisively relevant to the issue than other facts about which our knowledge is vague and scanty.[1] [Keynes, 1936, p. 148]

Although they share the same basic information, participants within each group of speculators interpret short-term movements

---

[1]As we argue in the next chapter, this focus on short-term changes in fundamentals helps explain why value speculators may also contribute to excessive price swings.

in fundamentals with a view to assessing returns at different time horizons. Short-term speculators attempt to assess what current short-term trends might mean for near-term returns, whereas value speculators attempt to project the meaning of these movements for longer-term prospects and cross-check and supplement these assessments with detailed company-specific information.

However, imperfect knowledge effectively limits the horizon that value speculators could reasonably be thinking about in forecasting future prospects and making trading decisions:

> [i]f we speak frankly, we have to admit that our basis for knowledge for estimating the yield ten years hence of a railway, a copper mine, a textile factory, the goodwill of patent medicine, an Atlantic liner, a building in the City of London amounts to very little and sometimes to nothing; or even five years hence. [Keynes, 1936, pp. 149–50]

Consequently, forecasting prospects over the entire life of an investment "is so difficult today as to be scarcely practicable" (Keynes, 1936, p. 158). Nevertheless, by basing their trading decisions in part on company-specific information, as well as by interpreting short-term trends from a longer-term perspective, value speculators impart to asset-price movements their interpretation of the unfolding longer-term prospects of companies and projects.

How Short-Term Speculation Facilitates Value Speculation

Despite the considerable difficulties and uncertainties inherent in attempts to speculate for the longer term, many financial market participants engage in this investment strategy. As we mentioned in Chapter 7, many mutual funds and hedge funds buy stocks that, given their assessments of future earnings and other prospects, they believe are undervalued. Such investors do not expect that these prospects will materialize soon (say, in the coming year), only that in addition to any dividends earned in the interim period, the market will bid up prices and deliver capital gains when they do materialize.

Although Keynes expressed doubt about the feasibility and profitability of value speculation, he recognized that there were market participants who engage in speculation for the longer term (Keynes, 1936, p. 156). Remarkably, Keynes also acknowledged, though perhaps unwittingly, that short-term speculation—which he, like many observers nowadays, considered a socially pernicious economic activity—might actually be the key to understanding the viability of value speculation as a profit-seeking activity.

Keynes offered a long list of reasons why the emergence of modern financial markets has rendered value speculation unviable. Nonetheless, he suggested that "there must surely be large profits to be gained from the *other players* in the long run by a skilled individual who, unperturbed by the prevailing pastime, continues to purchase investments on the best genuine long-term expectations he can frame" (Keynes, 1936, p. 156, emphasis added).

The "other players" must, of course, be short-term speculators. As the future becomes the present, what were longer-term prospects quarters or years back become current short-term trends in company earnings and other fundamentals. These trends are the news that short-term speculators react to in their trading decisions. If some of the predictions that value investors made in fact materialize in superior company performance, the positive news will lead short-term speculators to bid up those companies' share prices.[2]

---

[2]Walter J. Schloss is a well-known example of such a value speculator; his investment firm generated a remarkable return of more than 15% per year between 1955 and 2000, compared to the return on the S&P 500 of just over 10%. Schloss described his strategy in a *Hindu Business Line* interview this way:

> One of the things we've done is hold over a hundred companies in our portfolio ... we can't project the earnings of these companies, they are secondary companies, but somewhere along the line some of them will work. Now I cannot tell you which ones, so I buy a hundred of them. Of course, it does not mean you own the same amount of each stock. [*Hindu Business Line*, 2007, p. 1]

Keynes feared that short-term speculation and market liquidity adds greatly to the instability of the system. But it is short-term speculators who buy value speculators' newly appreciated shares. Paradoxically, then, short-term speculation is precisely what enables value speculators to earn a handsome profit on their painstaking research and their patience in holding assets.

In fact, the distinction between short-term and value speculation is not sharp. Although value speculators trade with a view toward longer-term returns, the time horizon over which they can estimate returns with a minimum degree of confidence is necessarily limited and varies by project and company. As Keynes emphasized, "our knowledge of the factors which will govern the yield of an investment some years hence is usually very slight and often negligible." Thus, value speculation is in general based on estimates of returns over periods usually not much longer than "five years hence."

The importance of imperfect knowledge is implied by the high frequency with which value speculators, like their short-term counterparts, trade in markets.[3] Thus, when making their trading decisions, value speculators place substantial weight on short-term trends in company earnings, interest rates, and a wide array of other fundamentals. And yet, although both short-term and value speculation are driven by short-term trends in fundamentals, financial markets select projects and companies that, on the whole, deliver far superior longer-term returns to investors and society than those produced by attempts to allocate capital without markets.

Value speculators, despite paying close attention to short-term trends in fundamentals, contribute in an important way to markets' superior allocative performance. Because they trade with a view toward longer-term returns, they examine short-term trends for clues about whether the longer-term prospects of assets

---

[3]For example, Chen et al. (2000) find that the annual turnover, measured by total stock purchases or sales divided by average total net assets, of 385 growth and income mutual funds was 73.3% in 1995.

in their portfolios have improved or worsened and increase or decrease their positions accordingly. By influencing value speculators' trading decisions, short-term trends in fundamentals cause asset-price movements to incorporate the unfolding prospects of past investments—embodied in existing capital—and to track the prospects of new investment projects that seek financing.

Even if the market were to be composed entirely of value speculators, it could not track perfectly the unfolding prospects of projects and companies, let alone their longer-term prospects. Asset-price movements are driven by participants' forecasts, and even if they all cared only about longer-term returns, imperfect knowledge would limit their ability to assess these returns anywhere near perfectly.

Of course, markets are not composed solely of value speculators. Indeed, much of the public debate on the crisis that began in 2007 has pinned blame for the malfunctioning of financial markets on short-term speculators. These proposals presume, as Keynes did, that short-term speculators play no role in helping markets to allocate capital according to the unfolding longer-term prospects of assets. This view overlooks factors—such as the quality and organization of relevant physical and human capital—that affect their performance in both the short and longer term. It thereby ignores the possibility that movements in short-term trends may reflect changes in longer-term prospects.

For example, if a company hires a better management team than it had, both its short-term performance and longer-term prospects are likely to improve. Thus, even if short-term speculators pay no attention to returns beyond the near term, by reacting to improved short-term performance, they help market prices track the company's unfolding (and inherently unknowable) longer-term prospects.

To be sure, as Keynes emphasized, short-term speculators tend to overreact to good (and bad) short-term news. But, as time passes, the effect of the new management on company performance is reflected in then-realized short-term trends. If change in these trends reveals that short-term speculators overreacted to the appointment of the new management, the weaker-than-anticipated short-term performance will lead speculators to bid down the share price, reversing all or part of the increase that they themselves caused. And if the future short-term trends in company earnings validate short-term speculators' confidence in the new management, the company's shares will remain elevated and may even increase further. In this sense, short-term speculators' ongoing reinterpretation and reactions to short-term trends in fundamentals may help the market better track longer-term prospects.

Speculation and Economic Dynamism

Even if the increased volatility caused by short-term speculators' trading behavior offsets the potential benefits of their role in tracking the performance of longer-term investments, their presence seems to play a crucial role in motivating other market participants to engage in speculation that aims for returns beyond the near term.[4] By bidding up prices of shares that value speculators bet on quarters or years ago, short-term speculators provide the returns needed to keep value speculators in the market, performing the highly uncertain and arduous task of assessing investments from the perspective of their longer-term prospects. This effort, in turn, enables financial markets to allocate capital to new investment projects.

After all, venture capitalists are longer-term value speculators par excellence. By facilitating such speculators' exit from ownership positions in new companies, financial markets are an important determinant of entrepreneurship at the startup phase. In fact, exit is important for both types of principals of a successful entrepreneurial business: the entrepreneur himself, who may want to cash out on his investment, and the venture capitalist, who may have identified better opportunities elsewhere, and whose role in the company is, in any case, likely to diminish over time.

[4]This section draws on Frydman et al. (2010a).

Indeed, although noncapital inputs, such as reputation, experience, and external monitoring, are extremely valuable to businesses in the early stages of their growth, as a business model succeeds, the relative value of the nonfinancial contributions of the venture capital firm declines. Exercising an exit option enables a venture capitalist to recycle her nonfinancial contributions to the success of the startup and reinvest in another early-stage portfolio company.[5] The exit of venture capital is also important to market participants generally, as it generates information about the relative success or failure of different fund managers, thereby enabling reallocation of capital from the less successful to the more successful—or to other investment vehicles (Berger and Udell, 1998; Black and Gilson, 1998).

Exit may occur through sale, initial public offering, or repurchase of a venture capitalist's stake by the company itself. In all these scenarios, the valuation provided by well-functioning equity markets plays a key role.[6]

But financial markets are particularly important in facilitating exit by initial public offering and thus motivating engagement in entrepreneurial activities and their financing. The original entrepreneur prefers exit by initial public offering, because, as the venture capitalist is replaced by dispersed shareholders, she regains control of the business, whereas a direct sale would leave her in a managerial role at best. The initial public offering option is also important to the venture capitalist, because it increases liquidity and allows additional returns at a time when the relative valuation of publicly traded securities is high (Lerner, 1994). Indeed, for these and other reasons, an initial public offering is much

---

[5]Exit is also important in spreading entrepreneurial experience throughout the economy. It leads to the creation of a pool of serial entrepreneurs, who, having exited from one venture, can use their abilities and experience in subsequent ventures. For an analysis of the role of serial entrepreneurship, see Wright et al. (1997). For a recent study of the entry and exit of entrepreneurial businesses as a major driver in the evolution of industries and economies, see Hessels et al. (2009) and references therein.

[6]For example, shares of the acquiring company are a typical means of payment in the trade sale of entrepreneurial ventures.

more profitable than other forms of exit: studies show that a U.S. firm that eventually goes public yields a 195% average return over a 4.2-year average holding period; the same investment in an acquired firm provides an average return of only 40% over a 3.7-year average holding period (Venture Economics, 1988; Bygrave and Timmons, 1992; Gompers and Lerner, 1997; Bienz and Leite, 2008).

Exit through an initial public offering is thus the linchpin of a dynamic entrepreneurial environment, and it is viable only in the presence of a large, vibrant equity market that has numerous providers of long-term capital, as well as short-term speculators, and permits new firms to issue shares easily. Such markets—indeed, all financial markets—allocate capital by translating the assessments and trading decisions of short-term speculators and value investors into price movements. They provide an ongoing evaluation of the unfolding longer-term prospects of prior investments while fostering and financing new companies and projects —the key to modern economic dynamism and innovation. As we discuss next, the process through which financial markets perform these essential functions inherently involves swings in asset prices and risk.

9

Fundamentals and Psychology in Price Swings

Bloomberg's market wrap reports indicate that short-term movements in a wide array of fundamental factors —from corporate earnings to the price of oil—underpin participants' trading decisions in equity and other asset markets. Participants interpret the impact of movements of fundamentals on the prospects and returns of companies over the near and longer term, causing their relative prices and thus their access to financial capital to change. As this allocative process unfolds over time, individual stock prices and broad price indexes also tend to undergo swings of unequal magnitude and duration away from and toward estimates of common benchmark levels.

These observations suggest that swings in asset prices and risk arise from the way that financial markets adjust relative prices and allocate capital. And because such swings depend on how market participants interpret fundamentals in forecasting outcomes, they are ultimately driven by short-term movements in fundamentals. But to account for swings in asset prices and risk on the basis of fundamental factors, we must jettison fully predetermined models. After all, profit-seeking participants revise their forecasting strategies in nonroutine ways, owing to news about fundamentals and to psychological considerations, such as confidence and optimism (which depend on fundamental factors but do not move in lockstep with them).

Whereas nonbubble Rational Expectations models ignore psychological considerations and select one fully predetermined fundamental relationship to account for asset prices, the fully predetermined Rational Expectations and behavioral bubble models recognize the importance of psychological considerations for understanding price swings but largely ignore the role of fundamentals. The problem is not only that both fundamental and psychological factors matter for asset-price fluctuations but also that they matter in ways that cannot be fully prespecified with mechanical rules. It is not surprising, therefore, that neither contemporary approach has been able to account for the swings in prices and risk that we actually observe in financial markets.

Imperfect Knowledge Economics eschews fully predetermined models and the presumption that market participants steadfastly rely on one overarching forecasting strategy. As we have argued throughout this book, in coping with ever-imperfect knowledge, profit-seeking market participants revise their forecasting strategies at times and in ways that they themselves, let alone an economist, cannot fully foresee—especially given that institutions, economic policies, and other features of the social context that underpin movements of fundamentals also change in nonroutine ways.

Although movements in fundamentals and revisions of forecasting strategies are nonroutine, there may be qualitative regularities that characterize them. Moreover, these regularities characterize change during the periods of time that no one can fully foresee. Our IKE account of asset-price swings and risk is based on such qualitative and contingent regularities.

One of the regularities that we formalize was emphasized by Keynes (1936, p.152): regardless of whether participants in financial markets are bulls or bears, they tend to assume that the "existing state of affairs will continue indefinitely, except in so far as we have specific reasons to expect a change." Even when a participant does "have specific reasons to expect a change," it is entirely unclear what new forecasting strategy, if any, she should adopt. Faced with this uncertainty, participants tend to revise their thinking about how fundamentals matter in "guardedly moderate ways": there are stretches of time during which they either maintain their strategies or revise them gradually. Such revisions do not generally alter, in substantial ways, the set of fundamentals that participants consider relevant and/or their interpretation of their influence on future outcomes. As we shall see, a price swing arises during stretches of time in which market participants on the whole revise their forecasting strategies gradually and fundamentals trend in unchanging directions.[1]

But like price swings themselves, the tendency toward guardedly moderate revisions are not only qualitative but also contingent. A participant's decision to revise her forecasting strategy depends on many considerations, including her current strategy's performance, whether she has "specific reasons to expect a change" in how fundamental factors are trending or how they are influencing prices, and the "*confidence* with which we . . . forecast" (Keynes, 1936, p. 148).

Moreover, market participants on the whole may not revise their strategies in guardedly moderate ways. There are occasions when news about fundamentals and price movements leads participants to radically revise their forecasting strategies. Such revisions can have a dramatic impact on prices and can spell the end of a price swing in one direction and the start of a new one in the opposite direction. Shifts in how fundamentals are trending can also lead to such reversals in price movements.

By formalizing Keynes's insight as a qualitative and contingent regularity, we can account for the importance of trends in fundamentals for driving price swings, and yet remain open to the nonroutine ways in which fundamentals and psychological factors matter over time. Moreover, because our IKE model fully prespecifies neither when the trends in fundamentals will change nor

---

[1]Whether a price swing continues or ends also depends on the degree of diversity in how trends in fundamentals affect participants' price forecasts. See Frydman and Goldberg (2010b).

when market participants will revise their strategies in guardedly moderate ways, it does not predict sharply when a swing in asset prices may begin or end. This feature of the model is what enables it to account for asset-price swings of irregular duration and magnitude and to remain compatible with the presumption that profit-seeking participants largely forecast in reasonable ways.

In Chapter 8, we discussed how the behavior of short-term speculators can distort relative prices. But we also argued that, because their trading decisions are based on fundamental factors, they help markets to allocate capital across companies and projects. Our IKE account of markets shows how both types of actors—short-term speculators and longer-term value speculators—also underpin the tendency of asset prices to undergo swings of irregular duration and magnitude. When speculators tend to revise their strategies in guardedly moderate ways and short-term movements in fundamentals unfold in unchanging directions, asset prices undergo a swing in one direction or the other.

Bulls, Bears, and Individual Forecasting

Market participants' trading decisions determine whether an asset price rises or falls. The central factor behind these decisions, of course, is an individual's forecast of future prices and risk. If, for example, individuals in the aggregate raise their forecasts of next month's price, they will buy the asset today and bid up its price. To account for asset-price swings, then, we must characterize how participants' forecasting behavior unfolds over time.[2]

---

[2]For a rigorous exposition of our approach to revisions of forecasting strategies and an account of swings in asset prices and risk based on Imperfect Knowledge Economics, see Frydman and Goldberg (2007, 2010b). Using a novel approach to connect theory with empirical analysis, Frydman et al. (2010b) show that an IKE model of currency swings accords significantly better with empirical evidence than a large, widely relied-on class of Rational Expectations models.

When forming her forecast of the future price and risk of a stock or other asset, a participant must choose which fundamental considerations are relevant and how much weight to place on each, as well as how much weight to place on an asset's current price. As Keynes emphasized, because forecasting "cannot depend on strict mathematical expectation" (Keynes, 1936, pp. 162–63) other considerations, such as one's confidence and intuition, play a role. But these other considerations are also, in part, related to movements in fundamental factors. We can thus portray a participant's forecasting strategy with a simple linear relationship that connects future prices and risk to a set of fundamentals with a corresponding set of weights.

News about the fundamentals that participants think are relevant drives their forecasts. But short-term movements in these factors can lead to changes in a participant's forecast without any change in her forecasting strategy. For example, suppose an individual interprets a fall in interest rates as positive news for a company's prospects over the near or longer term. If such news was reported, and she maintained her assessment of the impact of interest rates, then, other things being equal, she would raise her forecast of the company's stock price.

News can also influence a participant's thinking and intuition about the fundamentals that are relevant and the weights that she attaches to them in forming her forecasts. For example, the uptrend in the inflation rate that began in 2004 was no larger than the downtrend that prevailed between 2001 and 2003. Nonetheless, Bloomberg News reported that the importance of inflation as a main driver of stock prices (measured by the average proportion of days each month that this factor was mentioned in Bloomberg's stories) changed dramatically, rising from below 5% during the earlier period to 45% by 2005 (see Chapter 7). This change suggests that during this period, many market participants revised their thinking about the importance of inflation for forecasting market outcomes, leading to movements in their price forecasts.

Of course, every market participant, regardless of whether she is a short-term or value speculator, formulates a forecasting strategy that reflects her own knowledge and intuition. Some participants look at recent trends in fundamental factors and, drawing on other considerations as well (for example, an understanding of certain historical economic episodes or information about companies' research projects), predict rising prices. Other participants, with different knowledge, intuitions, and thus forecasting strategies, look at the same trends in fundamentals and predict falling prices. Indeed, given imperfect knowledge, bullish views about the future may be no less reasonable than bearish ones (and vice versa). What matters, then, for how asset prices move over time is how fundamentals—and the aggregate of participants' bullish and bearish forecasts based on them—move over the same period.

PERSISTENT TRENDS IN FUNDAMENTALS

We have already seen that corporate earnings can trend in one direction or the other for extended periods (see Figure 7.1). In fact, economists have long observed that many basic fundamental factors that market participants rely on to form their forecasts of asset prices and risk, such as overall economic activity, employment, and interest rates, exhibit this pattern.[3] No one can fully foresee how long or steep such trends may be. At any point in time, changes in the economy can cause these trends to reverse, beginning a countertrend in the other direction.

The tendency of many basic fundamental factors to trend in one direction for stretches of time is a key reason that asset markets are prone to price swings. To see this, consider a period during which the trends that participants consider to be relevant for forecasting the price of a particular stock (say, interest rates

---

[3]See Juselius (2006) and Johansen et al. (2010) and references therein, who find that the persistence of trends in many macroeconomic variables is much greater than commonly believed. Although discussing why this is so is beyond the scope of this book, we suspect that imperfect knowledge plays a key role.

and company earnings) remain unchanged.[4] Suppose each quarter during this period, interest rates and company earnings tend to rise—negative and positive news, respectively, for a stock's price. Some participants attach greater relative weight to higher interest rates, leading them to lower their price forecasts, while others, attaching greater relative weight to higher earnings, raise theirs.

And, of course, no one knows with certainty beforehand how trends in these variables will unfold. Some participants might conclude that a rise in earnings over the most recent quarter implies their subsequent fall and thus attach a negative weight to higher earnings when forecasting prices. For these individuals, higher earnings and interest rates would lead them to lower their price forecasts.

However, regardless of the diversity of participants' views, the unfolding of their price forecasts may, for a time, entail no revisions in their forecasting strategies. During such periods, the impact of developments in fundamentals on individuals' forecasts would not change. If the trends in fundamentals also remained unchanged, these forecasts would tend to move one specific direction during the period. The aggregate of these forecasts, and thus the stock price, would also tend to move in one direction—that is, undergo a swing.

Guardedly Moderate Revisions

Keynes's insight that market participants tend to assume that the existing state of affairs will continue suggests that they tend to stick with a forecasting strategy for stretches of time. Indeed, it is often unclear whether an individual should alter her strategy. A quarter or two of poor forecasting performance may be the result of ephemeral chance events and not an indication of a failing strategy.

---

[4]For now, we consider a situation in which participants' assessments of risk do not vary. In Chapter 10, we explain how movements in these assessments play a key role in the ultimately self-limiting character of asset-price swings.

So unless an individual has specific reasons to expect a change in the market, she may leave her current strategy unaltered, even if its performance begins to flag over several periods.

If a market participant does have reasons to suspect or anticipate a genuine change, she cannot be sure about her beliefs, let alone about the precise nature of the change. When and how she decides to revise her strategy depends on her intuition about how market relationships may be unfolding and on her confidence in this intuition. In such uncertain situations, it is often reasonable for an individual to reinterpret the implications of recent trends in fundamentals or prices for future outcomes in guardedly moderate ways, in the sense that the impact of these revisions on her forecast does not outweigh the influence stemming from the trends themselves.

Continuing with our example, consider an individual who interprets the trends in interest rates and earnings in such a way that would lead her to raise her price forecast over the period without any revisions in her forecasting strategy. If she decided to revise her strategy at some point, the impact of her revisions on her forecast would either reinforce or impede the positive change stemming from the direct effect of trends in fundamentals.

In our example, reinforcing revisions would, by definition, lead an individual to increase her price forecast, as they would tend to reinforce the positive impact of fundamentals. This is not generally the case for impeding revisions in forecasting strategies. These revisions could be quite substantial: a participant may alter her set of relevant fundamentals or her interpretations of them so significantly that she updates her price forecasts in ways that outweigh the impact of trends in fundamentals. Nevertheless, owing to her imperfect knowledge and uncertainty about the future, she is reluctant to revise her strategy so radically. Consequently, we would expect stretches of time during which impeding revisions remain guardedly moderate—smaller—in their impact on a participant's forecast. During such periods, the impact of trends in fundamentals would dominate and lead the individual's price forecast to move on average in one direction.

As noted earlier, we do not assume that such guardedly moderate revisions characterize participants' forecasting strategies at all times. Indeed, that revisions can sometimes be radical plays a key role in our IKE account of price reversals. However, our model's ability to account for persistent swings in asset prices crucially depends on whether guardedly moderate revisions adequately characterize forecasting during periods that are comparable with the irregular duration of price swings.

Direct empirical evidence that would support viewing guardedly moderate revisions as a qualitative regularity that holds during the upswing (or downswing) still needs to be gathered and examined.[5] But psychologists have uncovered experimental evidence indicating that when individuals change their forecasts about uncertain outcomes, on average they tend to do so gradually, relative to some baseline.[6] This observation is consistent with Keynes's insight and our characterization of guardedly moderate revisions: the impact of participants' revisions on their forecasts is evaluated relative to the baseline change that would have resulted if they had left their strategies unchanged and updated their forecasts solely on the basis of trends in fundamentals. Because it is qualitative, this portrayal of individual decisionmaking is open to myriad possible nonroutine ways in which a market participant might revise her forecasting strategy.[7]

Our qualitative and contingent characterization of individual decisionmaking is not only open to nonroutine changes in

---

[5]For example, one could survey market participants with qualitative questions about how much they revised their forecasting strategies from one point to another during price swings.

[6]See Edwards (1968) and Shleifer (2000) and references therein.

[7] For a rigorous formulation of qualitative and contingent conditions characterizing guardedly moderate revisions, see Frydman and Goldberg (2010b). In sharp contrast, formalizations by behavioral economists of the experimental evidence on so-called "conservatism" presume that market participants never revise their forecasting strategies. Instead, individuals are assumed to underreact to new information in a mechanical way relative to what the economist's overarching probability model would imply. See Barberis et al. (1998).

bulls' and bears' forecasting strategies, but is also consistent with the diverse ways in which this change occurs. Regardless of the precise way in which a participant revises her strategy or whether she is a bull or a bear, her price forecast tends to move in an unchanging direction for as long as her revisions are guardedly moderate and trends in fundamentals remain unchanged.

What matters for whether an asset price undergoes a swing is how participants' diverse price forecasts, in the aggregate, change over time. If trends in fundamentals lead the market's forecast to rise, say, during some stretch of time, and participants on the whole revise their strategies in guardedly moderate ways, the asset price will also tend to rise, regardless of whether bulls become more bullish or bears become less bearish.

Price Swings in Individual Stocks and the Market

Some of the basic fundamentals on which market participants rely are company specific, such as corporate earnings and sales. Short-term trends in these factors vary across companies and provide clues to their differing prospects and returns over the near and longer term. Other fundamental factors, such as overall economic activity and interest rates, are interpreted more broadly to have an impact on many companies. But trends in these fundamentals also have differing implications for companies' prospects and future returns. Consequently, periods characterized by persistent trends in the basic fundamentals and guardedly moderate revisions of forecasting strategies will not only involve swings in individual stock prices but will also entail changes in relative prices between companies—and thus their relative access to capital.

However, as this allocative process unfolds, the prices of many companies often undergo swings in the same direction, because market participants interpret many of the basic fundamentals' influence on future outcomes in a qualitatively similar way. For example, positive trends in overall economic activity and employment are often viewed bullishly for many companies, whereas rising interest rates are usually interpreted bearishly. Moreover, trends in company-specific fundamentals tend to be related to overall economic activity. For example, the earnings and sales of many companies generally rise and fall along with the economy. These observations, together with persistent trends in economy-wide macrofundamentals and guardedly moderate revisions, imply that broad stock price indexes will tend to undergo swings.

Price Swings, Genuine Diversity, and Rationality

Beyond accounting for the pattern of asset-price swings in real-world markets, the contingency of IKE models renders them compatible with the coexistence of bulls and bears in asset markets and the rationality of both positions, despite their contradictory predictions of price movements.

Our IKE model explains the presence of both bulls and bears in the market at every point in time by the fact that no participant can predict with certainty when trends in fundamentals may switch directions, or when other participants may cease to revise their forecasting strategies in guardedly moderate ways. Because a price swing may continue or end at any time, betting one way or the other does not involve any obvious irrationality on the part of participants who hold either bullish or bearish views.

Sustained Reversals

Even if trends in fundamentals continue in the same broad direction, the qualitative regularity of guardedly moderate revisions in forecasting strategies may cease to hold at moments that neither market participants nor anyone else can fully foresee. Participants may revise their set of relevant fundamentals, or the weights that they attach to them, so drastically that the effect of

their updated forecasts outweighs the impact of trends in fundamentals. If a sufficient number of participants revises their forecasts in such radical ways and bets their wealth on such a reversal
in their forecasts, stock and other asset prices themselves will also
undergo a reversal.

Non-moderate revisions of forecasting strategies are often
proximate to points at which trends in fundamentals also reverse
or there is a major change in economic policies or institutions.[8]
After all, as Keynes pointed out, recent or impending changes in
the way fundamentals are trending provide specific reasons to expect a change, which is why profit-seeking individuals pay a great
deal of attention to them.

If there are indications that fundamentals may unfold in
new directions, participants will decide on what weights to attach
to them in forecasting the future. But once they do, they are likely
to resume revising their strategies in guardedly moderate ways.
Again, if sufficient wealth is bet on such forecasts, a sustained reversal in the upswing or downswing ensues. The swing in the new
direction continues until market participants again lose confidence that the new trends in fundamentals will persist or until
they have reason (or intuition) to believe that others are about to
revise their strategies in radical ways. At such points in time, the
market experiences another reversal, which may or may not turn
into a sustained movement of prices in the opposite direction.

We thus expect that the duration and magnitude of asset-
price swings will vary in irregular ways, as the stretches of time in
which fundamentals trend persistently and revisions are guardedly moderate also vary in similarly irregular ways. Figures 5.1 and
5.2 not only reveal such irregular price swings but also show that
instability in asset prices is bounded: price swings sometimes end
too late, but they do eventually undergo sustained reversals. We
next show how this excess can be explained and develop an IKE
model of risk that explains why price instability is bounded.

[8]For econometric evidence related to this point, see Frydman and Goldberg (2007, chapter 15).

10

Bounded Instability:

Linking Risk and Asset-Price Swings

WE HAVE DISCUSSED how trends in fundamentals and guardedly moderate revisions of participants' forecasting strategies, and the contingency of such qualitative characterizations of change can account for the price swings observed in asset markets. We also sketched how swings in broad price indexes arise from movements in the relative prices of assets. In this chapter, we explain how these swings play an indispensable role in the process by which financial markets allocate capital to alternative projects and companies. However, we also show why, owing to imperfect knowledge, price swings can sometimes become excessive: prices move beyond a range of values that reflect what most value speculators would consider consistent with the longer-term prospects of projects and companies. We illustrate our arguments in the context of developments in U.S. equity markets in the 1990s and early 2000s.

If markets were entirely populated with value speculators, they would self-correct any excess in prices relatively quickly once it was generally perceived. With the presence of short-term speculators, however, the correction may be considerably delayed, resulting in substantial misallocation of capital. The possibility of a prolonged excessive price swing is further enhanced by what Soros (1987, 2009) calls "reflexive" relationships, or channels through which, for a time, an asset-price swing and fundamental trends reinforce each other.

However, as the housing- and equity-price booms of the 2000s show, even with short-term speculators and reflexive relationships, markets eventually correct excessive price swings on their own. The problem, we now see, is that the reversal, when it eventually comes, may be as sharp as the price swing was excessive, inflicting enormous damage on the financial system and the broader economy. Moreover, it may take years to correct misallocations resulting from the distortions that excessive swings cause.

In accounting for the self-limiting nature of asset-price swings, we build on another insight of Keynes (1936): participants' assessments of the potential losses—the risk—associated with their speculative positions move either in line with or counter to the price swing, depending on whether they are bulls or bears. We combine this insight with Kahneman and Tversky's (1979) prospect theory and formalize, in a way that recognizes imperfect knowledge, their observation that participants' well-being is more sensitive to potential losses than to potential gains of the same magnitude. By relating risk from trading and holding assets in financial markets to the gap between an asset price and estimates of its benchmark level, our approach results in very different measures of risk from those implied by contemporary models, which relate risk to the short-term volatility of an asset price.[1]

Our IKE model of risk implies that as asset prices rise well above or fall far below most participants' perceptions of historical benchmark levels, those who are betting on further movements away from benchmark levels raise their assessments of the riskiness of doing so. Eventually, these assessments lead participants to revise their forecasting strategies in radical and nonreinforcing ways. When that happens, even the most excessive price swings come to an end and are followed by sustained reversals back toward benchmark levels.

---

[1]As we show in Frydman and Goldberg (2007, chapters 9–13), our IKE model provides a significantly better account of risk in the foreign-exchange market than do Rational Expectations models.

THE INDISPENSABLE ROLE OF ASSET-PRICE SWINGS IN ALLOCATING CAPITAL

Consider the U.S. equity market in the 1990s. During this period, particularly before 1998, corporate earnings, gross domestic product, employment, exports, and productivity levels were rising strongly, while inflation was declining. Political and institutional developments, accompanied by loose monetary policy, were also conducive to growth. Given the widespread view at the time that the U.S. economy and others were in the midst of an information-technology revolution, both value and short-term speculators likely interpreted these persistent trends bullishly.

Value speculators focused on these short-term trends to assess how individual companies' longer-term prospects might be unfolding. They interpreted these trends in the context of in-depth company-specific and industry analyses, buying companies that they anticipated would generate a steady stream of earnings over the longer term or those thought to be undervalued, and reducing positions in companies for which confidence in earnings and value potential had fallen. These trading decisions thus contributed to the movement of relative prices and helped society to allocate its scarce capital.

As the bullish trends in economy-wide and company-specific fundamentals unfolded in the 1990s, value speculators no doubt reevaluated and possibly revised their assessments of the differing longer-term prospects of many companies. But because market participants tend to revise their thinking about the future in guardedly moderate ways or leave their strategies unaltered, value speculators' trading decisions not only influenced relative prices, but also likely contributed, at least early on, to the decade-long upswing in broad price indexes.

Of course, these speculators' assessments of the longer-term prospects of the companies that underlie, say, the S&P 500 price index spanned a range of values. Many observers would argue that this range likely shifted up, and thus, that at least for a time, the upward climb in stock prices was not a swing away from the range of values consistent with perceived longer-term prospects but was merely a reflection of its rise. Although the bullish perceptions of the information-technology revolution's longer-term benefits did—and still do—seem warranted, this does not mean that the market correctly appraised the effects on companies' longer-term prospects, even during the early phase of the 1990s upswing.

For one thing, short-term speculators also contributed to the movement of relative prices, as they, too, focused on unfolding trends in fundamentals to forecast the returns on individual companies. Because they were concerned with near-term returns, they generally did not rely on the type of extensive fundamental analysis that their longer-term counterparts undertook. Consequently, they no doubt overreacted to the trends in fundamentals when assessing some companies, pushing prices up or down excessively and distorting relative prices compared to those that would have been generated if the market were composed solely of value speculators.

However, as we discussed in Chapter 8, the performance of companies over the short term, whether positive or negative, is a harbinger of longer-term performance. By reacting to trends in fundamentals and the performance of companies over the near term, short-term speculators help the market assess companies' differing, and inherently unknowable, longer-term prospects.

During the first half of the 1990s, for example, new and old companies alike were finding and using novel applications of information technology to lower their production costs, improve their existing services or products, or develop new ones. Dell, Microsoft, and Google are prime examples of firms for which favorable short-term trends in macroeconomic and company-specific fundamentals presaged longer-term performance.

To be sure, no one knew beforehand whether any company's development strategy would succeed or fail. But as the bullish trends in fundamentals unfolded in the 1990s, short-term and value speculators were most likely buying many of the same companies. And, because short-term speculators, like value speculators, tend to revise their forecasting strategies in guardedly moderate ways or leave them unaltered, as the bullish trends in fundamentals persisted, their trading decisions, too, not only influenced relative price movements but also contributed to the general upswing in stock prices.

This and many other historical episodes demonstrate that swings in broad price indexes are integral to the process by which financial markets assess the ever-changing near-term and longer-term prospects and returns of companies—and thus to how they allocate society's capital. It is also true, however, that such swings may eventually become excessive relative to most participants' assessments of the longer-term prospects of companies and projects.

HISTORICAL BENCHMARKS AS GAUGES OF LONGER-TERM PROSPECTS

The dynamism of modern economies implies that, however careful one's analysis of a stock's prospective value might be, any light that it may shed on the longer term will be dim at best. Who in the late 1970s could have predicted the phenomenal rise of the personal computer and the internet, let alone their impact on economic outcomes, in the 1980s and 1990s?

Forecasting the longer-term prospects of a basket of companies, such as the one underlying the S&P 500 price index, is also difficult. But history tells us that irregular swings in broader price indexes tend to revolve around estimates of benchmark levels. Market participants, therefore, look to them as an imprecise but useful gauge of whether stock prices are consistent with assessments of companies' longer-term prospects.

Common benchmark levels in equity markets are based on historical averages of price-earnings or price-dividend ratios. Figure 10.1 plots the stock price relative to a 10-year moving average of earnings and its historical average (which was also plotted in Figure 5.1), as well as an example of a historically based range

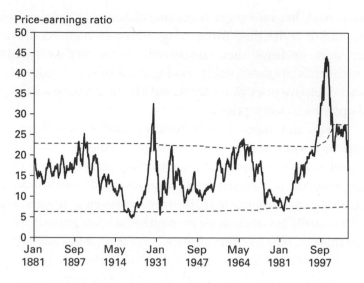

Price-earnings ratio

Fig. 10.1. Range of historically moderate price-earnings valuations
Source: Data are from Robert Shiller's website: www.econ.yale.edu/~shiller.

within which most of the fluctuations in the price-earnings ratio have occurred. Price-earnings ratios are often based on a moving average of current and past earnings, because such averages provide a better measure of companies' longer-term prospects than do current earnings in any given quarter. To derive the lower and upper bands of the range, we first find the fifth and ninety-fifth percentiles of price-earnings ratios during the first fifty years of the sample (1881–1931). After 1931, we move the fifty-year window forward one month at a time and again find the high and low price-earnings ratios that imply a 90% range of moderate values.

The price swings away from and toward the benchmark level in the figure are of irregular duration and magnitude; when a price swing might begin or end cannot be predicted solely on the basis of mathematical calculation. But the empirical record shows that when stock prices move beyond a range of historically moderate levels relative to current and past earnings, the high valuations are likely not sustainable. Eventually, stock prices undergo sustained countermovements back toward the historically moderate range.[2]

The range of historically moderate values plotted in Figure 10.1 is just one possible example of such a span. No one can fully foresee what upper or lower threshold would, if crossed, imply excessive values and a greater likelihood of unsustainability. Given the dynamism of modern economies, these thresholds no doubt change over time.[3]

Nonetheless, because growing departures from common benchmark levels are eventually not sustainable, market participants rely on the historically moderate values around them to evaluate the plausibility of their own assessments of longer-term prospects. How individuals come to decide on a particular notion of the benchmark and estimate it is an open question. Keynes (1936) suggests that conventions and the historical record play an important role. For example, price-earnings ratios and purchasing power parity exchange rates have long influenced how market participants and policymakers assess the sustainability of prices in equity markets and currency markets, respectively.

A market participant's assessment of companies' longer-term prospects will generally differ from her assessment of the historical benchmark. After all, historical benchmarks are backward looking and, by definition, cannot account for the longer-term impact of innovative activities and nonroutine change on companies. At each point in time, a participant who trades with a view to the longer term devises her own forecast of prospects, generally draw-

---

[2]There is much formal research, which we discuss in Chapter 11, showing that stock prices do tend to revert back toward historically moderate levels based on recent and past earnings or dividends. Of course, there are many ways to calculate a benchmark price-earnings level. For example, a moving average of this ratio would deliver a different estimate of the benchmark level than would a fixed historical average. Likewise, price-dividend ratios and other indexes would deliver different benchmark values. But research shows that sustained countermovements also eventually follow departures from historically moderate levels that are based on these alternatives measures.

[3]This issue is addressed in Chapter 12, when we discuss the policy implications of our IKE account of asset-price swings and risk.

ing on historical information (including her assessment of the historical benchmark), current information about fundamentals, and any innovations and other changes in the social context that she deems relevant. Indeed, current information might—and likely does—lead individuals to think that future returns could turn out to be different from what is implied by the historical benchmark.

It seems uncontroversial to suppose that the difference between an individual's forecast of companies' longer-term prospects and her assessment of the historical benchmark is limited. After all, there is a floor and a ceiling, relative to current and past earnings, to the value of U.S. equities as a whole, say, ten or twenty years hence.[4] Consequently, when stock prices rise above or fall below historically moderate values, they have likely moved beyond the range that is consistent with most participants' assessments of companies' longer-term prospects.

Such excessive price swings can arise from the trading decisions of both short-term and value speculators. However, it is short-term speculators whose trading can sustain an excessive price swing, even though they and their longer-term counterparts understand that prices are already historically high and inconsistent with most assessments of longer-term valuations.

The Unfolding of Excessive Price Swings

Price swings may unfold more or less quickly than do current earnings. Figure 7.1 (reproduced here as Figure 10.2 for convenience) shows that the upswing in equity prices in the 1990s was steeper than the rise in current earnings, whereas the opposite was true for the upswing and downswing that occurred between 2003 and 2007. However, as Figure 10.1 reveals, the price swings that we observe in financial markets tend to involve persistent movements away from or toward moving averages of earnings, which change much more slowly than current earnings do.

[4]Similar limits, though based on different considerations, exist in other markets.

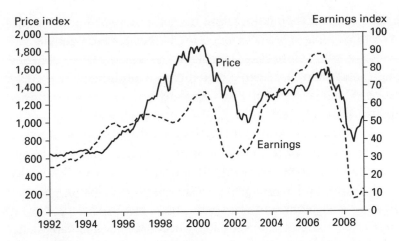

Fig. 10.2. S&P 500 stock price and current earnings, 1992–2009
Source: Data are from Robert Shiller's website: www.econ.yale.edu/~shiller.

Consider again the U.S. stock market in the 1990s. Given the positive perceptions of the information-technology revolution's longer-term benefits during this period and the bullish trends in many of the basic fundamental factors, value speculators likely raised their assessments of the capacity of many companies' to generate greater future earnings—and thus of the price-earnings multiples that these companies deserved. Short-term speculators also focused on the bullish trends in fundamentals in the context of the information-technology revolution. Because both groups of participants tend to revise their forecasting strategies in guardedly moderate ways, both contributed to the upswing in the stock prices relative to current and past earnings.

Reflexivity, Speculation, and Excess

Of course, assessments of companies' longer-term prospects, relative to their current and past earnings, cannot grow without bound. Eventually, value speculators will realize that companies' prospects do not warrant higher price-earnings multiples, despite persistent bullish trends in the basic fundamentals. The length of time before value speculators as a group come to believe that such a point has been reached can be prolonged by the existence of feedback, or reflexive relationships, between stock prices and trends in fundamentals.

Most individuals hold their wealth entirely or mostly in their house and/or in the stock market. When equity and housing prices rise, so does individual wealth. As a result, they feel less need to save and are also able to borrow more, leading them to increase their consumption spending. Likewise, as stock prices increase, businesses gain greater access to finance capital, enabling them to increase their investment spending on new plant and equipment. Rising consumption and investment spending stimulates overall economic activity, thereby enhancing the favorable trends in company earnings and other basic fundamental factors on which both value and short-term speculators rely in forecasting market outcomes. The persistence of bullish trends, in turn, exerts positive feedback on stock prices. And, of course, a rising stock market and overall economy boosts the confidence and optimism of consumers, businesses, and financial market participants about the future, further adding to the positive reflexive effects.

Eventually, if it continues long enough, this reflexive process reverses itself, as consumers find themselves financially overextended and firms begin to see that capital expenditures have resulted in excess capacity.[5] Of course, no one knows when debt levels and capital expenditures may become unsustainable. Value speculators must take into account reflexive considerations, along with their painstaking company-specific research, when interpreting the consequences of short-term trends in fundamentals for companies' longer-term prospects.

----

[5]This unsustainability is the key mechanism in Soros's account of how price swings eventually end after a period during which reflexive feedbacks dominate their movements. For example, see Soros (2009).

The difficulty that reflexive relationships pose suggests that a point may have been reached in the 1990s when value speculators came to believe that their own assessments of the longer-term impact of short-term trends in fundamentals, and of the benefits of the information-technology revolution, had risen too far. At that point, they came to believe that the weights attached to the bullish short-term trends in fundamentals were incorrect, and they revised them in radical ways that reflected lower longer-term assessments.

Short-Term Speculation and Excess

If the market were composed entirely of participants who traded with a view to the longer term, their non-moderate revisions of forecasting strategies would lead them to correct their excessively positive assessments of the impact of fundamental trends on companies' prospects, thereby bringing the upswing to an end. However, short-term speculators have a significant influence on market prices. Their main concern is whether recent trends in fundamentals will continue for another few months or quarters rather than whether they are sustainable over the longer term. Consequently, as long as the basic fundamentals continue to unfold with unchanging trends and short-term speculators continue to revise their strategies in guardedly moderate ways, they will bid stock prices beyond the range of values consistent with their longer-term counterparts' assessments of companies' prospects.

The empirical record suggests that the 1990s upswing was characterized by such excess. Indeed, already by the end of 1996, Robert Shiller's price-earnings ratio stood at 28—almost twice the contemporary historical average of 15. The last time the market had seen price-earnings multiples that high was during the six months prior to the Great Crash of 1929.

Nevertheless, the trends in many basic fundamentals, including current earnings, continued to unfold in favorable directions for another three years. Of course, at each point in time, no one knew whether the favorable trends in fundamentals would continue or whether the revisions of other participants would remain guardedly moderate. At any point during the decade-long upswing, the trends in fundamentals could shift direction or revisions could become radical, which implies that some short-term speculators forecasted rising prices, while others predicted a fall at every point in time.

But, as we argued in Chapter 9, the key to explaining asset-price movements is how the price forecasts of market participants unfold over time. Given favorable trends in fundamentals and the tendency of short-term speculators toward guardedly moderate revisions, short-term bulls and bears in the aggregate raised their forecasts and continued to bid up prices well beyond what they themselves knew was likely to be consistent with most value speculators' assessments of longer-term prospects.

In Chapter 8, we discussed how the trading decisions of short-term speculators contribute positively to the ability of financial markets to allocate society's scarce capital, and yet they can also distort relative prices, because their decisions are not based on the painstaking research undertaken by value speculators. Within a range of values that is consistent with most speculators' assessments of longer-term prospects, the distorting influence of short-term speculators is likely to be relatively muted. Indeed, during the early phase of the 1990s upswing in stock prices, the favorable trends in basic fundamentals most likely led them to buy many of the same companies that value speculators bought.

In contrast, once a price swing becomes excessive, say, from above, the benefits of value speculators' trading decisions disappear as short-term speculators drive ballooning valuations. Moreover, reflexive relationships in the economy imply that bullish trends in fundamentals eventually will send incorrect and unsustainable signals concerning the differing longer-term prospects of companies. As short-term speculators largely base their trading decisions on these signals, there is much more room for the market to distort relative prices and misallocate capital. Overinvestment in technology stocks in the 1990s is indicative of such misallocation.

Of course, the process by which upswings sometimes become excessive also applies to downswings, which are equally likely to misallocate capital by providing incorrect signals concerning which companies should be started, expanded, restructured, scaled down, or liquidated. But another, even more serious danger associated with excessive downswings, which Keynes (1936) emphasized, is that the overall volume of investment falls precipitously and remains depressed for a protracted period of time (see Chapters 7 and 8).

However, although short-term speculators sometimes bid stock prices far beyond the range of non-excessive values, they do not continue to do so without bound. Our IKE account of risk implies that eventually they, too, will radically revise their forecasting strategies, leading to a sustained price reversal—even if fundamentals continue to trend in unchanging directions. This process helps explain why markets eventually self-correct.

LINKING RISK TO DISTANCE FROM BENCHMARK LEVELS

Financial economists typically portray the riskiness of holding speculative positions with standard measures of short-term volatility, such as the variance of returns. They use these models to account for the premium—a positive expected excess return—that market participants demand for holding speculative positions. As we discussed in Chapter 5, the empirical performance of economists' risk-premium models has been extremely poor.

Keynes's (1936) ideas about speculation in asset markets lead to an alternative characterization of how participants assess financial risk. He argued that speculators are aware of the tendency of asset prices to undergo uneven swings, and that speculators use this feature of their social context when attempting to forecast market outcomes. In discussing why an individual might hold cash rather than risky interest-bearing bonds, Keynes observed that "what matters is not the absolute level of [the interest rate] but the degree of its divergence from what is considered a fairly safe [benchmark] level, having regard to those calculations of probability which are being relied on" (Keynes, 1936, p. 201).[6]

This insight suggests that a short-term speculator focuses on the gap between stock prices and her perception of the historical benchmark level when assessing the potential capital loss from her speculative position:

> Unless reasons are believed to exist why future experience will be very different from past experience, a . . . rate of interest [much lower than the safe rate] leaves more to fear than to hope, and offers, at the same time, a running yield which is only sufficient to offset a very small measure of fear [of capital loss]. [Keynes, 1936, p. 202]

This insight leads to an alternative characterization of market participants' risk premiums.[7] Of course, how a participant interprets the gap between asset prices and benchmark values in assessing risk changes over time in ways that neither she nor an economist can specify fully in advance. Indeed, we present evidence below that the importance individuals attach to the gap when it is historically large is much greater than when it is historically small. However, no one can fully foresee the thresholds above or below which participants might consider the magnitude of the gap to be

---

[6]For an early formalization of this insight in a model of speculators' decision to apportion their wealth between cash and bonds, see Tobin (1958).

[7]In Frydman and Goldberg (2007, chapter 9), we develop what we refer to as endogenous prospect theory, which builds on Kahneman and Tversky (1979) and assumes endogenous loss aversion: an individual is not only loss-averse (her disutility from losses is greater than her utility from gains of the same magnitude), but endogenously so (her degree of loss aversion increases with the size of her open position). More importantly, as Kahneman and Tversky themselves pointed out, their original formulation of prospect theory was based on an experimental setting that, by design, ignored imperfect knowledge. Remarkably, other behavioral economists do not acknowledge this fundamental difficulty. Endogenous prospect theory explicitly addresses this problem and provides a way to formalize all of Kahneman's and Tversky's experimental findings without disregarding the imperfection of knowledge.

large or small or how the crossing of these thresholds might affect their assessments of the potential losses from speculation. Consequently, we formalize Keynes's insight as a qualitative regularity: depending on which side of the market a short-term speculator takes, she either raises or lowers her assessment of the potential losses—and thus her risk premium—as prices move farther away from or closer to her perception of benchmark levels.[8]

Consider, for example, an upswing in stock prices, say, farther above participants' assessments of benchmark levels. A short-term bull forecasts that the price swing will continue over the near-term, whereas a bear forecasts the opposite. Nonetheless, both contemplate the potential losses that they would incur if the asset price were to move against them. If trends in fundamentals persuade bulls to raise their forecasts of future prices, they will want to increase their open positions. "Unless reasons are believed to exist why future experience will be very different from past experience," they will also raise their assessments of the potential losses of being wrong: the greater the gap from their estimate of the benchmark, the more concerned they tend to be about a reversal. Bears, however, respond in the opposite way to a further rise in prices: they tend to become more confident about an eventual reversal and thus lower their assessment of the potential losses from their open positions.

How Markets Ultimately Self-Correct

If a market participant's risk premium depends on the gap between the asset price and her assessment of the benchmark level, she will alter the premium that she requires for holding an open

---

[8]There are no doubt other factors that speculators rely on when assessing the riskiness of their open positions. In currency markets, for example, participants may focus on the size of current-account imbalances and countries' international debt positions when assessing risk. See Frydman and Goldberg (2007, chapter 12), where we incorporate such considerations into an IKE model of risk.

position during a price swing—in one direction if she is a bull, in the other if she is a bear. These changes in premiums help account for the fact that long swings in asset markets are ultimately bounded.

To see how they are limited, suppose that persistent trends in fundamental factors and guardedly moderate revisions of forecasting strategies lead bulls to raise their forecasts of future prices; that is, they expect that the return to buying stocks has increased. Acting on this belief, they increase their speculative positions and bid up prices, say, farther above the range of values consistent with most estimates of the companies' longer-term prospects and thus most assessments of benchmark levels.

Even though bulls expect a greater return, they understand that such excessive price swings eventually end, so they increase their assessments of the risk of a reversal and capital losses. The resulting rise in their premiums acts to temper their inclinations to increase their speculative positions. If trends in fundamentals continue, thereby prolonging the excessive price swing, a threshold is eventually reached at which bulls become so concerned about a reversal that they no longer revise their forecasting strategies in guardedly moderate ways. At that point, they either reduce their long positions or abandon them altogether, which precipitates a price reversal. Bears will also change their premiums, but in the opposite direction, likewise contributing to the self-limiting nature of long swings away from benchmark levels.

Our IKE account of risk implies that the market premium in the aggregate is equal to the premiums of the bulls minus those of the bears. As mentioned in Chapter 5, the market premium thus depends positively on participants' assessments of the gap relative to estimates of benchmark levels. Figure 5.4 shows that this qualitative prediction is borne out in currency markets,[9] whereas Figure 5.3 suggests that the connection is much less clear in stock markets.

---

[9]Time plots for other major exchange rates show a similar pattern, and formal statistical analysis supports the conclusion of a positive relationship. See Frydman and Goldberg (2007, chapter 12).

However, Mangee's (2011) Bloomberg data, discussed in Chapter 7, provides evidence that participants in stock markets pay attention to the divergence of stock prices from historical valuation levels when this gap grows large. Three excerpts illustrate how Bloomberg News reported the importance of this consideration:

> U.S. stocks fell in a late-day slide amid concern that share prices may have overshot earnings prospects.... "There are an increasing number of people who think this market is overvalued," said David Diamond, a money manager at Boston Company Asset management with $17 billion in assets. The Standard and Poor's 500 index is trading at 19 times 1997 earnings, based on a Zacks Investment research survey, 25% higher than its average price-to-earnings ratio of 15.2 since 1980. [February 19, 1997]

> "Investors are looking for a reason to sell," said Gene Grandone, director of investment counseling at the Northern Trust Co., which oversees $130 billion. "With the market in the 7,900 area, people see a market that is a little rich." ... Many investors are uncomfortable with the market's price-to-earnings ratio, which is near the high end of its historic range. [July 7, 1997]

> U.S. stocks were mixed.... Companies are being punished for any shortfalls because stocks are at historic highs relative to profit forecasts. The S&P 500, for example, trades at 35 times earnings. [April 7, 1999]

Figure 10.3 plots a 12-month moving average of the proportion of days in each month that such gap considerations were mentioned as having influenced the market. For much of the period, they were unimportant, meriting mention on only 2% or fewer of the days each month on average. However, starting in 1997, the importance of gap considerations rose, with the proportion of mentions each month reaching roughly 10% by the end of 1999—precisely during the most excessive phase of the market's upswing. A similar rise occurred starting in the second half of 2008, when the financial crisis led to a sharp and prolonged down-

Frequency (%)

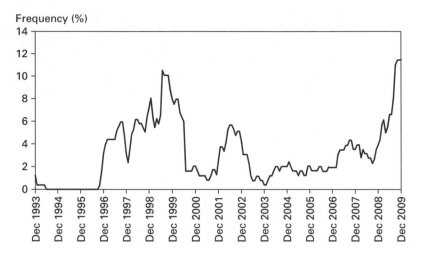

Fig. 10.3. Average monthly frequency of mentions in wrap reports: The price gap from benchmark values.

swing, sending the price-earnings ratio from 21 in August of that year to 13 by March 2009.

THE RETURN OF FUNDAMENTALS

Market participants' assessment of financial risk in terms of the gap between prices and historical benchmark levels points to movements in fundamental factors as the key to understanding the main features of financial markets. In Chapters 8 and 9, we showed how trends in fundamentals, such as corporate earnings and interest rates, influence the allocation of capital among projects and underpin swings in asset prices. In this chapter, we showed how trends in fundamentals may lead the market to bid prices up or down to excessive levels. We also showed how these trends, through their influence on asset prices—and thus on the price-benchmark gap—affect financial risk and help explain the fact that markets eventually self-correct.

What enabled us to uncover the key role of fundamentals for understanding financial markets is that, in sharp contrast to extant approaches, we do not assume away nonroutine change and imperfect knowledge. Moreover, by placing these features at the center of our analysis, we are able to recognize the role of psychological factors in driving outcomes. In Chapter 11, we show how a return of fundamentals enables us to avoid the two extreme views of markets held by contemporary economists: that they set prices nearly perfectly at their supposedly true values or that they are prone to psychologically driven bubbles that push prices far from levels that are consistent with fundamental considerations.

11

Contingency and Markets

ACCORDING TO OUR IKE model, prices and risk tend to undergo swings when trends in fundamentals persist for some time, which they do quite often, and market participants have no specific reasons to expect a change, and thus they are likely to revise their forecasting strategies in guardedly moderate ways. We would expect, therefore, that fundamental factors play an important role in driving asset-price swings and risk. We would also expect the set of fundamental factors and their influences to change over time.

Yet nearly all of the literally thousands of empirical studies make no allowance for any change in the way that fundamentals might matter for monthly or quarterly movements in asset prices. Instead, these studies estimate statistical models with fixed parameters over long stretches of time (in many cases, decades). Unsurprisingly, these empirical studies fail to find evidence that fundamentals matter.

The only sensible conclusion to draw from such fixed-parameter studies is that looking for overarching relationships in asset markets is futile. Instead, economists have largely concluded that factors other than fundamentals must move markets. Those who argue that bubbles and irrationality drive asset prices routinely appeal to these results to support their position.

Economists who continue to embrace the Efficient Market Hypothesis largely recognize that "we don't have . . . [a Rational Expectations] model yet" (Cassidy, 2010b, p. 3) that can account for asset-price swings and risk. But they point to an enormous amount of statistical research that they believe provides strong empirical support for the claim of the Efficient Market Hypothesis that available information cannot be used to earn above-average returns consistently (for review articles, see Fama, 1970, 1991). Researchers in the 1960s and 1970s examined short-term (daily, weekly, and monthly) asset returns and generally reported no discernable correlations in the data that could be used to beat the market. Researchers also found that mechanical trading rules based on past price trends were generally unable to produce profits on average and that mutual fund managers, as a group, were unable to generate average returns higher than those of passive funds based on a broad index. Economists concluded from this early evidence that "there is no other proposition in economics which has more solid empirical evidence supporting it than the Efficient Markets Hypothesis" (Jensen, 1978, p. 95).

More recent studies, which use more powerful statistical procedures and longer samples, have produced results that contradict the Efficient Market Hypothesis. Researchers have found what appear to be strong correlations in stock returns over the short term and long term (three to five years).[1] They have also found that when stock prices relative to earnings or dividends are high compared to historical averages, returns tend to be below average over the subsequent three to ten years, which is just a reflection of the tendency of asset prices to undergo wide swings around benchmark levels (see Campbell and Shiller, 1988; Fama and French, 1988). In currency markets, studies report that future currency returns are correlated with available information on the forward premium (which we will define shortly) and suggest that a simple rule of betting against the prediction implied by the forward rate would deliver above-average returns.

[1]For short-term correlations, see Jegadeesh and Titman (1993) and Lo and MacKinlay (1999). For long-term correlations, see De Bondt and Thaler (1985) and Fama and French (1988).

Financial economists have engaged in an intensive search for an REH-based risk-premium model that could rationalize the more recent empirical results. They have failed so far, but they continue to hold out the possibility of eventual success. As the University of Chicago's John Cochrane put it, "That's the challenge. That's what we all work on" (Cassidy, 2010b, p. 3).

But that is not the challenge (and it is not what we all work on). Indeed, beyond its inability to account for asset-price swings and risk, there is something fundamentally absurd about the Efficient Market Hypothesis. It is based on the idea that individuals are profit-seeking, but it supposes that the masses of market participants who do use available information in an effort to earn above-average returns are merely wasting their time.

In contrast, behavioral economists point to the supposedly systematic patterns in returns, and the failure of standard risk-premium models to explain them, as additional evidence that asset markets are grossly irrational. But there is a fundamental absurdity here, too. Behavioral economists would not deny that professional participants in asset markets are not only profit-seeking but also extremely clever and highly compensated to find ways to outperform the market. Yet their theories suppose that markets offer profit opportunities—as simple to exploit as betting against the forward rate—which these masters of the universe somehow overlook.

As with the bizarre conclusion that fundamentals are unimportant for asset prices, the absurdities of both the Efficient Market Hypothesis and behavioral views stem from searching for fully predetermined models of asset returns. Almost all empirical evidence that both camps invoke to buttress their positions is based on seeking fixed patterns in the data. However, new technologies, institutional and policy developments, fresh ways of thinking about markets and the economy, and myriad other possible nonroutine changes lead to temporary but significant correlations in the data.

The temporary above-average returns that come from anticipating these correlations or spotting them early enough provide huge incentives for individuals to use available information to do so. To assume away these temporary returns, as proponents of the Efficient Market Hypothesis do, is to disregard the very basis for making profits in financial markets. Moreover, the importance of nonroutine change implies that there are no stable patterns in returns, and the claims of behavioral economists that they have discovered mechanical rules that deliver easy profits, yet participants leave them unexploited, are simply bogus.

CONTINGENT MARKET HYPOTHESIS

Markets play an essential role in modern economies precisely because change is "contingent"—it is "affected by unforeseen causes or conditions" (*Webster's Unabridged Dictionary*)—and knowledge is imperfect. This leads us to propose the Contingent Market Hypothesis as an alternative to the Efficient Market Hypothesis. Like the latter hypothesis, the Contingent Market Hypothesis supposes that

• The causal process underpinning price movements depends on available information, which includes observations concerning fundamental factors specific to each market.

However, in sharp contrast to the Efficient Market Hypothesis,

• This process cannot be adequately characterized by an overarching model, defined as a rule that exactly relates market outcomes to available information up to a fully predetermined random error at all time periods, past, present, and future.

Chapters 8, 9, and 10 showed how, with contingent change, asset-price swings are inherent to the process by which financial markets allocate capital and yet they sometimes become excessive. The Contingent Market Hypothesis has three additional implications. In presenting each, we discuss more fully how this alternative hypothesis accounts for the empirical evidence that has confounded the standard theory and how it leads to an intermediate view of the role of asset-price swings.

CONTINGENCY AND INSTABILITY OF ECONOMIC STRUCTURES

Significant changes in the process driving asset prices occur at moments and in ways that cannot be fully foreseen. Such contingent change implies that the statistical estimates of fully predetermined models of asset prices vary in significant ways as the time period examined is changed. Correlations between price changes and informational variables that might be found in the data over some stretch of time eventually change or disappear and are replaced with new relationships.

Temporal instability is not difficult to find in asset markets. For example, Fama and MacBeth (1973) and others report favorable estimates of the Capital Asset Pricing Model, which is widely used in academia and industry, over a sample that runs until 1965. However, when the sample was updated to include the 1970s and 1980s, and additional variables were added to the analysis, the results led Fama to refer to the Capital Asset Pricing Model in a *New York Times* interview as an "atrocious . . . empirical model" (Berg, 1992, p. D1). Commenting in an interview with *Institutional Investor* on the temporal instability of correlations in asset-price data, Nobel laureate William Sharpe quipped that "[i]t's almost true that if you don't like an empirical result, if you can wait until somebody uses a different [time] period . . . you'll get a different answer" (Wallace, 1980, p. 24).

Given such temporal instability, looking for stable correlations between asset prices and variables in any information set, as most empirical researchers do, merely draws data from different subsamples, each involving distinct correlations. Doing so is likely to conceal the nature of the correlations that might exist in the data during stretches of time between significant shifts in the causal process.

The Exchange-Rate Disconnect Puzzle

Nowhere is the futility of searching for the role of fundamentals with fully predetermined models more apparent than in currency markets. International macroeconomists routinely estimate fixed exchange-rate relationships in samples that run longer than two or three decades. Such empirical analysis presumes that market participants never revise their forecasting strategies, and that the policy and institutional framework remains unchanged. The results of this research are dismal, leading most researchers in the field to conclude that "exchange rates are moved largely by factors other than the obvious, observable, macroeconomic fundamentals" (Dornbusch and Frankel, 1988, p. 16).[2]

Meese and Rogoff's (1983) study is perhaps the most often cited as showing the supposed disconnection between exchange rates and fundamentals. They examined the performance of the most popular models, which relate the exchange rate to interest rates, national income, trade balances, and other fundamentals that are widely believed to underpin currency fluctuations. The authors estimated each model over an initial sample that ran from March 1973 through November 1976. They were interested in how well a model that was estimated on the basis of data during the initial period captured the influences of fundamentals outside of that period.

To answer this question, they used their initial parameter estimates to forecast the exchange rate over short horizons of one, six, and twelve months. A real forecasting exercise would, of course, also need to project the values of the fundamentals for the future dates of the forecasts. But to keep the focus of the exercise on whether the in-sample estimates could account for the influence of fundamentals out of sample, they used the actual future values of the fundamentals to obtain exchange-rate predictions. To produce a series of short-term exchange-rate forecasts from

---

[2]See Frankel and Rose (1995) and Frydman and Goldberg (2007, chapter 7) for overviews of this literature.

the models, Meese and Rogoff added to their initial sample observations beyond November 1976, one month at a time until June 1981, and at each step, they combined their in-sample parameter estimates with the actual future values of the fundamentals.

Meese and Rogoff's results had a profound impact on the literature. They found that none of the models examined produced exchange-rate predictions that would enable a forecaster to do any better than merely flipping a fair coin. This was the case even though the predictions of these models were based on the actual future values of the fundamentals. The results thus suggested that possession of such information provided absolutely no benefit to a forecaster. The implication drawn by most researchers in the field seemed obvious: fundamentals play absolutely no role in currency fluctuations.

There are literally hundreds of studies that have extended Meese and Rogoff's (1983) analysis to include newer exchange-rate models, more powerful statistical techniques, longer sample periods, and additional exchange rates. The results are largely the same as those of the original study (for a review, see Cheung et al., 2005). Appealing to such evidence, many international macro-economists continue to argue that short-term fluctuations in currency markets do not depend on macroeconomic fundamentals.

The Contingent Market Hypothesis implies a more plausible interpretation of the empirical record. Time-invariant and other fully predetermined probabilistic models simply provide an inadequate lens for examining the importance of fundamental factors for price fluctuations in financial markets. In these markets—where the imperfection of knowledge and psychological considerations underpin participants' trading decisions, and the policy and institutional framework undergoes nonroutine change—fundamentals matter, but in different ways during different stretches of time.

Contingent Change in Currency Markets

Although the causal process driving outcomes in currency markets changes at times and in ways that no one can fully prespecify, there may be extended periods during which the non-routine change that does occur is sufficiently moderate that a relatively stable relationship between the exchange rate and a set of fundamental variables results. No one can foresee when such distinct periods might occur or how long they might last, let alone the precise nature of the fundamental relationships during those periods.

In fact, there are no strictly objective criteria, statistical or otherwise, to determine the precise nature of the fundamental relationship and points of change—breaks in the data when a new relationship arises—in the historical record. Different models and testing procedures will lead to different break points and estimated relationships. As with estimates of the Capital Asset Pricing Model in the stock market, empirical estimates of economists' exchange-rate models depend on the sample period used.

For example, in Frydman and Goldberg (2007, chapter 15) we suppose that the fundamental relationship driving the German mark–U.S. dollar exchange rate in any given period entails one or more of the fundamental variables implied by the exchange-rate models examined in Meese and Rogoff (1983). We use statistical procedures that enable us to approximate when this relationship may have changed over our sample without prespecifying the timing or nature of this change. Figure 11.1 plots the exchange rate and reports results of change tests; dotted vertical lines indicate break points.[3]

In all, we find six break points in our sample, which includes the 1970s, 1980s, and 1990s.[4] Some of the breaks are proximate to major shifts in economic policy. For example, in October 1979, the U.S. Federal Reserve deemphasized the federal funds rate in favor of monetary aggregates as its primary operating target, and October 1985 was the month following the Plaza accord,

---

[3]The analysis makes use of the CUSUM test of Brown et al. (1975). For more details, see Frydman and Goldberg (2007, chapters 12 and 15).

[4]Many other studies also find temporal instability in currency markets. See Boughton (1987), Meese and Rogoff (1988), Goldberg and Frydman (1996a,b, 2001), Rogoff and Stavrakeva (2008), and Beckman et al. (2010).

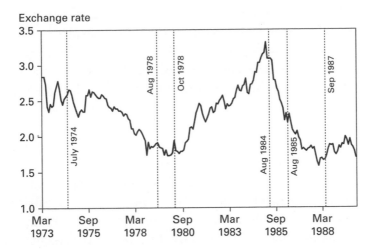

Fig. 11.1. Structural change results: German mark–U.S. dollar exchange rate relationship

which aimed at lowering the dollar's value. But other break points are not. No one can fully foresee shifts in monetary or fiscal policies, let alone the factors underpinning the other break points.

The Disconnect Puzzle as an Artifact of the Contemporary Approach

The results of the structural change tests suggest that there are distinct subperiods in the data or regimes during which the exchange-rate process is approximately stable. It thus makes little sense to estimate any fixed exchange-rate model over our entire sample. Indeed, doing so produces the same dismal results found by earlier researchers, suggesting that fundamentals do not matter at all.

However, a very different picture emerges when we examine separately the distinct fundamental relationships in the two extended regimes of the 1970s and 1980s. In each regime, we find that many of the fundamentals implied by economists' exchange-rate models matter in ways that are consistent with the qualitative

predictions of these models.[5] We also find that different fundamentals with different influences drive the exchange rate across
the two regimes.[6]

The structural change results in Figure 11.1 show that
three break points occur during the sample period underlying
Meese and Rogoff's (1983) forecasting exercise. Their results,
therefore, have little significance for understanding exchange-
rate fluctuations. Indeed, our estimated fundamental relationship for the 1970s regime (which runs from July 1974 through
September 1978) outperformed the coin-flipping strategy for
forecasting by considerable margins, but only if we restrict the
analysis to the 1970s regime. For example, the fundamental
model was able to predict correctly the direction of change of the
exchange rate 100% of the time at the six-month, nine-month,
and 12-month forecasting horizons.[7]

Figure 11.2 shows the basic problem posed by instability for
the Meese and Rogoff (1983) analysis. The figure plots a measure of
the forecasting error at the three-month horizon of the fundamental model estimated for 1970s regime.[8] Prior to the regime change in
October 1978, the model's forecasting error is consistently less than
2.5%, which is less than half the 6% forecasting error produced by
flipping a coin. However, after the point of change, another set of

---

[5]To specify these qualitative predictions, we make use of the Theories-
Consistent Expectations Hypothesis proposed by Frydman and Phelps (1990).
This hypothesis is based on the idea that economists' models summarize their
qualitative insights concerning the causal mechanism underpinning market outcomes and that, presumably, these insights are shared by market participants.
Economists usually have several models of an aggregate outcome. Thus, representations of forecasting behavior based on this hypothesis make use of several
economic models rather than relying on just one. In Frydman and Goldberg
(2007, chapter 10) we show how this can be done, even if the qualitative features
of a set of extant models conflict with one another.

[6]For a recent study that also finds that different fundamentals matter
during different periods, see Beckman et al. (2010).

[7]For a recent study that also finds forecasting performance to depend
on the period studied, see Rogoff and Stavrakeva (2008).

[8]The figure is based on root mean square error. See Meese and Rogoff
(1983) for details.

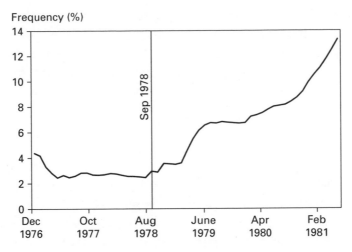

Fig. 11.2. Pre- and post-break performance of the fundamental model

fundamentals with different influences drives the exchange rate. Unsurprisingly, the forecasting error of the estimated model prior to the break point deteriorates markedly once change occurs, far surpassing the error from coin flipping.

Meese and Rogoff (1983) report only the average of the forecasting errors generated by exchange-rate models over the entire sample, which combines the stellar forecasting performance prior to the point of change with the dismal errors that followed it. This practice merely conceals the significance of fundamentals in driving currencies in nonroutine ways both before and after the point of change.

THE FLEETING PROFITABILITY OF MECHANICAL TRADING RULES

As with estimated relationships between asset prices and fundamentals, contingent change implies that any fully prespecified trading rule that generates above-average returns over some past stretch of time, after accounting for risk, will eventually cease to do so. This implication goes a long way toward resolving one of the core "puzzles" in financial economics.

Early studies of the performance of trading rules that extrapolate past price trends found little evidence that they delivered any profits at all (for a review, see Fama, 1970). However, more recent studies, which have looked at a much wider array of technical rules and trading horizons, claim that rules based on intraday horizons do generate above-average returns after accounting for risk.[9] Economists have also estimated fixed-parameter models of asset returns and report apparently stable patterns in the data that could be used to earn above-average returns after accounting for risk.

According to the Efficient Market Hypothesis, all such trading-rule profits and patterns should be quickly arbitraged away. Economists' apparent discovery of them suggests that they are not. Conventional economists have been searching for decades for an REH-based risk-premium model that could rationalize the supposed profitability of their rules and stable patterns in returns. Having accepted the Rational Expectations Hypothesis as the standard of rationality, behavioral economists have interpreted the failure of this effort as another indication of the irrationality of asset markets. They have also been at work over the past two decades developing an array of fully predetermined accounts of such behavior.

Of course, one can search for fixed trading rules that are profitable and for correlations between asset returns and available information during some past stretch of time, and find what looks like profitability and stable patterns. But the contingent change that characterizes markets (and capitalist economies more broadly) implies that fixed trading rules will eventually lose their profitability, and past correlations will eventually change at times and in ways that no one can fully foresee.

To be sure, many participants in financial markets use technical trading rules. However, there is much evidence that these rules are used in nonmechanical ways. Even dealers in cur-

---

[9]See Schulmeister (2006). For a review, see Menkhoff and Taylor (2007).

rency markets, who trade over very short horizons, combine them with considerations based on fundamental and psychological factors in ways that change over time.[10] Using technical rules requires intuition and the skill to know which rules to use and when to use them: as Menkhoff and Taylor (2007, p. 947) conclude in their review article, "the performance of technical trading rules is highly unstable over time."

This result is not surprising, given that economists' fixed-parameter models of returns are also temporally unstable. Fama and French (1988), for example, report that stock portfolios with positive returns over the preceding three to five years tend to produce negative returns over the subsequent three to five years, and vice versa.[11] However, when they deleted the first part of their sample, the negative relationship largely vanished.

Campbell and Shiller (1988) report that when stock prices relative to earnings or dividends are high compared to historical averages, real returns tend to be below average over the subsequent three to ten years.[12] But these results do not provide a mechanical way to beat the market. For example, the price-earnings ratio on the S&P 500 basket of stocks in January 1997 stood at a record-high 28. Campbell and Shiller (1998) report that at this level, their analysis implied a prediction of a negative 40% real return on holding the S&P 500 stocks over the next ten years. Although stock prices fell considerably from 2000 to 2003, they were back up by January 2007: over the ten-year period, an investor would have earned a respectable real annual return of 4.6%. Timing when to buy and sell is essential, and one would not want to rely solely on a mechanical relationship between price-earnings ratios and returns based on historical data.

What appear to economists to be easy ways to make money are nothing more than temporary mirages. That participants in financial markets do not avail themselves of these sup-

[10]See the survey studies of Cheung et al. (1999), Cheung and Chinn (2001), and Menkhoff and Taylor (2007).
[11]De Bondt and Thaler (1985) showed much the same result.
[12]Fama and French (1988) find similar results.

posed opportunities is a testament not to their irrationality, but to common sense: they simply cannot afford to stick to one fixed rule endlessly. The enormous amount of time, energy, money, and other resources that economists have devoted to explaining their findings on returns is a prime example of how economists' insistence on searching for fully predetermined models has impeded progress in economics.

The Forward-Discount Anomaly

Perhaps the best illustration of the fleeting nature of the profitability of fixed trading rules—and of how insisting on fully predetermined models leads to an intellectual cul de sac—is found in the literature on modeling returns in currency markets.

In hundreds of studies, international macroeconomists have looked for a fixed correlation in monthly data between the value of the forward premium at the beginning of the month and the future return on holding foreign exchange over the month.[13] Almost all these studies report a significantly negative correlation between these variables. As two of the leading researchers in the field put it, "What is surprising is the widespread finding that realized [currency returns] . . . tend to be, if anything, in the opposite direction to that predicted by the forward premium" (Obstfeld and Rogoff, 1996, p. 589; for reviews, see Lewis, 1995; Engel, 1996).

To see what this result would mean if it were consistently true, consider a typical forward contract for a currency. This contract enables its holder to lock in today the price at which she buys or sells a certain dollar value of foreign exchange in the future, for example, in one month. This price, say, $1.20 per euro, is called the forward rate. If today's forward rate is higher than today's spot

[13]Most studies in the literature examine the correlation between the forward premium and the future change in the spot exchange rate. However, the correlation with returns, which depend on changes in the spot rate, provides an exactly equivalent way to present the forward-discount anomaly while simplifying our discussion.

rate, then foreign exchange (the euro in our example) is said to be trading today at a forward premium. For example, if one could enter into a spot contract today to buy the euro for $1.00—the spot rate—then the euro would be trading at a forward premium of 20%. If this premium were negative instead of positive, the euro would be said to be trading at a forward discount.

Whether one could make profits on average by using forward contracts depends on how the forward premium covaries over time with the future one-month return on holding foreign exchange. If a rise in the forward premium tends to be associated with a negative return, and if this correlation is stable, as economists claim it to be, then "one can make predictable profits by betting against the forward rate" (Obstfeld and Rogoff, 1996, p. 589). The trading strategy is particularly simple: if the forward premium is positive, one should bet on a fall in the spot rate over the coming month, whereas if the opposite is the case, bet on a rise in the spot rate. This rule involves no sophisticated statistical analysis and the collection of only one piece of information, the forward premium.

International economists have undertaken an enormous effort to rationalize the supposedly negative correlation between returns and the forward premium with an REH-based risk-premium model. However,

> there is no positive evidence that the forward discount's [correlation] is due to risk. . . . Survey data on exchange rate expectations suggest that the bias is entirely due to expectational errors. . . . Taken as a whole, the evidence suggests that explanations which allow for the possibility of market inefficiency should be seriously investigated. [Froot and Thaler, 1990, p. 190]

As a result, economists have developed several fully predetermined accounts of the supposed irrationality of currency markets (for example, see Mark and Wu, 1998; Gourinchas and Tornell, 2004).

But it is such efforts, not the profit-seeking motive in currency markets, that should be questioned. Consider that the foreign-exchange market is the largest financial market in the world, with a daily volume now estimated to be more than $3 trillion. The stakes in this market, as in any other large asset market, are extremely high. Financial institutions, which hire many of the participants who move the markets, pay large sums of money to attract the best and the brightest. Is it really possible that these individuals can make money by following a rule as simple as betting against the forward rate, and that they are either unaware of this opportunity or fail to exploit it?

In fact, currency returns do not unfold in conformity with an overarching rule. Instead, revisions of participants' forecasting strategies or shifts in the process driving the forward premium lead to nonroutine changes in the correlation between returns and the forward premium (and any other informational variable, for that matter).[14] Unsurprisingly, the data bear this out: the correlation is largely negative during some stretches of time and largely positive during others, implying that always betting against the forward rate will sometimes deliver profits and at other times losses.[15] No one can precisely specify ahead of time when the correlation might be negative and for how long, so no one can foresee when it might be profitable to bet against or with the forward rate.

As we would expect with such contingent change, successful speculation in currency markets is not as simple as suggested by the voluminous academic literature on international finance. Indeed, we report in Frydman and Goldberg (2007, chapter 13) that "predictable profits" cannot be made by simply betting against the forward rate. Although this rule delivers profits in some subperiods for some currencies, it stops being profitable at moments of time that cannot be foreseen by anyone. And we find that any

[14]We show this result formally in Frydman and Goldberg (2007, chapter 13).

[15]We find such instability in the British pound, German mark, and Japanese yen markets over a sample period that includes the 1970s, 1980s, and 1990s. Other studies that also find results that depend on the subperiod examined include Bekaert and Hodrick (1993), Lewis (1995), Engel (1996), and Mark and Wu (1998).

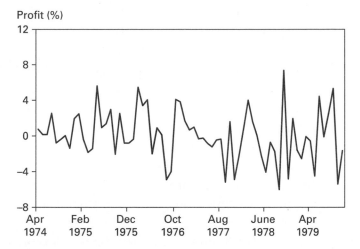

Fig. 11.3. Profits in the British pound market, 1970s
Source: Frydman and Goldberg (2007).

profits delivered by the rule are not large enough to provide reasonable compensation for uncertainty.

Figure 11.3 illustrates the fleeting nature of the profitability of
economists' forward-rate rule. It plots the monthly profits that one
would have earned by betting against the forward rate in the British
pound market during the 1970s. There are periods of profitability, but
they are fleeting. Over the entire period, the average return is zero.

Of the hundreds of studies that have reported a supposedly negative correlation between currency returns and the forward premium, very few examine the behavior of this correlation
over separate subperiods of the data sample, let alone formally test
whether it is stable over the entire sample. Of course, those that do
so find evidence of instability.[16] But as with the evidence of unstable exchange-rate relationships, the insistence on considering
only fully predetermined, mostly invariant relationships has led
economists to ignore their own findings.

[16]Studies that split their samples include Bekaert and Hodrick (1993),
Lewis (1995), Engel (1996), and Mark and Wu (1998). Only Bekaert and Hodrick
(1993) formally test for stability.

Temporary Profit Opportunities

Although contingent change implies that mechanical trading rules will eventually cease to be profitable, such change alters the correlations in the data, which for a time opens up temporary profit opportunities. Those who gather information and have the skill and flexibility to revise their thinking in ways that enable them to spot or anticipate these opportunities are able to earn above-average returns after adjusting for risk.

When modeling asset price swings in Chapters 9 and 10, we made use of Keynes's (1936, p. 152) insight that when forecasting future prices and risk, participants rely on "a convention . . . [of] assuming that the existing state of affairs will continue indefinitely, except in so far as we have specific reasons to expect a change." But because the process driving market outcomes undergoes contingent change, it is unclear how much past data a participant should use to understand the existing state of affairs, let alone forecast how long it might continue. As we saw, even the most sophisticated statistical techniques do not automatically pinpoint when the current state of affairs began. Of course, the choice among various alternative models also requires subjective judgments. Even when describing the past, interpretations vary among individuals, depending on their personal knowledge, experience, and intuitions.

Participants understand that "the existing state of affairs" will eventually change. In stock markets, for example, a company's prospects evolve over time in nonroutine ways that become more difficult to assess as one looks farther into the future. Movements of fundamentals—such as earnings, interest rates, and overall economic activity—provide clues to potential changes in these prospects. As investors alter their understandings and assessments about the future, they influence the process driving prices. Such contingent change leads to new states of affairs: new correlations between fundamentals and future outcomes emerge, and old ways of thinking lose their forecasting power.

Spotting such new correlations even after they have oc-curred is no easy task. A participant might rely on statistical tech-niques, but it is unclear which ones to use and how to apply them. Moreover, some amount of time must elapse after a change has oc-curred for these techniques to have a chance of picking it up. Par-ticipants, therefore, may want to rely more on their intuition about recent news in discerning whether significant change has occurred.

Anticipating change is even more difficult. As Keynes (1936, p. 163) so clearly understood, we "[calculate] where we can," in making decisions, but participants fall back on other consider-ations, including intuition, "*confidence* with which we . . . forecast," and optimism.

New correlations imply above-average returns for those who can discern them quickly using available information, and even higher returns for those who can anticipate them to some extent. The promise of above-average returns provides the incen-tive to comb over company data, study industry trends, and pur-chase the services of Bloomberg LP and other companies devoted to providing news and market analysis. Participants often com-bine quantitative models with their own insights concerning other traders' behavior, the historical record on price fluctuations, and their evaluations of the impact of past and future decisions by pol-icy officials. And because they act on the basis of different experi-ences, interpretations of the past, and intuitions about the future, they adopt different strategies to spot and anticipate contingent change. Doing so consistently is extremely difficult, but not im-possible. Warren Buffet and George Soros immediately come to mind as two investors who have shown such skills.

For proponents of the Efficient Market Hypothesis, such informational gathering and fundamental analysis is a waste of time and resources; individuals should instead invest in a well-diversified portfolio. They readily admit that many participants do engage in fundamental analysis, and that some have been able to earn above-average returns consistently. As Michael Jensen, a lead-ing proponent of the Efficient Market Hypothesis, argued in a de-bate with Warren Buffet, "if I survey a field of untalented analysts all of whom are . . . flipping coins, I expect to see some . . . who have tossed ten heads in a row" (Lowenstein, 1995, p. 317).

Warren Buffet rejected the coin-flipping story as an explanation of his success. As he put it, "if 225 million orangutans had engaged in [stock picking] . . . the results would be much the same [as flipping a coin]," but too many of the successful orangutans, "came from the 'same zoo'" (Lowenstein, 1995, p. 317).

To be sure, Buffet would not claim that the mere fact of using fundamental analysis necessarily implies an ability to beat the market. Ultimately, good forecasting is much like good entrepreneurship: it involves one's own knowledge, intuition, and hard work to spot and anticipate the profit opportunities that come from contingent change. The insight that such endeavors cannot be preprogrammed lay behind Hayek's argument that central planning is impossible in principle.

Thus, we would not expect that all or even most mutual fund managers could anticipate correctly future changes in the market or the economy consistently over time, which is exactly what the literature has found. But the fact that it is possible, and that some individuals do succeed, provides powerful incentives to look for signs of change and attempt to speculate on them.

AN INTERMEDIATE VIEW OF MARKETS AND A NEW FRAMEWORK FOR PRUDENTIAL POLICY

Once we recognize that fundamentals matter, but in non-routine ways, markets are seen as neither near-perfectly rational and efficient, as supposed by the Efficient Market Hypothesis, nor grossly irrational and inefficient, as implied by the behavioral finance models.

Our intermediate position has allowed us to uncover the key importance of nonroutine movements of fundamentals and the mediating role of psychology for understanding price swings and risk in financial markets. In addition, it enables us to show that many empirical puzzles that have been identified by researchers are not anomalies—they are merely artifacts of the disconnect between fully predetermined models and what markets in the real world do.

Our intermediate view of markets not only sheds new light on the supposed empirical puzzles implied by fully predetermined models, but it also leads to a new way of thinking about the relationship between the market and the state. The nonroutine role of fundamentals in driving swings and financial risk and our analysis of its implications for the instability, excessiveness, and allocative function of financial markets lead to a new rationale for state intervention. Our view also opens up new channels for policymakers to limit the magnitude of long swings in asset markets and leads to a new way for regulators to assess systemic and other risks in the financial system.

12

Restoring the Market-State Balance

IN MUCH-TALKED-ABOUT testimony before the U.S. Congress in October 2008, former Federal Reserve Chairman Alan Greenspan revealed his "shocked disbelief" that market participants' self-interest had failed so spectacularly in "protecting" society from the financial system's gross excesses, culminating in the worst crisis since the Great Depression.[1] Greenspan went on to acknowledge that he had "found a flaw" in the ideology that unfettered financial markets would limit their own excesses.

Although the crisis that started in 2007 has vividly exposed the dangers inherent in relying on financial markets to self-regulate, policy reforms adopted around the world have largely excluded measures requiring the state to attempt to wield direct influence over asset markets' price-setting process. Despite the recognition that excessive swings in housing, equity, and other markets triggered the crisis, there is a widespread belief that the state cannot effectively influence asset-price movements, and that, even if it could, its actions would ultimately result in even more severe misallocations of capital and other undesirable economic and political consequences.

[1] As reported in Faisenthal (2008).

THE IMPORTANCE OF POLICY REFORM FOR FINANCIAL MARKETS

Contemporary macroeconomic and finance theory, with its fully predetermined foundations, has been of little relevance in guiding the debate about whether and to what extent the state should play a more active role in asset markets. In the eyes of many observers, the crisis has discredited orthodox rational expectations models, which imply that the state should stay out of financial markets. The behavioral approach's seductive claim that the problem with orthodox theory is its lack of psychological realism has gained it many adherents in the aftermath of the crisis. But although psychological considerations, such as market participants' confidence and intuition, do play a role in decisionmaking, they do not by themselves provide a basis for formulating sensible financial reform and prudential policy measures.[2]

Beyond the inherent difficulty in formulating policies to influence the psychology of markets, behavioral finance models formalize psychological insights with mechanical rules. Such formalizations not only miss how these insights matter for outcomes, but they also lead to policy implications that, if adopted, would jeopardize the allocative performance of financial markets.

The policy implications of behavioral bubble models are a case in point. According to these models, swings are largely unrelated to movements in economic fundamentals. Their occurrence therefore implies a massive distortion of relative prices and a gross misallocation of capital. As such, extant bubble models place no limits on the scope and intrusiveness of state intervention in financial markets. No matter how strong the measures required to extinguish asset-price swings, the bubble models imply that im-

---

[2]For an early discussion of this point, see Friedman's (2009) review of important books that have examined the financial crisis and its aftermath from the perspective of behavioral economics.

plementing them as quickly as possible would unambiguously improve long-term capital allocation.

Policymakers, however, have not been inclined to heed the guidance of bubble models. As Bernanke (2002, p. 6) has reminded us, pricking bubbles early is likely to have unambiguous social costs rather than the unambiguous benefits implied by theory:

> [T]he problem of a bubble-popping Fed is much tougher than just deciding whether or not a bubble exists. . . . In my view, somehow preventing the boom in stock prices between 1995 and 2000, if it could have been done, would have throttled a great deal of technological progress and sustainable growth in productivity and output.

Bernanke's argument against popping bubbles as soon as they begin seems uncontroversial. However, it ignores the possibility that beyond a certain point, an asset-price swing may become excessive: its continuation is more likely to misallocate capital than to help society allocate it on the basis of ever-changing long-term fundamental values. Indeed, as the crisis that started in 2007 shows, one of the main triggers of financial crises (including banking and currency crises) are excessive upswings in key asset prices—those for equity, housing, and currency—which are followed by sharp and prolonged downturns.[3]

Even before the financial crisis began in 2007, there was growing awareness among policymakers and researchers that the success of monetary policy in achieving low-inflation environments in many countries was far from sufficient to protect the fi-

---

[3]In a seminal study, Reinhart and Rogoff (2009) look at data going back as far as eight centuries for sixty-six countries spanning six continents. They find that the top two predictors of banking crises are excessive movements in real exchange rates and real housing prices, with excessive short-term capital inflows, current-account imbalances, and movements in real stock prices rounding out the top five predictors. Borio and Lowe (2002a,b) also find that excessive movements in equity prices are a key predictor of financial crises, especially when they are associated with excessive growth in overall credit.

nancial system from excessive asset-price swings and crisis. There is widespread understanding in policymaking circles that systemic risks in the financial system grow as upswings in the economy and asset markets continue for prolonged periods, and that significant reforms to the Basel 2 regulatory framework for banks are needed to address this pro-cyclicality.[4]

Indeed, the Basel Committee is set to announce Basel 3 at the November G-20 meeting in Seoul, South Korea, and preliminary reports (as of September 2010) suggest that it will call for increasing capital requirements beyond Basel 2 levels.[5] The requirements may include a countercyclical component that builds up banks' defenses during economic upturns and draws on them during downturns.[6] These and other macro-prudential measures are aimed at actively limiting the buildup of risks in the banking system and strengthening its resilience to adverse aggregate developments.[7]

Reducing systemic risk has been an important concern for financial reform in both the United States and Europe. Both the

[4]See Borio (2003), Borio and Shim (2007), and BIS (2010). The Bank for International Settlements defines systemic risk in the financial system as the "risk of disruption to financial services that is caused by an impairment of all or parts of the financial system and has the potential to have serious negative consequences for the real economy" (BIS, 2010, p. 200). Basel 2 revised the set of rules known as Basel 1, which was promulgated in 1988 by the Basel Committee (which is associated with the Bank for International Settlements and is composed of banking regulators from industrialized countries) to harmonize bank regulation across countries. The Basel accords are not formal treaties, and countries do not always implement them fully, though most base their banking regulation on the Basel rules. In the European Union, they are implemented fully by directives and regulations and for all credit institutions.

[5]The Group of Twenty is composed of finance ministers and central bank governors from nineteen countries with the largest economies plus the European Union.

[6]Spain has been implementing such a dynamic system for loan-loss provisioning since 2000. See Fernández de Lis et al. (2001).

[7]Many countries, particularly in Europe and Asia, began implementing macro-prudential measures in the early 2000s. The aim was to limit the amount of credit supplied to specific sectors seen as prone to excessive credit growth, especially property investment and development. See BIS (2010) and Borio and Shim (2007), who report that many of these countries have found the measures useful.

Dodd-Frank Act, recently signed into law by President Obama, and European Union reform proposals, which are planned to take effect by January 2011, create independent regulatory agencies—the Financial Stability Oversight Council and the Systemic Risk Board, respectively—charged with monitoring and addressing systemic risk. A range of additional macro-prudential measures also will be required.[8]

On the whole, these reforms are important steps in reducing the banking and credit system's vulnerability to crisis. But Basel 3's focus on strengthening the system's resilience to adverse aggregate developments, rather than attacking these developments directly, means that the accord largely misses the need for the state to dampen excessive upswings and downswings in key asset markets when they occur.[9]

Dodd-Frank and the European Union reform proposals also ignore this need for state action. Instead, they address information-related distortions, such as the use of off-balance-sheet structured instruments, which obscure the market exposures and overall leverage of financial institutions. They also address the opacity and complexity of such instruments and other highly engineered derivative products, and they impose constraints on over-the-counter derivatives markets, such as those for credit-default swaps, which conceal the interconnectedness of financial institutions' risks.

To be sure, rules to limit banks' over-the-counter derivatives trading and to require much of it to be channeled through clearinghouses will help lower the financial system's vulnerability to crisis. Many other provisions, including the Volcker rule, which

[8]The U.S. reform bill was named after Senator Chris Dodd and Representative Barney Frank. Among its many provisions, it authorizes regulators to implement Basel 3 in full. This authorization is significant, because, although U.S. regulators played a major role in developing Basel 2, the U.S. Congress never approved it.

[9]Credit growth is a key fundamental in driving housing and other asset prices. Consequently, Basel 3's countercyclical capital requirements may work indirectly to dampen excessive price swings in these markets. We come back to this point later in this chapter.

prohibits banks from proprietary trading, and the Financial Stability Oversight Council's authority to break up large financial firms, will similarly reduce systemic risks. But none of these measures tackles directly the grave threat that excessive price swings in key asset markets pose to the financial system.

Beyond reducing the vulnerability of the financial system to crisis, our IKE approach and empirical evidence point to another important reason for the state to dampen excessive swings in key asset markets. In Chapters 8 and 10 we discussed how such swings are associated with distorted relative prices and misallocation of financial capital. Overinvestment in technology companies in the late 1990s and in the housing sector in the mid-2000s are just two examples of the misallocation that results when asset-price swings become excessive. History suggests that the more excessive a price swing, the greater the problems. When excessive upswings in equity and housing prices reach levels that cause misallocation of capital in key sectors, they are often followed by sharp and costly reversals. Even when these reversals do not trigger a financial crisis, they often lead to painful economic downturns, which are typically associated with prolonged periods of depressed investment spending and thus significantly lower the long-run growth potential of modern economies.[10]

A Focus on Dampening Excess

Imperfect Knowledge Economics provides an alternative conceptual framework for thinking about how capitalist econo-

---

[10]For example, Bordo (2003) looks at two centuries of U.S. and UK data and finds that most stock market crashes (defined as a 20% or greater decline in prices from peak to trough) are associated with recessions. Bordo and Jeanne (2004) find that the sharp and prolonged downturns in house and equity prices in fifteen countries belonging to the Organization for Economic Cooperation and Development are associated with sharp falls in output. Such downturns follow excessive upswings in these prices.

mies should deal with price swings in key asset markets, such as those for equities, housing, and currencies. Because price swings are inherent to how markets help society search for worthy investments, IKE-inspired policy reform suggests that so long as swings in broader market indexes or in key sectors remain within a guidance range of reasonable values, the state should limit its involvement to setting and enforcing the basic institutional framework for market transactions. It would also stand on guard to implement, cautiously and gradually, measures to dampen price swings if they moved beyond the state's guidance range, either from above or below. The purpose is not to defend at all costs the bounds of the state's guidance ranges but rather to ameliorate the magnitude and duration of departures when they occur.

By reducing the magnitude and duration of excessive asset-price swings—one of the key aggregate developments that underlie financial and economic crises—our proposed excess-dampening measures would lower systemic financial risks. This connection between excessive asset-price swings and systemic risk suggests that when devising a dynamic framework of capital requirements, regulators should link changes in these requirements not only to movements in the overall economy but also to price swings in the assets to which banks are heavily exposed.

The principle of dampening only excessive price swings is important in implementing such a dynamic framework. Raising banks' capital requirements increases their cost of capital, at least in the short-run, and may lead them to raise the interest rates they charge their borrowers and reduce new lending.[11] In designing

---

[11]The Macroeconomic Assessment Group, established under the auspices of the Basel Committee on Banking Supervision and the Financial Stability Board, has estimated the short-run costs of raising banks' capital and liquidity requirements to be small. For example, a 1% increase in the capital requirement is estimated to lower real gross domestic product by 0.04% per year over four years (see Macroeconomic Assessment Group, 2010). Of course, industry groups have estimated these costs to be significantly higher (see Institute of International Finance, 2010). Over the longer term, higher capital requirements should

countercyclical buffers, regulators would not want to begin raising them in the early phase of an economic upturn. Doing so would not only hamper recovery but would also, as Bernanke (2002, p. 6) put it, likely "throttle a great deal of technological progress and sustainable growth in productivity and output."

Instead, the dynamic component of banks' capital buffers should kick in only when the economic expansion begins to show signs of excess in asset markets and credit growth. One could also imagine that conducting macro-stress tests at such points of excess would help authorities in communicating to banks and the broader economy growing dangers to the financial system.[12]

By focusing anti-swing and countercyclical measures only on excessive price movements, the policies suggested by our IKE-based conceptual framework would likely help lower the potential for gross misallocations of financial capital, sharp and protracted downturns in overall economic activity, and future financial crises. Equally important, these policies are unlikely to impair capitalist economies' key advantage over other economic arrangements— their ability to spur innovation and sustained growth.

Informational Distortions and Imperfect Knowledge

Viewing the financial crisis that started in 2007 through the lens of fully predetermined models has led many economists to emphasize informational problems, poor incentives, and inad-

---

make banks less risky, thereby lowering their cost of funds, as well as lowering the frequency and severity of financial crises. The Basel Committee on Banking Supervision estimates that over the long term, the proposed increase in banks' capital and liquidity requirements would lead to large net economic benefits.

[12] Although they do not explicitly mention the notion of excess dampening, Borio and Shim's (2007) proposal that regulators first provide warnings when signs of overextension occur and then undertake additional steps, such as stress testing and tightening standards, is very close to our proposal. See also Borio (2003).

equate competition. To be sure, woefully insufficient transparency and distorted incentives for key financial market participants contributed significantly to the unfolding crisis. The regulatory reforms aimed at addressing them are essential for markets to perform their allocative role.

But even if all these distortions were eliminated, market participants, as well as regulators and credit raters—all of them essential to a properly functioning modern economy—interpret information with a necessarily imperfect understanding of how asset prices and risk unfold over time. Given imperfect knowledge, market participants have no hope of adequately deciding whether and how to revise their forecasting strategies—and thus no hope of pricing assets well—without good information. Indeed, when one recognizes the centrality of imperfect knowledge, transparency becomes more important to the market's indispensable function of adjusting relative prices and allocating capital to alternative uses.

Nevertheless, pro-transparency reforms, while necessary, are insufficient for preventing excessive asset-price swings or future financial crises. We not only propose a range of excess-dampening measures to deal with these problems, but we also suggest revamping how rating agencies communicate to the public the riskiness of all asset classes by requiring that they make their imperfect knowledge more transparent.

The Necessity of Discretion

A key feature of our proposals is the discretion that, owing to the imperfection of knowledge, policy officials must be given over how they implement excess-dampening measures over time. In contrast, academic economists have spent the past three decades arguing that policymakers' exercise of discretion is likely to result in inferior macroeconomic performance (according to a given social welfare criterion). Their belief in the scientific status of the fully predetermined models on which they base this conclusion has been so strong that leading economists have advocated far-reaching institutional changes to eliminate all discretion on the part of policymakers.[13] In a seminal paper, for example, Nobel Laureates Finn Kydland and Edward Prescott advocate

> institutional arrangements which make it difficult and time-consuming to change the policy rules in all but emergency situations. One possible institutional arrangement is for Congress to legislate monetary and fiscal policy rules and these rules to become effective only after a 2-year delay. This would make discretionary policy all but impossible. [Kydland and Prescott, 1977, p. 487]

Although the macro-prudential reforms that will ultimately be implemented may include built-in stabilizers, policymakers recognize that "each new financial cycle has unique as well as generic characteristics . . . [and that they] will need to exercise judgment and give weight to qualitative factors . . . [and vary] the timing and intensity of policy interventions . . . with some discretion" (BIS, 2010, p. 6).[14] As Governor Mervyn King of the Bank of England once put it, "Our understanding of the economy is incomplete and constantly evolving, sometimes in small steps, sometimes in big leaps" (King, 2005, p. 8). Policymakers' imperfect knowledge implies that their ability to ascertain, with any degree of confidence, whether asset prices have moved beyond a range of values consistent with participants' assessments of longer-term

---

[13]To avoid misunderstanding, we stress that what we question here is the scientific status of proposals for rules based on fully predetermined models. Nevertheless, some guidelines, intended to influence the decisions of market participants, may play a useful role in policymaking. For example, Atkins (2006) reports on how the Norwegian central bank uses guidelines and announces long-term forecasts in an attempt to influence market participants' decisions. However, to shed light on the consequences of such policy tools for individual decisionmaking and aggregate outcomes, they would have to be analyzed in models that are not fully predetermined.

[14]The Bank for International Settlements report mentions that one central banker in their survey stated that he "deliberately avoids the term 'macro-prudential policy measures,' on the grounds that the tools required to deal with financial instability constantly evolve and vary for each episode of financial instability" (BIS, 2010, p. 9).

prospects, or whether credit growth and other imbalances are excessive, is likewise imperfect. As knowledge and the economy evolve, they will need to reevaluate their judgments of excess and how they implement measures to dampen it.

RATIONALE FOR ACTIVE STATE INTERVENTION IN FINANCIAL MARKETS

In his 2002 speech on asset-price bubbles and monetary policy, Ben Bernanke argued forcefully against a Fed that was an "arbiter of security speculation or values":

> [T]o declare that a bubble exists, the Fed must not only be able to accurately estimate the unobservable fundamentals underlying equity valuations, it must have confidence that it can do so better than the financial professionals whose collective information is reflected in asset-market prices. I do not think this expectation is realistic, even for the Federal Reserve. [Bernanke, 2002, p. 5]

Bernanke concluded from this important insight that monetary policy should not be used to prick bubbles and thus replace the market's judgment concerning asset values, which although imperfect, is superior to that of any person or committee. Of course, recognizing imperfect knowledge would lead one exactly to this view. Although the imperfection of knowledge precludes the Fed's role as arbiter of values, it does not imply the state should simply do nothing.

The need for state intervention in key asset markets arises not because policy officials have superior knowledge about asset values, but because profit-seeking market participants do not internalize the huge social costs associated with excessive upswings and downswings in these markets. Chapter 10 showed how persistent trends in fundamental factors can lead short-term speculators as a group to bid stock prices beyond levels that most participants would consider to be consistent with the longer-term prospects of companies. For example, Bernanke (2002, p. 6) recounts how "in December 1996 ... John Campbell of Harvard and Robert Shiller of Yale made a presentation at the Fed, in which they used dividend-price ratios and related measures to argue that the stock market was overvalued."[15] And yet stock prices climbed higher relative to estimates of common benchmark levels for another three-and-a-half years.

Our IKE account of asset prices and risk implies that short-term speculators continued to bid up stock prices not because they were unaware of the departures from benchmark values. By 1997, anyone could see that they were historically very large. Rather, short-term speculators are concerned with making profits over the next month or quarter. As the end of the 1990s unfolded, corporate earnings, overall economic activity, and other fundamentals continued to trend in bullish directions. These trends led speculators to raise their short-term forecasts, and, because profits were their main concern, bid up stock prices.

No one can know precisely when an asset price swing becomes excessive, and as we argue shortly, policymakers will need to consider more than just departures from historical benchmark values. But the overinvestment in technology and communication companies and the sharp and prolonged downturn in stock prices that began in 2000 show that the upswing in stocks had indeed reached excessive levels. The market did eventually self-correct, but it did so too late. This boom-bust dynamic led to economic recession and a prolonged period of subpar rates of private investment and employment. Only the state and collective action can minimize the social costs of such delayed corrections to excessive asset price swings.

We have argued throughout this book that financial markets are essential precisely because they are the best institutions on offer to help society deal with the problems of nonroutine change and imperfect knowledge. Once imperfect knowledge is

---

[15]This analysis was published in Campbell and Shiller (1998).

placed at the center of analysis, we see that it produces swings of irregular duration and magnitude in the normal course of setting prices and allocating scarce capital. Eliminating this instability would amount to replacing the judgment of the market with that of the state.

However, the very fact that knowledge is imperfect makes markets imperfect: asset-price swings can sometimes reach excessive levels, and this excess can grow for prolonged periods, implying huge social costs. The state should attempt to limit these costs through policy and regulatory measures that are designed to dampen the magnitude and duration of excessive swings in key asset markets. As long as interventionist measures are aimed at dampening excess in market fluctuations, rather than at pricking the bubble early, the state can help markets function better without presuming that it knows more than they do.

Excess-Dampening Measures and Guidance Ranges

To implement excess-dampening measures in any asset market, policy officials must be able to judge with reasonable confidence when prices have moved beyond a range of values that is consistent with most participants' diverse assessments of the market's longer-term prospects. Like market participants, officials must cope with imperfect knowledge about the long term. But when implementing excess-dampening measures, their task differs from that of market participants with longer-term time horizons, who speculate in particular stocks, houses, or other assets. Officials are concerned with markets more broadly and with whether aggregate measures of value (such as price indexes in the overall stock or housing markets or in some key sectors) have departed excessively from participants' assessments of longer-term values.

The imperfect knowledge of policy officials implies that their guidance ranges need to be wide; no one knows the market values that would be consistent with the longer-term prospects of stocks or other assets. Officials need to be reasonably confident that their excess-dampening measures do not cut off a price swing that stems from changes in the market's assessments of these prospects, and that they instead target price movements that reflect departures from these assessments.

History as an Imperfect Guide to Assessing Excess

There is ample evidence that making use of historical benchmark levels when setting guidance ranges for asset prices is a good place to start. In Chapter 10, we presented an example of a 90% range of historically moderate price-earnings ratios for the U.S. stock market, reproduced here as Figure 12.1. Recall that the upper and lower bands of the guidance range (the dotted lines) refer to the fifth and ninety-fifth percentiles of a fifty-year moving window. This moving window provides a baseline estimate of how excessive values may have changed over time. The empirical record shows that once these historically extreme values were reached, the market itself concluded that prices had been pushed too far and self-corrected.

The guidance range in Figure 12.1 is just an example of a historical baseline assessment of non-excessive values. There are alternative ways to calculate a price-earnings ratio and the moving window, as well as alternative notions of the benchmark level (for example, the price-dividend ratio), not to mention alternative bandwidths.[16] Moreover, research by Borio and Lowe (2002a) and others suggests that when designing guidance ranges, authorities should take into account excessive credit growth.

Policy officials need to devote considerable resources to learning how best to take into account historical data when con-

---

[16]For example, Borio and Lowe (2002a) use departures from a real-time sample trend in asset prices and credit growth. They find that an asset-price gap of 40% and a credit gap of 4% provide the best combined threshold values in predicting financial crises.

Fig. 12.1. A historically based guidance range for the price-earnings ratio

Source: Data are from Robert Shiller's website: www.econ.yale.edu/~shiller.

structing guidance ranges for key markets or sectors. But they cannot rely solely on such analyses.

Nonroutine Change and Guidance Ranges

The dynamism of modern economies implies that historical benchmark values, although important, should not be the sole criterion for setting guidance ranges. Officials need to consider that new technologies and other nonroutine economic, political, and social changes can render a range of historically moderate values, however arrived at, a poor indicator of participants' assessments of longer-term prospects. Although economies change in new ways all the time, occasionally there are periods in which change is particularly far-reaching. During these periods, it might be especially difficult to know how much to deviate from a range of historically moderate values in setting a guidance range.

The 1990s are a case in point. As Figure 12.1 indicates, stock valuations had moved beyond the top band of our historically based guidance range by June 1995, rising to 23.7 times earnings—a level seen only three times in the previous one hundred years (the early 1900s, 1928–1929, and the mid-1960s). If history were our only guide, it would be reasonable to conclude that valuations were above most participants' assessments of longer-term prospects. But perceptions at the time of the longer-term benefits of the information-technology revolution and subsequent rapid productivity growth in many economic sectors suggest that this was not the case. Instead, assessments of longer-term prospects most likely rose beyond the levels of earlier epochs.

This was the view that Ben Bernanke espoused in the 2002 speech quoted earlier. According to Bernanke, standard valuation ratios, such as those based on Shiller's price-earnings ratio, were too pessimistic at "the start of 1997 [because] at least some of the run-up in stock prices in the latter 1990s *was* apparently justified by fundamentals, as evidenced by the remarkable growth in output and productivity in recent years, the recent recession notwithstanding" (Bernanke, 2002, p. 6).

As it turns out, evidence that participants' assessments of longer-term prospects in the 1990s did in fact rise relative to those of earlier periods can be found in Bloomberg's market wrap reports, discussed in Chapters 7 and 10. In Chapter 10, we plotted a twelve-month moving average of the number of days in each month Bloomberg reported that perceptions of the gap between asset prices and historical valuations were important in moving the market, reproduced here as Figure 12.2. The figure shows that these gap considerations played no role prior to the end of 1996, even though price-earnings ratios throughout that year were at levels not seen since 1929. The importance of gap considerations started rising sharply only at the end of 1996, when the price-earnings ratio was already more than 27, which suggests that at this point, market participants' assessments of longer-term prospects no longer supported a further rise in valuations.

Interestingly, the Bloomberg data indicate that this upward shift in the range of valuations consistent with participants' assessments of longer-term prospects has not been reversed by

Frequency (%)

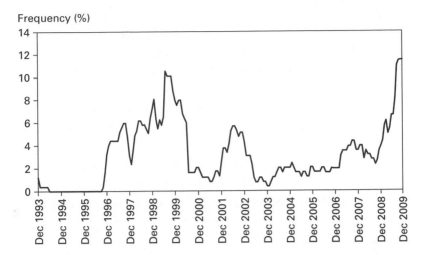

Fig. 12.2. Average monthly frequency of mentions in wrap reports:
The price gap from benchmark values

market and economic developments in the 2000s. By March 2009,
the price-earnings ratio had fallen to 13.3, which was not far below
its historical average of 16.3.

Bloomberg data suggest, however, that participants' concern about excessively low valuations nonetheless started rising
and continued rising during all of 2009, even though stock valuations by December implied a price-earnings ratio of 20.3. According to Bloomberg's reports, many market participants still considered valuations that were 25% higher than the historical benchmark
level excessively low. This observation suggests that the range of
participants' longer-term assessments had remained at its higher
level attained in the 1990s.

Market participants are always on the lookout for technological innovation and other nonroutine change and revise their
assessments of longer-term prospects when they perceive or anticipate its influence. So, too, must policy officials remain mindful
of these factors when devising useful guidance ranges for key markets. Authorities must undertake their own painstaking analyses
of the current level of such change and its impact on participants'

views about longer-term prospects, and they weigh their assessments against earlier historical epochs of change.

Of course, like market participants themselves, officials cannot rely on calculation alone. They must fall back on their own intuition and practical experience when analyzing the past and interpreting the impact of news and recent trends in fundamental factors on the longer-term prospects of companies. As officials' understanding and confidence evolve in nonroutine ways, so, too, must their guidance ranges. Consequently, they must be given discretion to alter the position and width of these ranges and latitude to implement prudential measures when asset prices move beyond them.

Guidance Range Announcements

A first step in dampening excessive asset-price swings would be for the central bank (or other institution charged with limiting instability, such as the U.S. Financial Stability Oversight Council or the European Systemic Risk Board) merely to announce on a regular basis a range of non-excessive values in these markets. How often authorities should revise their guidance ranges for key markets, how much lead time markets should be given before revisions are made, and the trade-off between more and less frequent changes are questions that require much analysis, which can be conducted only on the basis of experience. However, there are good reasons to believe that announcements of nonroutine guidance ranges would help markets to self-correct excess sooner than they would otherwise.

The imperfect knowledge of market participants when forecasting longer-term prospects implies that regular policy announcements may help coordinate their views around official assessments in much the same way that the inflation targets set by central banks do for inflation expectations.[17] Greater coordination

---

[17]The implications and merits of inflation-targeting regimes, which have been implemented in many developed and developing countries, are mostly

would lead market participants to bid prices to levels more consistent with the guidance range. To be most effective, regular official announcements of a range should be accompanied by a detailed explanation of the underlying analysis.

Bulls, Bears, and Excess Dampening

As we have pointed out throughout this book, market participants' ever-imperfect knowledge leads them to hold diverse forecasts of prices and risk. The market contains both bulls and bears who want to bid prices in opposite directions at every point in time. This obvious fact implies an important principle for devising policy to dampen excessive price swings:

- Interventionist measures should moderate the trading behavior of those market participants whose forecasting leads them to bid assets prices in the direction of greater excess. They should strengthen the trading behavior of those participants who are bidding prices back toward moderate levels.

Nearly all contemporary economic models disregard this straightforward idea altogether, because they attempt to account for asset-price fluctuations with the behavior of a representative agent.

Announcing a guidance range and its analytical underpinning would follow this key principle: it would reduce the confi-

---

studied in the context of Rational Expectations models, which do not provide any coordinating role for central bank inflation targets. However, once the Rational Expectations Hypothesis is jettisoned, such a role becomes essential for the success of inflation-targeting monetary policy. For a recent empirical study showing that central bank inflation targets are important for coordinating inflation expectations, see Gűrkaynak et al. (2006). Orphanides and Williams (2007) and references therein support this conclusion in non-REH models that make use of mechanical learning algorithms. Although these models point to the coordinating role of policy announcements, this issue as well as other tenets of the current policymaking framework need to be in reexamined in models that recognize the importance of nonroutine change.

dence of participants who bet on a continuation of an excessive swing and increase the confidence of those who bet on its reversal.

One of the most famous examples in recent years of an official announcement about asset valuations that influenced prices was Alan Greenspan's warning, on December 5, 1996, of "irrational exuberance" in U.S. equity markets. Initially, Greenspan's pronouncement led to a sharp drop in equity prices. Of course, prices soon resumed their upward climb. But had officials announced a guidance range, the magnitude of this swing would most likely have been dampened. A guidance range would work not only by coordinating participants' views about longer-term prospects but also by encouraging participants with short-term horizons to place greater weight on benchmark levels in assessing the riskiness of holding speculative positions.

Recall that market participants with shorter time horizons may knowingly bid asset prices beyond levels consistent with widespread perceptions of benchmark and longer-term values, and that, as they do, they increase their assessments of the potential losses. As discussed in Chapter 10, if the swing were to continue, an invisible threshold would eventually be reached, beyond which participants would consider their positions too risky, and they would begin bidding prices back toward perceived benchmark levels. The problem is that this threshold could be a long way off if short-term players' assessments of risk rose too slowly with the swing—that is, if they placed too little weight on departures from perceived longer-term values.[18]

This opens up the possibility that official announcements of a guidance range in a market, along with the underlying analysis, might lead individuals to place greater weight on gap considerations in assessing risk.[19] The higher risk assessments would then moderate participants' willingness to bid prices farther away from benchmark levels. They would also lend greater confidence to mar-

[18]Of course, a continuation of the reflexive relationships between prices and fundamentals in the same directions would also prolong an excessive price swing. See Chapter 10.
[19]We proposed this new policy channel in Frydman and Goldberg (2004).

ket participants who, despite having short horizons, bet on a reversal. The resulting fall in their assessments of the riskiness of their positions would lead them to strengthen those positions, further dampening an excessive swing.

Our IKE account of price swings and risk suggests that, had a framework of nonroutine guidance ranges been in place in the equity and housing markets in the 1990s and 2000s, markets would likely have self-corrected much sooner than they did, even without implementation of the additional prudential measures that we sketch next. Earlier correction would have avoided the worst excesses in these markets and perhaps even averted the global financial crisis that started in 2007.

ACTIVE EXCESS-DAMPENING MEASURES

Although announcing guidance ranges has the potential to dampen excessive asset-price swings, it is uncertain how effective this measure, taken by itself, might be. The ability of policy officials to dampen excess would be significantly strengthened if they announced beforehand that they were prepared to back up their guidance ranges with active prudential measures. These measures would have several key features.

Foremost, active measures would kick in only if prices in a key market moved beyond the official guidance range. As long as prices fluctuate within this range, the authorities would allow them to do so freely. Official guidance ranges should be wide, and the additional measures we propose would attempt to dampen only excessive price movements, implying that they would be used quite infrequently.

Moreover, the aim of active excess-dampening measures is not to confine asset prices to official guidance ranges. The resources available to market participants are so huge that if their trading decisions led them to bid prices farther into the excessive range, despite the authorities' efforts, the market would have its way. Consequently, a policy aimed at confining asset prices to official ranges is not only doomed to failure, but also to crisis when the failure eventually comes.[20] In contrast, our policy measures based on Imperfect Knowledge Economics are not designed to prevent excessive price swings in key asset markets but to reduce their frequency and dampen their magnitude.

As with guidance ranges, nonroutine change and imperfect knowledge imply that officials must fall back on their intuition, experience, and confidence in applying additional excess-dampening measures. Consequently, they need discretion to alter the measures that they would employ in particular markets and to phase them in at appropriate times. Again, the impact of these measures on market prices and how best to implement them can be understood only with experience.

Our IKE account implies that trends in fundamental factors drive fluctuations in asset prices and risk in nonroutine ways, and in Chapters 7 and 11 we discussed statistical and less formal evidence from the equity market supporting this view. The connection between asset-market outcomes and fundamentals provides an important channel through which to dampen excessive price swings. However, depending on the market, our account implies other channels as well.

A New Bretton Woods Agreement for Currency Markets?

Although we have not emphasized currency markets in this book, floating exchange rates are notorious for their tendency to undergo long swings around levels that are consistent with competitiveness in the international trade of goods and services. Such swings

---

[20]Many countries over the years have attempted to confine their currencies to prespecified ranges, often called "target zones." With few exceptions, speculators eventually attack these arrangements with huge amounts of capital, precipitating a currency crisis. The collapse of the European Monetary System in 1992 and East Asian currency arrangements in 1997–1998 provide notable examples.

lead to large shifts in a country's competitiveness and share of global output and demand, implying huge adjustment costs and trade frictions among countries. As market participants are profit seeking, they do not internalize these costs in their trading decisions.

Consequently, many countries, large and small, attempt either to fix their exchange rates (the European Monetary Union being a notable example) or to implement a target zone or other semi-pegged regime. One of the problems with fixing the exchange rate is that monetary authorities give up the use of monetary policy to achieve other objectives, namely, low inflation and economic growth. And, of course, attempts to fix exchange rates or implement a semi-pegged regime almost always end in failure and crisis.

In Frydman and Goldberg (2004, 2009), we sketch a new policy framework for currency markets that would provide an alternative to letting currencies float freely or fixing them completely. Its aim is to dampen excessive exchange-rate swings, while leaving monetary policy free to pursue inflation and economic-growth objectives. Our proposed framework entails the central bank regularly announcing a guidance range of non-excessive values and declaring its concern about departures from this range. It would then stand ready to buy or sell currency if such departures were to occur. To be most effective, it would intervene at unpredictable moments to bolster or weaken the exchange rate as appropriate.[21] It is important to emphasize that the aim is not to confine the exchange rate to a target zone, but to dampen departures from the official guidance range. Consequently, unlike target zones and fixed-rate regimes, our excess-dampening framework is not vulnerable to crisis.

International coordination would substantially strengthen the impact of regular announcements of the guidance range and interventions to push a currency back toward this range. This pol-

[21]Unpredictability of the timing of interventions is important, because it increases participants' uncertainty about the potential losses that would occur from betting on greater excess, thereby dampening their willingness to engage in such speculation.

icy could serve as the basis for a new Bretton Woods–type agreement on floating but managed exchange rates. Unlike its predecessor, it would not force countries to agree to a set of single parity levels or to defend a band around them. Agreement on a wide range of non-excessive values could accommodate many differing views about the appropriate benchmark. Asking countries to intervene only to dampen over- and undervalued currencies, rather than to defend chosen exchange-rate bands, would also be much easier for them to accept.

Monetary Policy and Excess-Dampening Measures

There have been calls for central banks or other regulatory bodies to buy and sell directly in other asset markets, such as those for equities (see, for example, Muelbauer, 2008; Farmer, 2009). Although this type of intervention is common in currency markets, it is not in equity and housing markets. Using this policy raises obvious political and other concerns that are not salient in currency markets. We leave this matter for future research.

One possibility for active excess-dampening measures in equity and housing markets would be for the central banks to use monetary policy and their influence over interest rates, both short-term and long-term. Bloomberg's market wrap stories report that although the importance for the stock market of interest rates and central bank communications (including Federal Open Market Committee minutes, testimony to Congress, and the Beige book) changes over time, they are among the main fundamental considerations that market participants watch in forecasting and making their trading decisions. The data presented in Table 7.4 shows that these considerations, combined, were mentioned as a driver of stock prices almost every other day on average. Mangee (2011) finds that the qualitative relationship between interest rates and stock prices was, unsurprisingly, a negative one on 98% of the days on which it was mentioned. That is, stock prices and interest rates almost always moved in opposite directions. Although central banks typically use their control over short-term interest rates to deal with inflation and unemployment, the importance of interest rates for equity prices implies that monetary policy could also be used to dampen excessive movements in stock markets.[22]

Of course, interest-rate considerations also play a key role in the housing market; as mortgage rates fall, real estate becomes more affordable, leading to greater demand and upward pressure on prices. Traditional monetary-policy tools have a much weaker and less predictable impact on mortgage and other long-term interest rates than on short-term interest rates. However, as the quantitative-easing measures that the Fed and other major central banks began undertaking in 2009 show, monetary authorities have the ability to influence long-term interest rates more directly.[23] As with short-term interest rates and the stock market, they could use this ability to dampen excessive price swings in the housing market. Indeed, many observers have argued that the low interest rates that prevailed for much of the 1990s and 2000s were responsible for the asset-price inflation during this period, and that the Fed should have used its influence over interest rates to fight it.

Economists have long debated the pros and cons of using monetary policy to influence asset prices. In his 2002 speech, Ben Bernanke argued that monetary policy is the wrong tool for the job, because it is too blunt, and that a central bank is best advised to focus its "policy instruments on achieving its macro goals—price stability and maximum sustainable employment" (Bernanke, 2002, p. 2).

[22]Others have advocated the use of monetary policy to influence asset prices, but in the context of pricking bubbles. See, for example, Cecchetti et al. (2000, 2002) and Bordo and Jeanne (2004).

[23]The Federal Reserve's quantitative-easing measures, including the purchase of longer-term Treasury bonds and mortgage-backed securities issued by government-sponsored companies like Fannie Mae and Freddie Mac, has a direct impact on mortgage rates. For an overview of these measures and their influence on long-term interest rates, see Sarkar and Shrader (2010) in the special issue of the *Federal Reserve Bank of New York Economic Policy Review* on "Central Bank Liquidity Tools and Perspectives on Regulatory Reform."

However, policymakers' conception of the relationship between monetary policy and asset prices has been based largely on fully predetermined bubble models. Relying on these models, Bernanke argues,

> The Fed can also contribute to reducing the probability of boom-and-bust cycles [in asset prices] occurring in the first place, by supporting such objectives as more-transparent accounting and disclosure practices and working to improve the financial literacy and competence of investors." [Bernanke, 2002, p. 3]

As we have argued, addressing transparency issues is crucial, but doing so will not eliminate excessive asset-price swings. A discussion of whether monetary policy is nonetheless best reserved for macroeconomic goals is beyond the scope of this book. There are, however, other excess-dampening measures that authorities could implement to strengthen the impact of official guidance ranges.

Differential Margin Requirements for Bulls and Bears

In equity markets, authorities could announce impending changes in margin and collateral requirements if prices were to become excessive. Our framework suggests that, to be effective, changes in margin and collateral requirements should be set differently for bulls and bears: they should increase for those who want to continue to bid prices away from the guidance range, and decrease for those who are betting the other way. Such adjustments in margin and collateral requirements would raise costs for the former and lower them for the latter, which would directly dampen the excessive price movement.

These measures would also work by influencing participants' assessments of risk. Participants betting on greater excess would increase their assessments of the potential losses, whereas those betting the other way would lower them. The resulting changes in risk premiums would help to dampen the excessive swing. This active policy, in conjunction with an official guidance range, would not be difficult for authorities to implement. Authorities in the United States and other countries already set margin and collateral requirements at fixed levels.

A similar policy would also help to dampen excessive price swings in the housing market. Many participants in the housing market, unlike those in stock markets, have little experience, as they are first-time homebuyers. Announcements of official guidance ranges in key regional markets may lead many of these participants to reconsider buying at excessive prices. At a minimum, it would strengthen their hand at the bargaining table.

During the upswing in housing prices in the 2000s, lenders often issued mortgages with no money down and in many cases required no proof of income or employment. There is little doubt that if U.S. and other authorities had announced guidance ranges and gradually raised capital requirements on mortgages in regional markets showing excess, they would have helped the market to self-correct much sooner than it did.[24]

EXCESSIVE PRICE SWINGS AND THE BANKING SYSTEM

On the most basic level, the financial crisis that began in 2007 is not difficult to understand. Originate-to-distribute financing and a world awash in U.S. dollars enabled banks and other financial institutions to become increasingly leveraged—so much so that much of their capital was vulnerable to loss even from moderate reversals in asset prices, especially for housing. The upswings in asset prices were unprecedented in the housing market.

---

[24]Indeed, with the aim of reducing risk in the banking system, many countries did implement measures to reduce available credit for property during the 2000s, such as lower loan-to-value and debt-service-to-income ratios. See Borio and Shim (2007) and BIS (2010).

The subsequent reversals, when they came, were thus particularly jarring, and financial institutions were forced to deleverage. When deleveraging is widespread and simultaneous, a financial crisis becomes inevitable.

This thumbnail sketch implies that containing systemic risks requires not only managing leverage in the system but also recognizing that these risks vary with the values of institutions' asset portfolios.[25] The run-up in housing and equity prices should have led financial institutions whose portfolios were heavily exposed to these markets to increase their measures of risk and raise their capital and loan-loss buffers. Unfortunately, it did not.

The reason is simple: the way that banks measure risk and determine the size of their capital and loan-loss provisions makes no explicit allowance for excessive price swings in asset markets. In assessing the riskiness of their trading books, where asset growth was concentrated in the run-up to the crisis (see Turner, 2009), banks rely on value-at-risk calculations, which link risk to short-term market volatility. The problem is that they implicitly assume that risk declines when markets are stable: less capital is required during calm periods, and more is required during volatile periods. Thus, such calculations disregard the potential losses (the risk) that mount as an upswing in prices becomes more excessive.

Indeed, in his analysis of the financial crisis, Turner (2009, p. 19) points out that in the run-up to the banking system's near-collapse, "VAR [value-at-risk] measures of the risk involved in taking propriety trading positions, in general, suggested that risk relative to the gross market value of positions had declined." And because capital buffers were based on these measures, "trading book capital was inadequate," leaving the banking system ill prepared for the oncoming crisis. The connection between risk and asset-price swings suggests

[25]Background documents for Basel 3 (see the Bank for International Settlements website: www.bis.org) emphasize the need to monitor banks' overall leverage and call for using a measure of banks' ratio of capital to total assets without any risk-weighting for assets. As of this writing, however, reports indicate that use of such a leverage ratio will be put off until further study is conducted.

that banks' risk-management measures would be substantially improved if they took it explicitly into account. Regulators could, for example, require banks whose trading books are heavily exposed to particular markets to include departures from estimates of benchmark levels in those markets in their risk calculations.

Banks' risk measures of their loan portfolios (nontrading assets) are based on the frequency of defaults over the recent past, called "default probabilities." Policy researchers and other observers have pointed out that these default probabilities fall when the economy is doing well and rise when it is not, implying that capital requirements and loan-loss provisions based on them tend to be pro-cyclical (see, for example, Borio, 2003; Heid, 2007; Repullo and Suarez, 2008; BIS, 2010). But as with price swings in financial markets, periods of economic expansion are followed by periods of contraction, during which default probabilities rise sharply. Consequently, just when risks were rising in the banking system prior to 2007, banks' capital buffers relative to total assets were falling.

Basel 3 is reported to call for revising the way banks' capital buffers are calculated so that they vary countercyclically with the overall economy. Spain's dynamic provisioning, which was implemented in 2000, provides an example of such a system. Spanish banks are required to build up loan-loss provisions during periods when default rates are below the average recorded in the preceding fourteen years. They can draw down these provisions when default rates rise above this average.

Although Spain's countercyclical provisioning is a step in the right direction to remedy the old system's problems, it does not benefit from an explicit connection between risk and asset-price swings. To be sure, the reinforcing reflexive relationship between asset prices and the overall economy, which plays an important role in our IKE account of excessive price swings, suggests that default rates may tend to rise and fall inversely with the upswings and downswings in equity and housing markets. Spain's dynamic provisioning may thus indirectly capture the connection between risk and price fluctuations in these markets.

Nevertheless, the sharp downswing in house prices fueled widespread insolvency among Spain's *cajas* (regional savings banks), which are heavily exposed to the country's housing market. This suggests that the variation in provisioning requirements for banks should be related not just to default rates but also directly to banks' exposure to particular markets (or sectors)—and to whether price swings in those markets are excessive.

IMPERFECT KNOWLEDGE AND CREDIT RATINGS

Lehman Brothers Holdings declared bankruptcy on September 18, 2008. Yet Standard & Poor's had maintained its solid investment grade of A until six days earlier, when it abruptly downgraded the firm to "Selective Default." Moody's waited even longer, downgrading Lehman one business day before it collapsed. How could the most reputable ratings agencies and an investment bank so experienced in issuing securities end up looking so bad?

Much attention has been focused on predatory practices in originating mortgages and on the "cozy" relationship between investment banks and the rating agencies entrusted to rate their structured assets. To be sure, these are important defects that need to be addressed. But there is a further, more basic, cause: the agencies' procedures for rating assets have not allowed for the potential severity of price-swing reversals. Thus, even if the agencies relied solely on state-of-the-art practices, rather than following their narrow commercial interests, their ratings would have substantially underestimated the risk of the securities that they rated.

This underestimation would have occurred because the statistical models on which the ratings agencies rely projected historical default patterns to continue into the future. These patterns showed very low loss rates, owing to ever-rising house prices. With low loss rates, AAA ratings appeared to be justified. But these models ignored the very nature of price swings in asset markets: they eventually reverse themselves, and the more excessive they are, the sharper the reversal. The longer the boom lasted, the more the ratings agencies trumpeted the superiority of structured finance over loans to businesses, and the more investors came to rely on these ratings. Brave new models, which largely ignored the changing structure of the processes driving risk, together with radical deregulation, tempted the mortgage industry into abandoning proven prudential procedures that combined their own judgments and more formal criteria. Instead of lending to "the man who shaved this morning" (to use Albert Camus's wonderful phrase), they lent mechanically to a FICO score.[26] And homebuyers responded by learning how to manipulate their FICO scores.

Of course, nobody knew when the reversal would begin. Had the ratings agencies been required to show how their ratings would change under the alternative assumption that house prices might fall dramatically once the inevitable reversal arrived, projected loss rates on investment banks' securities would have been much higher—and their ratings and prices would have been much lower. Instead, by assigning single ratings to assets, the agencies failed to convey the necessarily contingent character of their models and the assumptions that underpinned them.

These observations lead to a simple proposal.[27] Ratings agencies should be required to report at least two ratings for each security, along with the methodology used to arrive at them: one assuming that historical patterns will continue, and at least one other assuming that there will be reversals in the trends of major variables and the prices of the underlying assets. To be sure, Moody's, S&P, and Fitch apply stresses to their current procedures. But these stresses are hidden in ratings reports, and, as recent events have painfully demonstrated, are woefully inadequate. Furthermore, requiring the agencies to rate securities under one or more pessimistic scenarios would make it harder for them to deliver rosy ratings in return for business from investment banks.

[26]We thank Richard Robb for this wonderful metaphor. Credit rating scores are often called "FICO scores" because they are produced from software developed by Fair Isaac and Company.

[27]We advanced this proposal, together with Edmund Phelps, in Frydman et al. (2008).

Of course, no single individual or institution can render a definitive judgment on the riskiness of securities. As Hayek compellingly argued, only markets can aggregate knowledge that is not given to anyone in its totality. Nevertheless, an effective regulatory regime should require that rating agencies and issuers of securities help, rather than hinder, asset markets in the performance of this function.

Epilogue

> If there is such a thing as growing human knowl-
> edge, then we cannot anticipate today, what we will
> only know tomorrow.
>
> —Karl R. Popper, *The Poverty of Historicism*

What Can Economists Know?

Market outcomes (such as asset prices) or overall levels of economic activity, consumption, or investment result from the decisions of many individuals. In analyzing how outcomes unfold over time, Hayek, Knight, Keynes, and other early modern economists related their accounts to individual decisionmaking. Their profound insight was to place nonroutine change and market participants' imperfect knowledge at the center of economic analysis. This focus led them to discover the limits of economists' *own* knowledge—and thus of economics itself.

Knight's arguments concerning the importance of "radical uncertainty" led him to question the relevance of standard probability theory for understanding profit-seeking decisions. He argued that such decisions "deal with situations which are far too [non-routine] . . . for any sort of [unique] statistical tabulations to have any value for guidance" (Knight, 1921, p. 198). The key implication of this claim is that standard probabilistic portrayals of individual decisions—which presume that their future consequences, and the likelihoods attached to each, can be fully specified in advance—cannot adequately characterize how profit-seeking individuals respond to change and how market outcomes unfold over time.

Keynes (1921, 1936) shared Knight's profound doubts concerning the usefulness of standard probability theory for understanding change in individual decisionmaking and market outcomes: we "cannot depend on strict mathematical expectation, since the basis for making such calculations does not exist" (Keynes, 1936, pp. 162–63). The importance that Keynes attached to the role of uncertainty concerning both outcomes and probabilities played a key role in his analysis of financial markets and their influence on the broader economy, particularly investment.

Likewise, Hayek (1945, p. 519–20) argued that "the economic problem of society is a problem of the utilization of knowledge which is not given to anyone in its totality," implying that no mathematical model can fully mimic what markets do. This observation led him, in his Nobel lecture, to refute the scientific pretense of economic analysis that purports to account for individual decisionmaking and market outcomes with models that assume away imperfect knowledge:

> Our capacity to predict will be confined to . . . general characteristics of the events to be expected and not include the capacity for predicting particular individual events. . . . [However,] I am anxious to repeat, we will still achieve predictions which can be falsified and which therefore are of empirical significance. . . . Yet the danger of which I want to warn is precisely the belief that in order to be accepted as scientific it is necessary to achieve more. This way lies charlatanism and worse . . . I confess that I prefer true but imperfect knowledge . . . to a pretense of exact knowledge that is likely to be false. [Hayek, 1978, pp. 29, 33]

THE SEARCH FOR OMNISCIENCE

Hayek's admonition was directed at the post-1945 Keynesian econometric models, which grew out of the purported formalization of Keynes's ideas and were estimated by statistical methods on the basis of historical data. Around the time of Hayek's Nobel lecture, the applicability of these models for policy analysis had come under severe criticism, either for portraying market participants' forecasting behavior with mechanical rules, which did not take into account contemplated changes in policy, or for disregarding such behavior's effects on aggregate outcomes altogether.[1]

Rational Expectations models, which were becoming highly influential at the time, were proposed by their advocates as a way to remedy this flaw in Keynesian econometric models. But the Rational Expectations models were as mechanical as their Keynesian predecessors.[2] Because their portrayal of individuals' forecasting behavior is woefully inadequate, Rational Expectations models were unsuitable for analyzing how market participants would respond to the contemplated changes in economic policy. Remarkably (given that they were developed by Hayek's successors at the University of Chicago), these models were, moreover, fully predetermined, and thus perpetuated "the pretense of exact knowledge" that Hayek criticized so scathingly in his Nobel lecture.

With the emergence of the Rational Expectations Hypothesis, macroeconomics and finance theory moved from the early modern position that standard probabilistic descriptions have hardly any value for understanding individual behavior and market outcomes to the opposite extreme. The contemporary approach presupposes that in principle there are no limits, beyond a few random error terms, to economists' knowledge. To be sure, economists do recognize that the current state of knowledge is not sufficiently advanced to yield a single probability distribution that would adequately capture "the mechanics of economic development" (Lucas, 2002, p. 21). But the discovery of such a fully pre-

---

[1]For a discussion of this revolutionary juncture in contemporary macroeconomics, see Lucas (1995).

[2]In contrast to his followers, Lucas (1995, p. 253) seems to recognize this point and traces his approach back to Tinbergen's (1939) development of macroeconometric models.

determined account of history remains the primary goal of the research program of contemporary economists.

Faith that better fully predetermined models hold the key to adequately predicting all future changes and their consequences is puzzling not only with respect to adherents of the Rational Expectations Hypothesis. When behavioral economists, who uncovered many important empirical failures of Rational Expectations models, formalized their insights, they followed their conventional predecessors by doing so with fully predetermined models.

Sharp versus Contingent Predictions

Contemporary economists' aim to find a model that could predict the complete set of future market outcomes and probabilities is not the first such endeavor in the social sciences. In his seminal refutation of the claim that "historicism" might one day enable social science to "predict the future course of history," Karl Popper pointed out that any such approach is futile "to the extent to which [historical developments] may be influenced by the growth of our knowledge" (Popper, 1957, pp. xi–xii).

Because market outcomes—especially outcomes in financial markets—crucially depend on changing understandings of the process and psychology that underpin those outcomes on both the individual and aggregate level, our critique of contemporary macroeconomics and finance theory can be viewed as further refutation of the historicist's vain ambition. Although Popper was strongly critical of attempts to develop fully predetermined accounts of history, he was quick to point out that his

> argument does not, of course, refute the possibility of every kind of social prediction; on the contrary, it is perfectly compatible with the possibility of testing social theories—for example economic theories—by way of predicting that certain developments will take place under certain conditions. It only refutes the possibility of predicting historical developments to the extent to

which they may be influenced by the growth of our knowledge. [Popper, 1957, p. xii]

RECOGNIZING OUR OWN IMPERFECT KNOWLEDGE

How can economic analysis remain open to the importance of market participants' revisions of their interpretation of outcomes while still generating predictions that are empirically significant? How can it recognize the importance of nonroutine change and imperfect knowledge while continuing to portray individual and aggregate behavior in mathematical terms? The continued relevance of macroeconomics and finance theory to real-world markets and policy analysis depends on its ability to articulate answers to these questions; Imperfect Knowledge Economics offers a response.

Early modern economic analysis, particularly that of Keynes, is sometimes interpreted as claiming that economic decisions, particularly those in financial markets, stem only from erratic "animal spirits." Of course, if this were the case, no economic theory that aims to account for outcomes in these markets with mathematical models and confront hypotheses rigorously with empirical evidence would be possible. As Edmund Phelps (2008, p. A19) put it, "animal spirits can't be modeled." Indeed, Akerlof and Shiller's (2009) book, which argues that animal spirits, broadly defined, are the key to understanding macroeconomic outcomes and swings in asset prices, does rely on a narrative mode of analysis instead of mathematical models.

Imperfect Knowledge Economics stakes out an intermediate position between erratic animal spirits and the contemporary presumption that change and its consequences can be adequately prespecified with mechanical rules. In contrast to the contemporary approach, the mathematical models of Imperfect Knowledge Economics explore the possibility that change and its consequences can be portrayed with qualitative and contingent conditions. These conditions are context-dependent, and as discussed in Chapter 9, the qualitative regularities that they formalize become manifest—or cease to be relevant—at moments that no one can fully predict.

Imperfect Knowledge Economics therefore does not adopt the extreme view, often associated with Knight, that uncertainty is so radical as to preclude economists from saying anything useful and empirically relevant about how market outcomes unfold over time. Indeed, departing from the position of Knight and Keynes, we make nonstandard use of probabilistic formalism.[3] This approach facilitates the formalization of qualitative conditions that make up Imperfect Knowledge Economics models and the mathematical derivation of their qualitative and contingent implications. However, Imperfect Knowledge Economics recognizes the importance of early modern arguments that market participants (and economists) have access to only imperfect knowledge of the causal factors that may be useful for understanding outcomes.

Because their restrictions on change are qualitative, IKE models represent outcomes at every point in time with myriad probability distributions. In this sense, every such model is open and reflects the fact that, as Popper put it, "Quite apart from the fact that we do not know the future, the future is objectively not fixed. The future is open: *objectively* open" (Popper, 1990, p. 18, emphasis added).

The qualitative and contingent predictions generated by our IKE model of asset-price swings exemplify what Popper would regard as a feasible goal for economic theory. Although our model predicts that, under "certain conditions," an asset price will undergo a sustained movement in one direction, it does not predict when such upswings or downswings will begin or end.

Beyond building on Popper's insights concerning the possibility, scope, and character of predictions in the social sciences, our model of asset-price swings exemplifies Hayek's (1978, p. 33) claim that, "Our capacity to predict will be confined to . . . general

---

[3]For a mathematical exposition, see Frydman and Goldberg (2010a).

characteristics of the events to be expected and not include the capacity for predicting particular individual events." Although an IKE model, by design, stops short of predicting "particular individual events," such as when the swing will begin and end, it does generate predictions concerning their "general characteristics"— for example, that they tend to be quite persistent. Thus, by examining the persistence and related features of swings in asset prices and risk implied by alternative models, an economist may compare explanations of economic phenomena. Johansen et al. (2010) and Frydman et al (2010b,c) develop such an approach to econometric testing and conclude that our IKE model of swings in currency markets provides a significantly better account of exchange rate movements than standard and bubble models based on the Rational Expectations Hypothesis.[4]

These studies show that, despite placing imperfect knowledge and nonroutine change at the center of economic analysis and limiting our ambition solely to generating qualitative predictions, Imperfect Knowledge Economics may still yield "predictions which can be falsified and which therefore are of empirical significance" (Hayek, 1978, p. 29).

IMPERFECT KNOWLEDGE ECONOMICS AS THE BOUNDARY OF MACROECONOMIC THEORY

In Frydman and Goldberg (2007) and our recent technical studies, we show how IKE models shed new light on salient features of the empirical record on asset prices and risk that have confounded international macroeconomists for decades. In this book, we focused on how recognizing the centrality of nonroutine change and imperfect knowledge enables us to understand better

[4]Our approach to testing the implications of Imperfect Knowledge Economics versus Rational Expectations models of swings makes use of Cointegrating VAR Methodology and Inference, developed by Soren Johansen and Katarina Juselius in many papers over the last two decades. For book-length treatments, see Johansen (1996) and Juselius (2006).

how financial markets, particularly equity markets, help society allocate capital, and why asset-price swings are an integral part of this essential process.

Imperfect Knowledge Economics also provides a new way to explain why asset-price swings sometimes become excessive, and shows how the hitherto neglected relationship between financial risk and price swings can help us to understand how excessive price swings come to an end. This analysis provides a conceptual framework for prudential policy aimed at dampening excessive price swings and thus reducing the social costs inflicted when they reverse direction.

Although the application of Imperfect Knowledge Economics to financial markets appears promising, it is too early to claim broader usefulness for this approach in macroeconomic and policy modeling. If qualitative and contingent regularities can be established in contexts other than asset markets, the nonstandard probabilistic formalism of Imperfect Knowledge Economics can show how to incorporate them into mathematical models and confront them with empirical evidence. However, when revisions of forecasting strategies (or more broadly, change on the individual and aggregate levels) cannot be adequately characterized with qualitative and contingent conditions, empirically relevant mathematical models of how market outcomes unfold over time may be beyond the reach of economic analysis. In this sense, Imperfect Knowledge Economics provides the boundary to what modern macroeconomics and finance theory can deliver. How far, and in which contexts, this boundary can be extended is the crucial open question suggested by this book.

References

Abreu, Dilip, and Markus K. Brunnermeier (2003), "Bubbles and Crashes,"
Econometrica 71: 173–204.

Akerlof, George A. (2001), "Behavioral Macroeconomics and Macroeconomic Behavior," Nobel lecture, Stockholm: Nobel Foundation.

Akerlof, George A., and Robert J. Shiller (2009), *Animal Spirits: How
Human Psychology Drives the Economy and Why It Matters for Global
Capitalism*, Princeton, NJ: Princeton University Press.

Allen, Franklin, and Gary Gorton (1993), "Churning Bubbles," *Review of
Economics Studies* 60: 813–36.

Atkins, Ralph (2006), "Central Banks Eye Norway's Clarity on Rates,"
Financial Times, May 25, p. 15.

Barberis, Nicholas C., and Richard H. Thaler (2003), "A Survey of Behavioral Finance," in George Constantinides, Milton Harris, and Rene
Stulz (eds.), *Handbook of the Economics of Finance*, Amsterdam: North-
Holland, 1052–121.

Barberis, Nicholas C., Andrei Shleifer, and Robert Vishny (1998), "A
Model of Investor Sentiment," *Journal of Financial Economics* 49:
307–43.

Beckman, Joscha, Ansgar Belke, and Michael Kuhl (2010), "How Stable
Are Monetary Models of the Dollar-Euro Exchange Rate? A Time-
Varying Coefficient Approach," forthcoming in *Review of World Economics*.

Bekaert, Geert, and Robert J. Hodrick (1993), "On Biases in the Measurement of Foreign Exchange Risk Premiums," *Journal of International
Money and Finance* 12: 115–38.

Berg, Eric N. (1992), "A Study Shakes Confidence in the Volatile-Stock Theory," *New York Times*, February 18, p. D1.

Berger, Allen N., and Gregory F. Udell (1998), "The Economics of Small Business Finance: The Roles of Private Equity and Debt Markets in the Financial Growth Cycle," *Journal of Banking and Finance* 22: 613–73.

Bernanke, Ben S. (2002), "Asset-Price 'Bubbles' and Monetary Policy," speech at the New York Chapter of the National Association for Business Economics, New York, October 15.

Bernanke, Ben S., and Mark Gertler (2001), "Should Central Banks Respond to Movements in Asset Prices?" *American Economic Review* 91: 253–57.

Bernanke, Ben S., Mark Gertler, and Simon Gilchrist (1999), "The Financial Accelerator in a Quantitative Business Cycle Framework," in John B. Taylor and Michael Woodford (eds.), *Handbook of Macroeconomics*, vol. 1, Amsterdam: Elsevier.

Bienz, Carsten, and Tore E. Leite (2008), "A Pecking Order of Venture Capital Exits," Social Science Research Network Working Paper, April.

BIS [Bank for International Settlements] (2010), "Macroprudential Instruments and Frameworks: A Stocktaking of Issues and Experiences," Committee on the Global Financial System Paper 38, May. Available at: http://www.bis.org/publ/cgfs38.htm.

Black, Bernard S., and Ronald J. Gilson (1998), "Venture Capital and the Structure of Capital Markets: Banks versus Stock Markets," *Journal of Financial Economics* 47: 243–77.

Blanchard, Olivier (2009), "The State of Macro," *Annual Review of Economics* 1: 209–28.

Bordo, Michael (2003), "Stock Market Crashes, Productivity Boom Busts and Recessions: Some Historical Evidence," background paper prepared for chapter on Asset Price Busts, *World Economic Outlook*, April. Available at: http://sites.google.com/site/michaelbordo/.

Bordo, Michael, and Olivier Jeanne (2004), "Boom-Busts in Asset Prices, Economic Instability and Monetary Policy," in Richard Burdekin and Pierre Siklos (eds.), *Deflation: Current and Historical Perspectives*, Cambridge: Cambridge University Press.

Borio, Claudio (2003), "Towards a Macroprudential Framework for Financial Supervision and Regulation," Bank for International Settlements Working Paper 128, Basel, Switzerland, February.

Borio, Claudio, and Philip Lowe (2002a), "Asset Prices, Financial and Monetary Stability: Exploring the Nexus," Bank for International Settlements Working Paper 114, Basel, Switzerland, July.

—— (2002b), "Assessing the Risk of Banking Crises," *BIS Quarterly Review*, December: 43–54.

Borio, Claudio, and Ilhyock Shim (2007), "What Can (Macro-) Prudential Policy Do to Support Monetary Policy?" Bank for International Settlements Working Paper 242, Basel, Switzerland, December.

Boughton, John M. (1987), "Tests of the Performance of Reduced-Form Exchange Rate Models," *Journal of International Economics* 23: 41–56.

Brown, R. L., J. Durbin, and J. M. Evans (1975), "Techniques for Testing the Constancy of Regression Relationships over Time (with Discussion)," *Journal of the Royal Statistical Society* B 37: 149–92.

Brunnermeier, Markus K. (2001), *Asset Pricing under Asymmetric Information: Bubbles, Crashes, Technical Analysis, and Herding*, Oxford: Oxford University Press.

Bygrave, William D., and Jerry A. Timmons (1992), "Venture Capital at the Crossroads," Cambridge, MA: Harvard Business School Press.

Camerer, Colin, George Loewenstein, and Matthew Rabin (2004), *Advances in Behavioral Economics*, Princeton, NJ: Princeton University Press.

Campbell, John Y., and Robert J. Shiller (1988), "Stock, Prices, Earnings, and Expected Dividends," *Journal of Finance* 43: 661–76.

—— (1998), "Valuation Ratios and the Long-Run Stock Market Outlook," *Journal of Portfolio Management* 24: 11–26.

Cassidy, John (2009), *How Markets Fail*, New York: Farrar, Straus and Giroux.

—— (2010a), "Interview with James Heckman," New York. Available at http://www.newyorker.com/online/blogs/johncassidy/2010/01/interview-with-james-heckman.html.

—— (2010b), "Interview with John Cochrane," New York. Available at http://www.newyorker.com/online/blogs/johncassidy/2010/01/interview-with-james-heckman.html.

Cavusoglu, Nevin, Roman Frydman, and Michael D. Goldberg (2010), "The Premium on Foreign Exchange and Historical Benchmarks: Evidence from 10 Currency Markets," mimeo, University of New Hampshire, Durham.

Cecchetti, Stephen, Hans Genberg, John Lipsky, and Sushil Wadhwani (2000), "Asset Prices and Central Bank Policy," Geneva Report on the

World Economy 2, International Center for Monetary and Banking Studies and Centre for Economic Policy Research.

Cecchetti, Stephen, Hans Genberg, and Sushil Wadhwani (2002), "Asset Prices in a Flexible Inflation Targeting Framework," in William C. Hunter, George G. Kaufman, and Michael Pomerleano (eds.), *Asset Price Bubbles: Implications for Monetary, Regulatory, and International Policies*, Cambridge, MA: MIT Press.

Chen, Hsiu-Lang, Narasimhan Jegadeesh, and Russ Wermers (2000), "The Value of Active Mutual Fund Management: An Examination of the Stockholdings and Trades of Fund Managers," *Journal of Financial and Quantitative Analysis* 35: 343–68.

Cheung, Yin-Wong, and Menzie D. Chinn (2001), "Currency Traders and Exchange Rate Dynamics: A Survey of the U.S. Market," *Journal of International Money and Finance* 20: 439–71.

Cheung, Yin-Wong, Menzie D. Chinn, and Ian Marsh (1999), "How do UK-Based Foreign Exchange Dealers Think Their Market Operates?" CEPR Discussion Paper 2230, London: Center for Economic Policy Research.

Cheung, Yin-Wong, Menzie D. Chinn, and Antonio Garcia Pascual (2005), "Empirical Exchange Rate Models of the Nineties: Are Any Fit to Survive?" *Journal of International Money and Finance* 24: 1150–75.

Christoffel, Kai, Günter Coenen, and Anders Warne (2010), "Forecasting with DSGE Models," European Central Bank Working Paper 1185, Frankfurt, Germany, May.

Cochrane, John H. (2009), "How Did Paul Krugman Get It So Wrong?" Available at http://faculty.chicagobooth.edu/john.cochrane/research/Papers/krugman_response.htm.

Crotty, James R. (1986), "Marx, Keynes, and Minsky on the Instability of the Capitalist Growth Process and the Nature of Government Economic Policy," mimeo.

De Bondt, Werner F. M., and Richard H. Thaler (1985), "Does the Stock Market Overreact?" *Journal of Finance* 40: 793–808.

De Grauwe, Paul, and Marianna Grimaldi (2006), *The Exchange Rate in a Behavioral Finance Framework*, Princeton, NJ: Princeton University Press.

DeLong, Bradford J., Andrei Shleifer, Lawrence H. Summers, and Robert J. Waldman (1990a), "Noise Trader Risk in Financial Markets," *Journal of Political Economy* 98: 703–38.

—— (1990b), "Positive Feedback Investment Strategies and Destabilizing Rational Speculation," *Journal of Finance* 45: 375–95.

Dominguez, Kathryn M., and Jeffrey Frankel (1993), *Does Foreign Exchange Intervention Work?* Washington, DC: Institute for International Economics.

Dornbusch, Rudiger, and Jeffrey A. Frankel (1988), "The Flexible Exchange Rate System: Experience and Alternatives," in Silvio Borner (ed.), *International Finance and Trade,* London: Macmillan, reprinted in Jeffrey A. Frankel (ed.) (1995), *On Exchange Rates,* Cambridge MA: MIT Press.

Dow, Alexander, and Sheila Dow (1985), "Animal Spirits and Rationality," in Tony Lawson and Hashem Pesaran (eds.), *Keynes' Economics: Methodological Issues,* Armonk, NY: M. E. Sharpe.

Edwards, Ward (1968), "Conservatism in Human Information Processing," in Benjamin Kleinmuth (ed.), *Formal Representation of Human Judgement,* New York: John Wiley and Sons.

Engel, Charles A. (1996), "The Forward Discount Anomaly and the Risk Premium: A Survey of Recent Evidence," *Journal of Empirical Finance* 3: 123–91.

Evans, George W., and Seppo Honkapohja (2005), "An Interview with Thomas J. Sargent," *Macroeconomic Dynamics* 9: 561–83.

Faisenthal, Mark (2008), "Greenspan 'Shocked' at Credit System Breakdown," Reuters.com, October 23: http://www.reuters.com.

Fama, Eugene F. (1965), "Random Walks in Stock Market Prices," *Financial Analysts Journal* 21: 55–59.

—— (1970), "Efficient Capital Markets: A Review of Theory and Empirical Work," *Journal of Finance* 25: 383–417.

—— (1976), *Foundations of Finance,* New York: Basic Books.

—— (1991), "Efficient Capital Markets: II," *Journal of Finance* 46: 1575–617.

Fama, Eugene F., and Kenneth French (1988), "Permanent and Temporary Components of Stock Prices," *Journal of Political Economy* 96: 246–73.

—— (1989), "Business Conditions and Expected Returns on Stocks and Bonds," *Journal of Financial Economics* 25: 23–49.

Fama, Eugene F., and James D. MacBeth (1973), "Risk, Return, and Equilibrium: Empirical Tests," *Journal of Political Economy* 81: 607–36.

Farmer, Roger (2009), "A New Monetary Policy for the 21st Century," FT.com, January 12: http://www.FT.com.

Fatum, Rasmus, and Michael M. Hutchison (2003), "Is Sterilized Foreign Exchange Intervention Effective after All? An Event Study Approach," *Economic Journal* 113: 390–411.

—— (2006), "Effectiveness of Official Daily Foreign Exchange Market Intervention Operations in Japan," *Journal of International Money and Finance* 25: 199–219.

Fernández de Lis, Santiago, Jorge Martinez Pagés, and Jesús Saurina (2001), "Credit Growth, Problem Loans and Credit Risk Provisioning in Spain," in *Marrying the Macro- and Microprudential Dimensions of Financial Stability*, Bank for International Settlements Discussion Paper 1, March. Available at: http://www.bis.org/publ/bppdf/bispap01.htm.

Fox, Justin (2009), *The Myth of the Rational Market*, New York: Harper-Collins.

Frankel, Jeffrey A. (1985), "The Dazzling Dollar," *Brookings Papers on Economic Activity* 1: 190–217.

Frankel, Jeffrey A., and Kenneth Froot (1987), "Understanding the U.S. Dollar in the Eighties: The Expectations of Chartists and Fundamentalists," *Economic Record* Special issue: 24–38. Reprinted in Jeffrey A. Frankel (ed.) (1995), *On Exchange Rates*, Cambridge, MA: MIT Press.

Frankel, Jeffrey A., and Andrew K. Rose (1995), "Empirical Research on Nominal Exchange Rates," in Gene Grossman and Kenneth S. Rogoff (eds.), *Handbook of International Economics*, vol. III, Amsterdam: North-Holland.

Friedman, Benjamin M. (2009), "The Failure of the Economy & the Economists," *New York Review of Books*, May 28, pp. 42–45.

Friedman, Milton (1953), *Essays in Positive Economics*, Chicago: University of Chicago Press.

Froot, Kenneth A., and Richard H. Thaler (1990), "Anomalies: Foreign Exchange," *Journal of Economic Perspectives* 4 (Summer): 179–92.

Frydman, Roman (1982), "Towards an Understanding of Market Processes: Individual Expectations, Learning and Convergence to Rational Expectations Equilibrium," *American Economic Review* 72: 652–68.

—— (1983), "Individual Rationality, Decentralization and the Rational Expectations Hypothesis," in Roman Frydman and Edmund S. Phelps (eds.), *Individual Forecasting and Aggregate Outcomes: "Rational Expectations" Examined*, New York: Cambridge University Press.

Frydman, Roman, and Michael D. Goldberg (2003), "Imperfect Knowledge Expectations, Uncertainty-Adjusted Uncovered Interest Rate Parity, and Exchange Rate Dynamics," in Philippe Aghion, Roman Frydman, Joseph Stiglitz, and Michael Woodford (eds.), *Knowledge, Information, and Expectations in Modern Macroeconomics: In Honor of Edmund S. Phelps*, Princeton, NJ: Princeton University Press.

—— (2004), "Limiting Exchange Rate Swings in a World of Imperfect Knowledge," in Peter Sorensen (ed.), *European Monetary Integration: Historical Perspectives and Prospects for the Future. Essays in Honour of Niels Thygesen*, Copenhagen: DJOEF.

—— (2007), *Imperfect Knowledge Economics: Exchange Rates and Risk*, Princeton, NJ: Princeton University Press.

—— (2008), "Macroeconomic Theory for a World of Imperfect Knowledge," *Capitalism and Society* 3(3): article 1, http://www.bepress.com/cas/vol3/iss3/art1/.

—— (2009), "Financial Markets and the State: Price Swings, Risk, and the Scope of Regulation," *Capitalism and Society* 4(2): article 2, http://www.bepress.com/cas/vol4/iss2/art2/.

—— (2010a), "The Imperfect Knowledge Imperative in Modern Macroeconomics and Finance Theory," prepared for the conference on Microfoundations for Modern Macroeconomics, Center on Capitalism and Society, Columbia University, New York, November 19, forthcoming in Roman Frydman and Edmund S. Phelps (eds.), *Foundations for a Macroeconomics of the Modern Economy.*

—— (2010b), "Opening Models of Asset Prices and Risk to Non-Routine Change," prepared for the conference on Microfoundations for Modern Macroeconomics, Center on Capitalism and Society, Columbia University, New York, November 19, forthcoming in Roman Frydman and Edmund S. Phelps (eds.), *Foundations for a Macroeconomics of the Modern Economy.*

Frydman, Roman, and Edmund S. Phelps (1983), "Introduction," in Roman Frydman and Edmund S. Phelps (eds.), *Individual Forecasting and Aggregate Outcomes: "Rational Expectations" Examined*, New York: Cambridge University Press.

—— (1990), "Pluralism of Theories Problems in Post-Rational-Expectations Modeling," paper presented at the 1990 Siena Summer Workshop on Expectations and Learning, Siena, Italy, June.

Frydman, Roman, and Andrzej Rapaczynski (1993), "Markets by Design," manuscript, New York.

—— (1994), *Privatization in Eastern Europe: Is the State Withering Away?* Budapest and Oxford: Central European University Press in cooperation with Oxford University Press.

Frydman, Roman, Cheryl Gray, Marek Hessel, and Andrzej Rapaczynski (1999), "When Does Privatization Work? The Impact of Private Ownership on Corporate Performance in Transition Economies," *Quarterly Journal of Economics* 114: 1153–92.

—— (2000), "The Limits of Discipline: Ownership and Hard Budget Constraints in the Transition Economies," *Economics of Transition* 8: 577–601.

Frydman, Roman, Marek Hessel, and Andrzej Rapaczynski (2006), "Why Ownership Matters: Entrepreneurship and the Restructuring of Enterprises in Central Europe," in Merritt B. Fox and Michael A. Heller (eds.), *Corporate Governance Lessons from Transition Economies*, Princeton, NJ: Princeton University Press.

Frydman, Roman, Michael D. Goldberg, and Edmund S. Phelps (2008), "We Must Not Rely Only on the Rosiest Ratings," *Financial Times*, October 20, p. 11.

Frydman, Roman, Omar Khan, and Andrzej Rapaczynski (2010a), "Entrepreneurship in Europe and the United States: Security, Finance, and Accountability," forthcoming in Edmund S. Phelps and Hans-Werner Sinn (eds.), *Perspectives on the Performance of the Continent's Economies*, Cambridge, MA: MIT Press.

Frydman, Roman, Michael D. Goldberg, Soren Johansen, and Katarina Juselius (2010b), "Why REH Bubble Models Do Not Adequately Account for Swings," mimeo, University of Copenhagen, Denmark.

—— (2010c), "Imperfect Knowledge and Long Swings in Currency Markets," mimeo, University of Copenhagen, Denmark.

Goldberg, Michael D., and Roman Frydman (1996a), "Imperfect Knowledge and Behavior in the Foreign Exchange Market," *Economic Journal* 106: 869–93.

—— (1996b), "Empirical Exchange Rate Models and Shifts in the Co-Integrating Vector," *Journal of Structural Change and Economic Dynamics* 7: 55–78.

—— (2001), "Macroeconomic Fundamentals and the DM/$ Exchange Rate: Temporal Instability and the Monetary Model," *International Journal of Finance and Economics* 19: 421–35.

Gollier, Christian (2001), *The Economics of Risk and Time*, Cambridge, MA: MIT Press.

Gompers, Paul, and Josh Lerner (1997), "Risk and Reward in Private Equity Investments: The Challenge of Performance Assessment," *Journal of Private Equity* 1: 5–12.

Gourinchas, Pierre-Olivier, and Aaron Tornell (2004), "Exchange Rate Puzzles and Distorted Beliefs," *Journal of International Economics* 64: 303–33.

Greenspan, Alan (2007), *The Age of Turbulence: Adventures in a New World*, London: Penguin.

Gromb, Denis, and Dimitri Vayanos (2010), "Limits to Arbitrage: The State of the Theory," *Annual Review of Financial Economics* 2: 251–75.

Grossman, Sanford, and Joseph E. Stiglitz (1980), "On the Impossibility of Informationally Efficient Markets," *American Economic Review* 70: 393–408.

Gürkaynak, Refet S., Andrew T. Levin, and Eric T. Swanson (2006), "Does Inflation Targeting Anchor Long-Run Inflation Expectations? Evidence from Long-Term Bond Yields in the U.S., U.K., and Sweden," Federal Reserve Bank of San Francisco Working Paper 2006-09, San Francisco, March.

Hamilton, James D. (1988), "Rational-Expectations Econometric Analysis of Changes in Regime: An Investigation of the Term Structure of Interest Rates," *Journal of Economics Dynamics and Control* 12: 385–423.

Hare, Paul G. (1981a), "Aggregate Planning by Means of Input-Output and Material-Balances Systems," *Journal of Comparative Economics* 9: 272–91.

—— (1981b), "Economics of Shortage and Non-Price Controls," *Journal of Comparative Economics* 9: 406–25.

Hayek, Friedrich A. (1945), "The Use of Knowledge in Society," *American Economic Review* 35: 519–30.

—— (1948), *Individualism and Economic Order,* Chicago: University of Chicago Press.

—— (1978), "The Pretence of Knowledge," 1974 Nobel lecture, in *New Studies in Philosophy, Politics, Economics and History of Ideas,* Chicago: University of Chicago Press.

Heid, Frank (2007), "The Cyclical Effects of the Basel II Capital Requirements," *Journal of Banking and Finance* 31: 3885–900.

Hessels, Jolanda, Isabel Grilo, and Peter van der Zwan (2009), "Entrepreneurial Exit and Entrepreneurial Engagement," Scientific Analysis of Entrepreneurship and SME's, Zoetermeer, The Netherlands, June.

Hindu Business Line (2007), "Investment Nuggets: Walter Schloss," January 14: http://www.thehindubusinessline.com.

Institute of International Finance (2010), "The Net Cumulative Economic Impact of Banking Sector Regulation: Some New Perspectives," October, Washington, DC.

Jegadeesh, Narasimhan, and Sheridan Titman (1993), "Returns to Buying Winners and Selling Losers: Implications for Stock Market Efficiency," *Journal of Finance* 48: 65–91.

Jensen, Michael C. (1978), "Some Anomalous Evidence Regarding Market Efficiency," *Journal of Financial Economics* 6: 95–101.

Johansen, Soren (1996), *Likelihood Based Inference on Cointegration in the Vector Autoregressive Model,* Oxford: Oxford University Press.

Johansen, Soren, Katarina Juselius, Roman Frydman, and Michael D. Goldberg (2010), "Testing Hypotheses in an I(2) Model with Piecewise Linear Trends: An Analysis of the Persistent Long Swings in the Dmk/$ Rate," *Journal of Econometrics* 158: 117–29.

Juselius, Katarina (2006), *The Cointegrated VAR Model: Methodology and Applications,* Oxford: Oxford University Press.

Kahn, James A. (2009), "Productivity Swings and Housing Prices," *Federal Reserve Bank of New York Current Issues in Economics* 15: 1–8.

Kahneman, Daniel, and Amos Tversky (1979), "Prospect Theory: An Analysis of Decision under Risk," *Econometrica* 47: 263–91.

Kaletsky, Anatole (2010), *Capitalism 4.0,* New York: Public Affairs.

Keynes, John Maynard (1921), *A Treatise on Probability,* London: Macmillan, reprinted in 1957.

—— (1936), *The General Theory of Employment, Interest and Money*, Harcourt, Brace and World.

—— (1971–1989), *The Collected Writings of John Maynard Keynes*, 30 vols., Cambridge: Macmillan and Cambridge University Press.

Kindleberger, Charles P. (1996), *Manias, Panics, and Crashes*, New York: John Wiley and Sons.

King, Mervyn (2005), "Monetary Policy—Practice Ahead of Theory," Mais Lecture 2005, Bank of England, London. Available at http://www.bankofengland/news/2005/056.htm.

Knight, Frank H. (1921), *Risk, Uncertainty and Profit*, Boston: Houghton Mifflin.

Krugman, Paul R. (1986), "Is the Strong Dollar Sustainable?" NBER Working Paper 1644, National Bureau of Economic Research, Cambridge, MA.

—— (2009), "How Did Economists Get It So Wrong?" *New York Times Magazine*, September 2, pp. 36–43.

Kydland, Finn E., and Edward C. Prescott (1977), "Rules Rather Than Discretion: The Inconsistency of Optimal Plans," *Journal of Political Economy* 85: 473–91.

—— (1996), "A Computational Experiment: An Econometric Tool," *Journal of Economic Perspectives* 10: 69–85.

Lange, Oscar (1967), "The Computer and the Market," in C. H. Feinstein (ed.), *Socialism, Capitalism and Economic Growth*, Cambridge: Cambridge University Press.

Lerner, Josh (1994), "Venture Capitalists and the Decision to Go Public," *Journal of Financial Economics* 35: 293–316.

Le Roy, Stephen (1989), "Efficient Capital Markets and Martingales," *Journal of Economic Literature* 27: 1583–621.

Lewis, Karen K. (1995), "Puzzles in International Financial Markets," in Gene Grossman and Kenneth S. Rogoff (eds.), *Handbook of International Economics*, vol. III, Amsterdam: North-Holland, 1913–17.

Lo, Andrew W. and A. Craig MacKinlay (1999), *A Non-Random Walk down Wall Street*, Princeton, NJ: Princeton University Press.

Lowenstein, Roger (1995), *Buffett: The Making of an American Capitalist*, New York: Random House.

Lucas, Robert E. Jr. (1973), "Some International Evidence on Output-Inflation Trade-Offs," *American Economic Review* 63: 326–34.

—— (1976), "Econometric Policy Evaluation: A Critique," in Karl Brunner and Allan H. Meltzer (eds.), *The Phillips Curve and Labor Markets*, Carnegie-Rochester Conference Series on Public Policy, Amsterdam: North-Holland.

—— (1995), "The Monetary Neutrality," Nobel lecture, Stockholm: Nobel Foundation.

—— (2001), "Professional Memoir," mimeo, University of Chicago. Available at http://home.uchicago.edu.

—— (2002), *Lectures on Economic Growth*, Cambridge, MA: Harvard University Press.

Macroeconomic Assessment Group (2010), "Interim Report: Assessing the Macroeconomic Impact of the Transition to Stronger Capital and Liquidity Requirements," Bank for International Settlements, Basel, Switzerland, August.

Mangee, Nicholas (2011), "Long Swings in Stock Prices: Market Fundamentals and Psychology," Ph.D. dissertation, University of New Hampshire, Durham, forthcoming.

Mark, Nelson C., and Yangru Wu (1998), "Rethinking Deviations from Uncovered Interest Parity: The Role of Covariance Risk and Noise," *Economic Journal* 108: 1686–786.

Marx, Karl (1981), *Capital*, vol. 3, London: Penguin.

Meese, Richard A., and Kenneth S. Rogoff (1983), "Empirical Exchange Rate Models of the Seventies: Do They Fit out of Sample?" *Journal of International Economics* 14: 3–24.

—— (1988), "Was It Real? The Exchange Rate-Interest Differential Relation over the Modern Floating-Rate Period," *Journal of Finance* 43: 993–48.

Mehra, Rajnish, and Edward C. Prescott (1985), "The Equity Premium Puzzle: A Puzzle," *Journal of Monetary Economics* 15: 145–61.

Melberg, Hans O. (2010), "A Note on Keynes' Animal Spirits," mimeo, Oslo, Norway.

Menkhoff, Lukas, and Mark P. Taylor (2007), "The Obstinate Passion of Foreign Exchange Professionals: Technical Analysis," *Journal of Economic Literature* 45: 936–72.

Minsky, Hyman (2008), *Stabilizing an Unstable Economy*, New York: McGraw-Hill.

Montias, Michael J. (1962), *Central Planning in Poland*, New Haven, CT: Yale University Press.

Muelbauer, John (2008), "The World's Central Banks Must Buy Assets," *Financial Times*, November 25, Asia edition 1, p. 11.

Muth, John F. (1961), "Rational Expectations and the Theory of Price Movements," *Econometrica* 29: 315–35.

Obstfeld, Maurice, and Kenneth S. Rogoff (1996), *Foundations of International Macroeconomics*, Cambridge, MA: MIT Press.

Orphanides, Athanasios, and John C. Williams (2007), "Inflation Targeting under Imperfect Knowledge," *Federal Reserve Bank of San Francisco Economic Review* 1–23.

Phelps, Edmund S. (1983), "The Trouble with 'Rational Expectations' and the Problem of Inflation Stabilization," in Roman Frydman and Edmund S. Phelps (eds.), *Individual Forecasting and Aggregate Outcomes: "Rational Expectations" Examined*, New York: Cambridge University Press.

—— (2008), "Our Uncertain Economy," *Wall Street Journal*, March 14, p. A19.

—— (2009), "Uncertainty Bedevils the Best System," *Financial Times*, April 15, p. 13.

Phelps, Edmund S., Armen A. Alchian, Charles C. Holt, Dale T. Mortensen, G. C. Archibald, Robert E. Lucas, and Leonard A. Rapping (1970), *Microeconomic Foundations of Employment and Inflation*, New York: Norton.

Popper, Karl R. (1946), *The Open Society and Its Enemies*, Princeton, NJ: Princeton University Press, reprinted in 1962.

—— (1957), *The Poverty of Historicism*, London and New York: Routledge.

—— (1990), *A World of Propensities*, Bristol, UK: Thoemmes Antiquarian Books.

—— (1992), *The Logic of Scientific Discovery*, London and New York: Routledge.

Prescott, Edward C. (2006), "Nobel Lecture: The Transformation of Macroeconomic Policy and Research," *Journal of Political Economy* 114: 203–35.

Rabin, Matthew (2002), "A Perspective on Psychology and Economics," *European Economic Review* 46: 657–85.

Reinhart, Carmen M., and Kenneth S. Rogoff (2009), *This Time Is Different: Eight Centuries of Financial Folly,* Princeton, NJ: Princeton University Press.

Repullo, Rafael, and Javier Suarez (2008), "The Procyclical Effects of Basel II," discussion paper, Centre for Economic Policy Research, London.

Rogoff, Kenneth S., and Vania Stavrakeva (2008), "The Continuing Puzzle of Short Horizon Exchange Rate Forecasting," NBER Working Paper 14701, National Bureau of Economic Research, Cambridge, MA.

Samuelson, Paul A. (1965a), "Some Notions of Causality and Teleology in Economics," in D. Lerner (ed.), *Cause and Effect,* Glencoe, IL: Free Press.

——— (1965b), "Proof That Properly Anticipated Prices Fluctuate Randomly," *Industrial Management Review* 6: 41–49.

——— (1973), "Proof That Properly Discounted Present Values of Assets Vibrate Randomly," *Bell Journal of Economics* 4: 369–74.

Sargent, Thomas J. (1987), *Macroeconomic Theory,* New York: Academic Press.

——— (1993), *Bounded Rationality in Macroeconomics,* Oxford: Oxford University Press.

——— (2001), *The Conquest of American Inflation,* Princeton, NJ: Princeton University Press.

——— (2010), "An Interview with Arthur J. Rolnick: Modern Macroeconomics Under Attack," Federal Reserve Bank of Minneapolis, September. Available at: http://www.minneapolisfed.org/publications_papers/pub_display.cfm?id=4526.

Sarkar, Asani, and Jeffrey Shrader (2010), "Financial Amplification Mechanisms and the Federal Reserve's Supply of Liquidity during the Financial Crisis," in "Special Issue: Central Bank Liquidity Tools and Perspectives on Regulatory Reform," *Federal Reserve Bank of New York Economic Policy Review* 16: 55–74.

Schulmeister, Stephan (2003), "Technical Trading Systems and Stock Price Dynamics," WIFO-Studie mit Unterstützung des Jubiläumsfonds der Österreichischen Nationalbank 2002, Vienna, Austria.

—— (2006), "The Interaction between Technical Currency Trading and Exchange Rate Fluctuations," *Finance Research Letters* 3: 212–33.

Shiller, Robert J. (1981), "Do Stock Prices Move Too Much to Be Justified by Subsequent Changes in Dividends?" *American Economic Review* 71: 421–36.

—— (2000), *Irrational Exuberance,* New York: Broadway Books.

Shleifer, Andrei (2000), *Inefficient Markets,* Oxford: Oxford University Press.

Simon, Herbert A. (1971), "Theories of Bounded Rationality," in Bruce McGuire and Roy Radner (eds.), *Decision and Organization,* Amsterdam: North-Holland.

Sims, Christopher A. (1996), "Macroeconomics and Methodology," *Journal of Economic Perspectives* 10: 105–20.

—— (2010), "How Empirical Evidence Does or Does Not Influence Economic Thinking," presentation at the inaugural conference of the Institute for New Economic Thinking, Cambridge, April 8–11. Available at http://ineteconomics.org/sites/inet.civicactions.net/files/INET Session5-ChristopherSims.pdf.

Skidelsky, Robert (1983), *John Maynard Keynes,* vol. 1, London: Macmillan.

—— (1992), *John Maynard Keynes,* vol. 2, London: Macmillan.

—— (2000), *John Maynard Keynes,* vol. 3, London: Macmillan.

—— (2009), *Keynes: The Return of the Master,* New York: Public Affairs.

—— (2010), "Keynes and the Social Democratic Tradition," Project Syndicate, June 10: http://www.project-syndicate.org.

Soros, George (1987), *The Alchemy of Finance,* New York: Wiley.

—— (2008), *The New Paradigm for Financial Markets: The Credit Crisis of 2008 and What It Means,* New York: Public Affairs.

—— (2009), "Financial Markets", lecture 2 of the Central European University Lectures, Budapest, Hungary, October 27. Available at http://www.ceu.hu/news/2009-10-26/the-ceu-lectures-george-soros-on-the-economy-reflexivity-and-open-society-0.

Spence, Michael A. (2001), "Signaling in Retrospect and the Informational Structure of Markets," Nobel lecture, Stockholm: Nobel Foundation. Available at: http://nobelprize.org/nobel_prizes/economics/laureates/2001/spence-lecture.pdf.

Stiglitz, Joseph E. (2001), "Information and the Change in the Paradigm in Economics," Nobel lecture, Stockholm: Nobel Foundation, Available at: http://nobelprize.org/nobel_prizes/economics/laureates/2001/stiglitz-lecture.pdf.

—— (2010), "The Non-Existent Hand," *London Review of Books,* April 22, pp. 17–18.

Stillwagon, Josh (2010), "Imperfect Knowledge and Currency Risk: A CVAR Analysis with Survey," mimeo, University of New Hampshire, Durham.

Tinbergen, Jan (1939), *Business Cycles in the United States of America, 1919–32,* Geneva: League of Nations.

Tobin, James (1958), "Liquidity Preference as Behavior Towards Risk," *Review of Economic Studies* 25(1): 15–29.

Trichet, Jean-Claude (2010), "Introductory Remarks," European Central Bank press conference, September 2. Available at: http://www.ecb.int/press/pressconf/2010/html/is100902.en.html.

Turner, Adair (2009), "The Turner Review: A Regulatory Response to the Global Banking Crisis," Financial Services Authority, London. Available at http://www.fsa.gov.uk/pubs/other/turner_review.pdf.

Vajna, Thomas (1982), "Problems and Trends in the Development of the Hungarian Economic Mechanism: A Balance Sheet of the 1970s," in Alec Nove, Hans-Herman Hohmannn, and Getraud Seidenstecher (eds.), *The East European Economies in the 1970s,* London: Butterworths.

Venture Economics (1988), *Exiting Venture Capital Investments,* Needham, MA: Venture Economics.

Volcker, Paul (2010), "The Time We Have Is Growing Short," *New York Review of Books,* June 24, pp. 12, 14.

Wallace, A. (1980), "Is Beta Dead?" *Institutional Investor,* July, pp. 23–30.

Wright, Mike, Ken Robbie, and Christine T. Ennew (1997), "Serial Entrepreneurs," *British Journal of Management* 8: 251–68.

Zaleski, Eugène (1980), *Stalinist Planning for Economic Growth, 1933–1955,* Chapel Hill: University of North Carolina Press.

Zheng, L. (2009), "The Puzzling Behavior of Equity Returns: The Need to Move Beyond the Consumption Capital Asset Pricing Model," Ph.D. dissertation, University of New Hampshire, Durham.

Index

Page numbers for entries occurring in figures are suffixed by an *f*; those for entries in notes, by an *n*; and those for entries in tables, by a *t*.